Western Imagination: Renaissance to the Great War

Edited by Gregory Murry

Invino Academic Publishing
Hanover, PA

Western Imagination: Renaissance to the Great War

ISBN: 978-1535176071

Table of Contents

The Making of the Modern West

Texts

The Making of the Modern West

A Very Short Interpretive History of Western Civilization from the Renaissance to the Great War

By Gregory Murry

With Additional Material by

Jamie Gianoutsos and Sean Lewis

Introduction

From an historical perspective, the modern western world is a pretty strange place. Because we live in it, we often take our way of life for granted, breathing in our assumptions about the world like the air around us and rarely stopping to consider the fact that life in the Modern West is not inevitable at all, but rather the product of millions of choices and changes that have been made over thousands of years, and especially over the last five hundred.

Until quite recently, the vast majority of Western peoples lived in the countryside, clustered around small villages that were usually no bigger than a few hundred people, eating mostly what they could grow themselves. For most people, change happened slowly, almost imperceptibly. Many medieval people lived on the same plot of land that their grandparents had, using the same tools that had been available to them. Most expected that their children would work the very same plot of land and probably expected they would use the very same tools. To a large degree, Westerners in the Middle Ages shared a wide range of beliefs about who held authority in the church (the pope) and who held authority in the state (the king). The often arbitrary nature of this authority was set off by the fact that both pope and king were usually relatively weak figures, reliant on local magistrates and possessing little ability to enforce their decisions over broad areas.

Today, almost all of this has changed. The majority of Westerners live in cities. We consume goods that are mass produced in factories and industrial farms half-way around the world, made by people we will never even meet. Few people expect that their children will work the same jobs, live in the same place, or use the same technology. Far from it. Today, our smartphones go out of date faster than our wardrobes.

Nor do we share a wide range of beliefs about either authority or knowledge. What once was considered knowledge is now mere opinion and what once was considered opinion is now considered knowledge. Almost all Western peoples live in democracies and enjoy many liberties that people in the Middle Ages did not, but we also live in nation-states with governments that have infinitely more control and influence over our daily lives than any medieval kingdom.

Another way to say all this is that life in the Modern West is pluralistic, democratized, urbanized, industrialized, and globalized. It is pluralistic in the sense that we collectively recognize very few common authorities or sources of knowledge outside of our own judgments, feelings, and beliefs. It has become democratized by the arrival of the democratic nation-state, by modern mechanisms for choosing leaders, and by ideological commitments to protecting individual liberties. It has been urbanized, industrialized, and globalized largely by rapidly advancing technologies, which we have harnessed to do many things, but mainly to satisfy our appetites for consumption.

All of this makes life in the Western world fairly different from all other historical periods, and this fact alone makes it imperative that we question how we got here and what we should do with the enormous powers we find ourselves with. Technological advancement, for instance, is often simply assumed to be unconditionally good. And no doubt, it is good. Technology has reduced the cost of this book to thirty five dollars, considerably less than the hundred dollars it would have cost five years ago and much less than the thousand dollars it would have cost five hundred years ago. But while technology might mean that we live in an age of plenty, as the twentieth-century Catholic historian Christopher Dawson noted, the age of plenty might simply mean we live in the age of the machine gun, "which [makes] a thousand bullets fly where only one flew before."[1]

Whether we consciously realize it or not, the way we imagine the world continues to be shaped by the characters, texts, and events that we will study in this course: to know this course material is to know ourselves more fully. By not taking our assumptions for granted, we can

---

[1] Christopher Dawson, *Religion and the Modern State* (London: Sheed and Ward, 1935), 111.

question the nature and value of the changes in authority, knowledge, liberty, and consumption that have occurred over the past five hundred years. What developments ought we to prize, cherish, and nourish? What seems to represent a wrong turn? Where is the Modern West complicit in outright evil? It is often too easy to accept that the way things are is the best of all possible worlds: this course challenges that easy assumption. Have the past five hundred years been a time of unquestionably positive progress? That is for you to decide. But to make an informed decision, we must analyze and interpret historical, literary, and artistic texts, argue about their value and significance, and reach some conclusion about this strange culture called the Modern West.

Chapter One

The Renaissance

The modern western world is typically thought to have begun in the Renaissance (c. 1350-1600), though this belief certainly overstates the case. Renaissance comes from a French word that means rebirth, a branding that suggests something had died. But what? Nineteenth-century scholars looking back on the period suggested that the Middle Ages had marked the death of Greek and Roman culture, while the Renaissance recovered classical civilization, overthrew religion, discovered the individual, and launched the West on its way to modernity.[1] However, those of you who have taken Origins and Classical Philosophy know that this isn't really true. For starters, it ignores many of the achievements of the Middle Ages, an era that produced Charlemagne, Thomas Aquinas, Dante, Chaucer, and Chartres Cathedral. It wasn't as if civilization simply disappeared during the Middle Ages; rather, the western world was busy constructing soaring Gothic cathedrals, composing works of epic literature, building great cities, and laying the foundation of modern governance. Besides, most renaissance people were not secular individualists, but rather remained deeply religious and communal.[2]

What, then, was the Renaissance about? It is true that during the Renaissance, scholars and artists grew more interested in classical civil-

---

[1] Especially Jakob Burkhardt, in *The Civilization of the Renaissance in Italy*, trans. S.G.C. Middlemore (New York: Harper Torchbooks, 1958).

[2] John Jeffries Martin, "The Myth of Renaissance Individualism," in *A Companion to the Worlds of the Renaissance*, ed. Guido Ruggiero (Malden: Blackwell, 2007) 208-224 and David Peterson, "Out of the Margins: Religion and the Church in Renaissance Italy," *Renaissance Quarterly* 53 no. 3 (2000): 835-879.

ization, though it bears repeating that classical civilization had not died in the Middle Ages only to be 'reborn' in the Renaissance. For instance, Thomas Aquinas had relied heavily on Aristotle, and Cicero remained one of the West's most popular writers throughout the Middle Ages. Yet, western intellectuals had largely lost the ability to read Greek in the original, and many of Plato's works had been completely lost to the West until renaissance scholars recovered and translated them in the four-teenth and fifteenth centuries. Scholars recovered many other Greek and Roman texts as well, finding in them an optimism about the human condition that had occasionally been lacking in the Middle Ages. Since they were interested in the same sort of things the Greeks and Romans had been interested in, they increasingly modeled their studies on topics that had been important to the Greeks and Romans: grammar, rhetoric, poetry, history, and moral philosophy. (Sound familiar?) To describe this course of studies, they borrowed a phrase from Cicero, calling them the *studia humanitatis*, or humanities. Those who taught them were known as humanists.[3]

This interest in Greece and Rome stimulated another key development of the Renaissance: the return to classical forms of art and architecture. Gothic cathedrals, as magnificent as they are, don't look much like Greek and Roman temples. Take a look at Saint Peter's Basilica, a church designed and built during the Renaissance. Does it remind you of anything? Take a look at Michelangelo's *David*. Notice anything about his stance? Does he remind you of anyone? If you suddenly felt transported back to Origins, perfect; this is exactly the sensation that renaissance artists wanted to provoke, as they based their own creations on the surviving works of the classical world, whose ruins they lived among. Finally, as Raphael's *School of Athens* and Michelangelo's *David* show, renaissance artists made a big leap forward in the ability to represent realism in painting and sculpture.

Though the Renaissance would eventually spread to the rest of Western Europe, its center was undoubtedly in Italy. Why Italy? For

---

[3] Charles G. Nauert, *Humanism and the Culture of Renaissance Europe* 2nd ed. (Cambridge: Cambridge University Press, 2006), 8.

Michelangelo's *David*, Courtesy of Dreamstime

Saint Peter's Basilica, Courtesy of Dreamstime

starters, artistic and academic achievement takes money, which was primarily to be found in cities. Renaissance Italy had more cities than anywhere else, so naturally it was the richest part of Europe. This was mainly due to its geographical position. The Italian peninsula juts out into the middle of the Mediterranean Sea, making it the perfect entry point for goods entering Europe from the east, goods like porcelain, silk, and spices. Italian merchants, bankers, churchmen and rulers took advantage of Italy's position, as well as the wealth that poured into Papal Rome, to pile up huge fortunes, which they then used to fund superstar artists like Michelangelo, Donatello, Leonardo, and Raphael.

In turn, the social status of artists changed. Before the Renaissance, artists were considered little better than craftsmen, and painters and sculptors enjoyed a status only slightly superior to other artisans. But as wealthy patrons and wealthy Italian city-states started competing for the artists who could paint the most lifelike images and build the most grandiose buildings, the status of artists, sculptors, and architects improved correspondingly. The best artists could now demand the freedom to experiment with their own personal styles. And even better, they could command much larger payments. One story illustrates the point. The sculptor Donatello once made a bronze bust for a merchant. When the merchant complained that the price was too high, Donatello asked his patron, Cosimo dei Medici, to settle the matter for them. Cosimo had the bust brought to the roof of his villa so that they could see it better. When Cosimo said that Donatello's bust was so good that he was actually asking too little for it, the merchant complained that Donatello had only worked on it for a month. Donatello angrily retorted that he could undo the work of a year in a single instant, whereat he knocked the whole bust off the roof and onto the street below, where it shattered into pieces. Donatello then turned to the merchant and angrily exclaimed, "You are obviously more used to bartering for beans than for art." The horrified merchant offered him double the asking price to redo the bust; an insulted Donatello refused.[4]

Italian thinkers also saw similarities between the classical world and their own political situation. Much like Classical Greece, Renaissance Italy was a patchwork of small city-states, each of which was experimenting with different forms of government. In the north, Milan was ruled by monarchs, dukes who dreamed of taking over the whole peninsula. In the northeast, the city-state of Venice was governed (as the Spartans and Romans had been centuries before) by a mixed constitution. In this case, the government consisted of a duke with limited powers (known as the doge), a large council, and a senate of aristocrats, who were chosen to fill various executive committees by the most complicated set of voting procedures ever devised by man.[5] In the south, the Kingdom of Naples formed part of the dominion of the Spanish monarchs. It was typically ruled by a vice-king. In the middle of the peninsula sat the Papal States, unusual because they were ruled by the Pope, essentially an elected monarch who was the spiritual head of all of Christendom but also the civil governor of Rome and its surrounding area.

The most turbulent and creative of all the Italian city-states was undoubtedly Florence, which produced far more than its fair share of the Renaissance's greatest artists and thinkers. Florence was technically a republic, in which power was theoretically shared between the city's major guilds and a revolving council of magistrates (known as the

---

[4] Giorgio Vasari, *Lives of the Artists*, trans. Julia Conway Bondanella and Peter Bondanella (Oxford: Oxford University Press, 1998), 153-154.

[5] John Julius Norwich, *A History of Venice* (New York: Vintage, 1989), 282-284.

Signoria), who were drawn from the guild class and whose tenure in office lasted an incredibly short two months! However, in reality the government was often controlled by powerful factions within the city, the most important of which was usually the Medici family. The Medici used all sorts of shenanigans to fix the selection of the *Signoria* in order to make sure that only individuals loyal to themselves were ever in power.[6] Thus, for much of the Renaissance, the Medici basically controlled republican Florence by themselves. Occasionally, however, the old republican spirit of the Florentines rose up, and they chased the Medici out. On multiple occasions, (1494-1512 and 1527-1530) the Florentines took to the streets, crying "People and Liberty," expelling the Medici and establishing more inclusive republican styles of rule. However, the Medici always found a way to wriggle their way back into power.

All of this political turmoil and political diversity stimulated renaissance Italians to a renewed interest in politics and political theory. Which form of government is the best? What are the responsibilities of citizens? Which is better: a contemplative life of thought and prayer or an active life of service to one's country? What is tyranny? What is justice? Fortunately, renaissance thinkers didn't have to start from scratch, and there was no better place to turn than to the history and thought of the West's classical past: to Plato, Aristotle, Plutarch, Cicero, Livy, and Thucydides and to democratic Athens and republican Rome.

One Florentine thinker who loved nothing better in life than shaking the mud off his boots to enter his study and converse with the great thinkers of antiquity was Niccolò Machiavelli, whose name has become synonymous with immoral power politics.[7] Machiavelli is best known for a little book titled *The Prince*, composed in political exile between 1513 and 1519. On the surface, the book is about how a prince, by which Machiavelli meant a monarch, should behave in order to hold on to power. In it, Machiavelli uses classical and contemporary examples to

---

[6] Niccolai Rubinstein, *The Government of Florence Under the Medici* (Oxford: Oxford University Press, 1998).

[7] One question you might pose when you are reading *The Prince* is whether or not Machiavelli really does or does not propose an "amoral" or "immoral" system of politics.

stand much of what had been received wisdom on its head. His main target is the political thought of the Roman philosopher Cicero.[8] In brief, Machiavelli argued that a new prince usually needed to do at least some immoral things in order to hold on to power and prevent political chaos, the so-called "ends justifies the means" doctrine. Because of its supposed realism, *The Prince* is often considered the first modern political work, but Machiavelli's own Christian contemporaries were shocked, especially by his suggestion that a ruler should imitate the wicked Cesare Borgia, son of Pope Alexander VI, whom Machiavelli had personally witnessed in action and whom most of his contemporaries considered an outright villain.

However, *The Prince* itself poses a bit of a mystery. The book, which was not published until after Machiavelli's death, shows monarchs how to maintain their power, but Machiavelli himself had spent most of his political life in the service of the Florentine Republic, and there were few patriots in Florence more committed to the idea that people were only really free when they could participate in government.[9] Machiavelli wrote *The Prince* in the years following the fall of the Florentine Republic and the return of the Medici. In those years, the Medici dismissed him from his government post, arrested him on charges of political conspiracy, and submitted him to judicial torture. Machiavelli's exile continued when the Medici cardinal Giovanni was elected Pope in 1513. Why then would he write a tract teaching a prince, with its specific focus on a new prince, about how to maintain power? Before you start reading *The Prince*, look at Machiavelli's dedication and the letter to Francesco Vettori. To whom did Machiavelli plan to dedicate the work? To whom did he end up dedicating it? Why might this matter?

The mystery gets more intriguing; at the same time that Machiavelli was writing *The Prince*, he was composing a much longer tract on republican governance: his *Discourses on Titus Livy*. *The Prince*, which comes in at a fairly brief hundred or so pages, is read by students all over

---

[8] You read parts of his *On Friendship* last year in Veritas Symposium.

[9] Mark Jurdjevic, *A Great and Wretched City: Promise and Failure in Machiavelli's Florentine Political Thought* (Cambridge, MA: Harvard University Press, 2014).

the world, whereas almost no one except historians reads the five hundred page *Discourses*. However, it is likely that Machiavelli considered *Discourses* the more important work. How then could a man write a book that praises republics while simultaneously writing another book that teaches a prince how to keep power? One theory (though a minority view) is that Machiavelli's *Discourses* is a serious work, whereas *The Prince* is a veiled satire, written to warn Florentines about the dangers of princely rule. So what is Machiavelli trying to tell us in *The Prince*? Is he seriously telling princes to commit immoral deeds to maintain their power, or is he warning his fellow republican Florentines that all princes behave immorally? That's for you to decide.

One other thing that you should know about *The Prince* is that some of Machiavelli's language is simply untranslatable, nothing more so than the word *virtù*. In Machiavelli's thought, *virtù* definitely does not mean virtue in the way we understand it; it clearly does not refer to the moral virtues of justice, prudence, temperance, and fortitude. Rather, *virtù* means the type of skill, power, force, excellence, or manly courage that allows one to accomplish great deeds.[10] In the text, I have simply left it untranslated. Moreover, one of the running dichotomies in *The Prince* is the relationship between *virtù* (what a prince can accomplish with his own power) and *fortuna* (good or bad luck). It is important to note that sometimes Machiavelli intends fortune to mean 'good luck,' but sometimes it can mean either good or bad luck. Nevertheless, Machiavelli sees both *fortuna* and *virtù* as essential for winning and keeping power.

By the beginning of the sixteenth century, renaissance culture had spread from the Italian city-states into northern Europe, becoming especially prevalent in France, England, and Germany. While Machiavelli's *Prince* became a highly notorious and controversial work during the late Renaissance, northern humanists eagerly consumed, debated and developed Italian Renaissance ideas concerning philosophy, politics, history,

---

[10] Felix Gilbert, *Machiavelli and Guicciardini: Politics and History in Sixteenth Century Florence* (Princeton: Princeton University Press, 1965), 179; and Quentin Skinner, *The Foundations of Modern Political Thought*, vol. 1 (Cambridge: Cambridge Unviersity Press, 1978), 138.

law, and science. The Renaissance most significantly shaped English education in grammar schools and universities. King Henry VIII was the first English prince to be schooled in the humanist educational tradition, and his daughter Elizabeth gained impressive skills in Latin, Greek, French, and Italian while studying the *bonae litterae* (good literature of the classical past) prized by renaissance scholars.[11]

In the late sixteenth century, English boys finishing grammar school (before attending university) had as much classical education as university students graduating with degrees in Classics today.[12] This is one reason why a small-town poet and playwright named William Shakespeare, who never attended university, could write so many excellent plays and poems, often based on stories of the classical and English past. After growing up in Stratford-upon-Avon as the son of a leather worker, Shakespeare first became a player (actor) and poet before writing plays for the London stage beginning in the 1590s. His plays, which included comedies, tragedies, and histories, developed a dramatic language never heard before in English theatre. They depicted the complexity of human thought and action through a number of memorable characters.

In 1623, seven years after his death, Shakespeare's achievements as a playwright were commemorated with the production of the *First Folio* (entitled *Mr William Shakespeares Comedies, Histories, and Tragedies*), which printed 36 of his plays in one large volume. The enduring celebration and reproduction of these plays worldwide have helped enshrine the learning and ideas of the Renaissance in the modern tradition.

In summary, the Renaissance was a literary, artistic, and cultural movement, centered in Italy and spreading with the humanists of northern Europe, in which urbanization stimulated a renewed interest in the thought and culture of the classical past.

---

[11] See Aysha Pollnitz, *Princely Education in Early Modern Britain* (Cambridge: Cambridge Univeristy Press, 2015).

[12] The curriculum at grammar schools would have included reading and translating the history of Livy, speeches of Cicero, comedies of Plautus and Terence, tragedies of Seneca, and poetry of Virgil and Ovid, who was Shakespeare's favorite poet.

Chapter Two:

The Encounter with the World

When the Spanish conquistadors, swords already bloodied in conflict with native Mexican tribes, finally approached the Aztec capital of Tenochtitlan in 1519, the conquistador Bernal Diaz wondered if perhaps it was all a dream. Here was a city of almost a million people, built on an island like Venice, but with massive pyramids seemingly rising straight out of the water.[1] Yet, it was no dream; indeed, for the Aztecs, the arrival of the Spaniards was more like a nightmare, for along with their steel swords and their dogs and their guns, the Spaniards brought a silent and tiny killer with them: smallpox, a Eurasian disease to which native peoples had almost no natural immunity. Before long, smallpox and other diseases would wipe out as much as 95 percent of the native population, leaving the survivors virtually defenseless against Spanish aggression.[2] So began the age of encounter.

But what were the Spanish conquistadors doing in Mexico in the first place? Like all the earliest explorers, the conquistadors were in search of wealth. However, unlike Christopher Columbus, who returned from his

---

[1] Bernal Diaz, *The History of the Conquest of New Spain*, ed. and trans. David Carrasco (Albuquerque, NM: University of New Mexico Press, 2008), 157. Scholars estimate that the island itself held around 200,000 people. Between half a million and a million people lived in what we would call the "metro area."

[2] Guy Settipane, "Columbus: Medical Implications," in *Columbus and the New World: Medical Implications*, ed. Guy Settipane (Providence, RI: OceanSide Publications, 1995), 1.

first voyage with little more than fool's gold,[3] the conquistadors actually found wealth, in fact a whole lot of it.

In 1519, a small conquistador army, under the command of an adventurer named Hernan Cortez, landed in Mexico. Shortly after landing, Cortez destroyed his ships, making it clear to his men that there was no turning back. He then led his men right into the heart of the Aztec empire, making alliances with other native peoples as he went. Shortly after reaching Tenochtitlan, he captured the Aztec Emperor. Then, after some fierce fighting, he captured the capital city and with it, the whole empire in the bargain. When the Aztecs fell, Cortez took their gold and their land, making sure to cut the Spanish crown in for its twenty percent.[4] When silver mines were discovered in the New World, it was clear that the Spaniards had really struck it rich.

On the other hand, the discovery of America could also be seen as a major failure for the Spanish since they had failed to find a quicker route to the Indies by going west. A few years later, the Portuguese explorer Vasco da Gama would succeed where Columbus had failed, finding the Indies by sailing around Africa.[5] The Portuguese had struck it rich too, not because they found lands to conquer, but because China, India, and Japan were the lands from which luxury goods came: namely, cinnamon, black pepper, silk, and china porcelain, the best dishware in the world, which Europeans had no clue how to make for themselves.[6] For centuries, these goods had passed through a dangerous land route through Muslim territory. Once Europeans found the sea route, they could bypass the Muslims and bring those goods to market more quickly and more cheaply; indeed, a single successful voyage could make a man's fortune overnight.

---

[3] William Bernstein, *A Splendid Exchange: How Trade Shaped the World* (New York: Grove, 2009), 166.

[4] Michael C. Meyer and William L. Sherman, *The Course of Mexican History*, 2nd ed. (New York: Oxford University Press, 1983), 99-137.

[5] Sanjay Subrahmanyam, *The Career and Legend of Vasco da Gama* (Cambridge: Cambridge University Press, 1997).

[6] David Arnold, *The Age of Discovery, 1400-1600* 2nd. ed. (London: Routledge, 2002), 13-15.

The discoveries of explorers and conquistadors alike were aided by many advancements in sailing technologies, including one of the marvels of the age: the round caravel (*carabela redonda*). This ship was a technological blend of two sailing traditions: a southern European tradition that used triangular sails, known as lateen sails, to give their ships high maneuverability amongst the rocky shores of

The Caravels of Columbus
From Nestor Ponce de Leon, *The Caravels of Columbus*, 1893.

the Mediterranean, and an Atlantic tradition, which used square sails that were particularly good at catching the wind and propelling boats in the open sea. Sometime in the late Middle Ages, the Iberians who sat at the crossroads of these two traditions put the two sails on the same ship.[7] The result? Ships that were perfectly suited for exploration, as they could fly swiftly across the open sea but could also steer near the shore in uncharted waters. For instance, Columbus' famous ships the Niña and the Pinta were both round caravels.[8]

By backing Columbus, the Spanish ended up with rights to the New World, granted to them by the Pope and ratified by the Treaty of Tordesillas in 1494.[9] Though the Portuguese were given Asia and Brazil by the same treaty, the two empires looked very different. The Spaniards were able to conquer major civilizations such as the Aztec and Inca; establish huge, land-based empires; and siphon off a massive amount of wealth. On the other hand, the Portuguese Empire in the Indian Ocean

---

[7] J.H. Parry, *The Age of Reconaissance: Discovery, Exploration, and Settlement* (Berkeley: University of California Press, 1963), 58-63.

[8] Malcolm Archibald, *Across the Pond* (Dubeath: Whittles, 2001), 21-22.

[9] Incidentally, the Pope at the time was Alexander VI, father of Machiavelli's model prince, Cesare Borgia.

was not much more than a chain of fortified towns, which the Portuguese would use to load their ships up with spices to bring back to Europe. Meanwhile, Portugal's main export to the Indian Ocean was violence; unlike the native bamboo vessels, sturdy Portuguese ships could be loaded with cannons, which Portuguese sailors used to blast away unprepared native vessels and dominate the Asian trading lines. Asian countries thought it cheaper to simply pay the Portuguese protection money rather than completely reconstruct their own fleets.[10] No wonder the Chinese called them the barbarians from the south.

However, Europeans did not just journey for gold; they journeyed for God as well. The Spaniards and Portuguese who made first contact were gradually followed by the English and French in North America. In the wake of the first English settlement at Jamestown, thousands of persecuted Christians came to North America seeking religious asylum, either a chance to coexist with others and practice their religion in peace (like the Quakers of Pennsylvania) or to find a place where they could practice their religion without bothering about tolerating others (like the Calvinist Pilgrims of Massachusetts). In America, Asia, and Africa, Catholic missionaries followed in the wake of explorers, seeking to bring the word of God to pagan lands.

Sometimes, these missionaries were passive conspirators in the quest for plunder; at other times, however, they played the part of Socrates' gadfly, complaining loudly about the brutal exploitation of conquest and violation of native rights. No one was a fiercer critic of the conquistadors than the Dominican Bartolome de Las Casas, who had been a part of the age of exploration from nearly the beginning. He had traveled to the New World for the first time during the age of encounter and later would return as Bishop of Chiapas.[11] Las Casas saw the havoc wreaked on native populations first hand, and it deeply offended him. In the opening pages of his *Brief Relation*, he described the conquistadors as famished

---

[10] Geoffrey Parker, *The Military Revolution: Military Innovation and the Rise of the West* (Cambridge: Cambridge University Press, 1988), 108.

[11] His first voyage to the New World was either on the third voyage of Columbus as some early biographers maintain, or as most modern scholars assume, in 1502.

wolves, lions and tigers, who do nothing in the New World but to tear "[the natives] in pieces, kill them, martyr them, afflict them, torment them and destroy them by all strange sorts of cruelties." Las Casas argued that the conquistadors' bad behavior made it much harder to convert the natives and save their souls. For instance, he told the story of one native Cuban leader who was asked if he wanted to go to heaven. In response, the native leader asked if the Spaniards went to heaven. When the Spaniards responded that they most certainly did, the native leader retorted that in that case he would rather go to hell.[12] Las Casas worked tirelessly on behalf of the Indians, and his work eventually paid off. In 1537, Pope Paul III issued the papal bull *Sublimis Deus*, which stated, in no uncertain terms, that native peoples were rational creatures who could not be enslaved. The Spanish kings also enacted several laws designed to protect the natives, though the conquistadors, protected by the distance between Spain and the New World, did all they could to avoid obeying them.[13]

In arguing against the enslavement of the natives, Las Casas proposed a nefarious idea, suggesting that the Spaniards replace their native laborers with African slaves.[14] Unfortunately, this is exactly what the Spaniards did. Since Christian theology did not forbid Christians from buying slaves captured in just wars, European slavers were still theoretically able to buy African slaves from African slave traders, so long as the slaves had been captured in 'just wars.' As one can imagine, the slave traders usually did not care to enquire too deeply into just how their slaves had been captured.[15]

Here, at the dawn of globalization then, African slaves would enter into one of the first truly worldwide systems of trade. European slavers exchanged guns and European goods for slaves in West Africa, crammed

[12] Bartolome de las Casas, *A briefe Narration of the destruction of the Indes, by the Spanyardes*, trans. Jacques de Miggrode (London, 1583), sig. A[1v].

[13] Meyer and Sherman, 149.

[14] Hugh Thomas, *The Slave Trade: The Story of the Atlantic Slave Trade: 1440-1870* (New York: Simon and Schuster, 1997), 98.

[15] Anthony Pagden, *Peoples and Empire: A Short History of Migration, Exploration, and Conquest, from Greece to the Present* (New York: Modern LIbrary, 2007), 106-108.

their cargo into dreadfully inhumane transport ships, and then sold them in the New World slave markets. Probably around one in five slaves never even made it there at all, since disease and death were frequent passengers on the vastly overcrowded slave ships, and slavers were known to throw diseased captives overboard to protect the rest of their cargo.[16] Those who did survive the passage were set to back-breaking work, often on sugar plantations.[17] New world products like sugar and cocoa were then loaded on boats and taken back to Europe for sale. Wealthy Europeans, who in the meantime had grown practically addicted to the combination of cocoa beans and sugar cane, either didn't know or didn't care about the human misery that went into making their new favorite dessert: chocolate. Back in Africa, the gun buyers would use their new firepower to enslave others, thus perpetuating the cycle.

Meanwhile, the exchange of food and animals (known as the Columbian exchange) affected the whole world, for good and for ill. We have already seen how Europeans' transmission of smallpox to the New World wreaked havoc on the natives. The natives had their revenge, however, by infecting European explorers with syphilis, which was already an epidemic in certain European cities before the end of the fifteenth century. However, smallpox and syphilis were not the only things that traveled across the oceans. New foodstuffs passed from Old World to New World and vice versa. The New World gave modern cuisine things like potatoes, corn, turkey, tomatoes, vanilla, cocoa, and tobacco.[18] As goods moved, they acquired new uses, sometimes not entirely positive ones. For instance, Native Americans had smoked tobacco ceremonially and occasionally; Europeans got themselves addicted to it and smoked it like a drug.[19] On the other hand, Europeans brought chickens, rice, apples, cattle and other large livestock to the New World. The introduction of the horse practically revolutionized life among the Great Plains Indian tribes years before Europeans themselves

---

[16] Thomas, 421-489.

[17] John Thornton, *Africa and Africans in the Making of the Atlantic World* (Cambridge: Cambridge University Press, 1996), 116-125.

[18] Settipane, 7.

[19] Peter Mancall, "Tales Tobacco Told in Sixteenth-Century Europe," *Environmental History* 9 no. 4 (2004): 648-678.

even got there.[20] Indeed, many of the foods that we associate with certain cultures (oranges in Florida, coffee in Columbia, Italian tomato sauce, the spicy chili peppers in Indian food) only arrived there in the age of encounter.[21]

In summary, beginning in the late fifteenth century, European explorers utilized nautical technologies to discover and connect the world in an effort to bring Christianity to other lands and to profit from trade and conquest. This globalized the world for the first time, with revolutionary effects.

---

[20] Settipane, 7.
[21] Arnold, *The Age of Discovery*, 54-58.

Chapter Three:

The Age of Religious Reformations

On October 31ˢᵗ, 1517, the eve of the Feast of All Saints, a fiery August-inian friar angrily made his way to the doors of Wittenberg Cathedral. He carried with him a list of grievances against the Church's teaching on penance and indulgence, the so-called Ninety-Five Theses, which he proceeded to post on the cathedral door. Though maybe a little brash, his actions were not at all unusual; the cathedral door was the customary place for professional and amateur theologians alike to offer their opinions up for debate.[1] Though he may have been burning with righteous indignation, Martin Luther probably had no idea what he had just started; his critique of the indulgences that were being hawked in his native Germany in order to fund the building of Saint Peter's in Rome would soon enkindle an overarching attack on Church structure, the nature of priesthood, and the authority to interpret revelation. Luther didn't see it yet; neither did many others. When the Pope in Rome heard of Luther's protest, he reportedly responded that it was simply the attack of a drunk German monk, who would come to his senses as soon as he sobered up. He could not have been more mistaken. Luther's protest ignited a firestorm of controversy that would burn well into the modern world.

---

[1] G.R. Elton, *Reformation Europe, 1517-1559* (Glasgow: Fontana Press, 1988), 15.

Luther was a brilliant and tormented soul. Though his father had long planned a career in law for him, Luther had other plans. When he was caught in a thunderstorm as a young man, he vowed to Saint Anne that if he were spared, he would become a monk. Yet, life in the monastery was not easy on Luther; he spent much of his time there tormented by his feelings of inadequacy before God. His moment of relief and insight came when he was meditating on Romans 1:17, a passage in which the Apostle Paul writes, "he who through faith is righteous shall live." Here was the solution to Luther's anguish. It was faith alone (*sola fide*), given as a free gift of God's grace alone (*sola gratia*) that justifies the Christian and thereby ensures his salvation. This did not mean that a Christian could do whatever he or she wanted; after being saved by faith, the Christian should practice charity for the love of God alone.[2] But no amount of good works could ever contribute to one's salvation. Luther's Catholic opponents would dispute this, affirming that although people were justified by the free gift of grace alone, the human will truly cooperated with God in the performance of good works. Thus, as people performed good works throughout their life, these helped to "increase justification" in them, thereby helping them to "merit" eternal life.[3]

Since both Catholics and Lutherans believed in justification by grace, and both agreed that good works were important, at first glance their doctrinal disputes may seem a bit like splitting hairs; however, the two sides were actually miles apart. One of the sticking points concerned the usefulness of indulgences, the doctrine that had angered Luther in the first place. In traditional Catholic theology, the forgiveness of sins required the sinner to feel contrition (be sorry), go to confession (say they were sorry), and perform satisfaction (do something to make up for it). If someone died with contrition but without satisfaction, Catholic theology dictated that he or she went to purgatory, a time of spiritual cleansing

---

[2] Roland Bainton, *Here I Stand: A Life of Martin Luther* (Nashville, TN: Abingdon Press, 1978); Robert Kolb,"Martin Luther and the German Nation," *A Companion to the Reformation World,* ed. Ronnie Po-Chia Hsia (Malden: Blackwell, 2006); and Patrick Collinson, *The Reformation: A History* (New York: Modern Library, 2003), 49-59.

[3] *Canons and Decrees of the Council of Trent,* trans. H.J. Schroeder (Rockford, IL, Tan Books and Publishers, 1978), 29-50.

before the soul could enter heaven.[4]   The Church also asserted that believers could pay their satisfaction forward (more or less) either for themselves or for family members in purgatory, by for instance, going on pilgrimage or by paying for an indulgence; in this case, the Church believed that the extra merit of Christ and the saints could be applied to the person for whom the indulgence was bought.[5] The church would then use that money to do things like feed the poor — or to build cathedrals like Saint Peter's.

Indulgences infuriated Luther, especially the way that they were cynically hawked by unscrupulous indulgence peddlers in Germany. Luther thought that people were wasting their money because no amount of good works could ever help to justify or save a person's soul. But the doctrinal issue quickly developed into something more. When Catholic opponents found out about Luther's protest, they pointed out that his argument went further than indulgences alone. If good works were not useful for salvation, if, as Luther came to suggest, the human will was so corrupted by original sin that it could not perform good works at all, what should we think of purgatory? The sacraments? Confession? The priesthood? Prayers for the dead? Relics? If Luther was right, the whole medieval Catholic machinery of salvation had to be tossed out. Luther's opponents suggested that his ideas sounded like those of the medieval heretic, Jan Hus, whom the Council of Constance had condemned to death in 1415.[6]

In some parts of Germany, Lutheran ideas spread like wildfire. Luther called on the German nobility to come to the aid of the new movement, and some of them, encouraged in some cases by true piety and in others by the vast tracts of church land for the taking, took him up on it.[7] In either case, his movement was aided by a technological development that Hus had not had: the printing press, which allowed Luther to spread

---

[4] In your Origins of the West course, some of you may have followed Dante on his literary journey up the mount of Purgatory.

[5] Thomas Aquinas, *Summa Theologicae* Suppl. IIIae, Q. 25.

[6] Collinson, 60-61.

[7] James Estes, *Peace, Order, and the Glory of God: Secular Authority and the Church in the Thought of Luther and Melanchthon, 1518-1559* (Leiden: Brill, 2005), 1-15.

his ideas so rapidly the Catholic Church was caught flat-footed. Meanwhile, Luther and other Protestant reformers continued to make converts, though historians continue to debate whether this was primarily a bottom-up movement fed by the widespread conviction that the Roman church was corrupt or a top-down movement imposed on common people by power-hungry rulers.[8]

Needless to say, many rejected Luther's ideas. In 1521, after Luther publically tossed the Pope's warning onto a bonfire, Pope Leo X officially excommunicated him. Rejected by the papacy and unlikely to see a general council, Luther articulated a new type of authority: the individual believer reading scripture on his own (*sola scriptura*). Since reading the Bible put the believer in direct contact with God, there really was no need to have a separate, hierarchical clergy; in its place, Luther insisted that all believers were priests. Both *sola scriptura* and the priesthood of all believers were like thunderbolts flung at the established church, since they denied the authority of the pope in resolving doctrinal disputes. Three months after the excommunication, Luther was hauled before an imperial court, the disgustingly named Diet of Worms,[9] and told to recant his opinions. Luther held firm, famously claiming:

> Unless I am convinced by scripture and plain reason, I do not accept the authority of the popes and councils, for they have contradicted each other. My conscience is captive to the Word of God. I cannot and I will not recant anything, for to go against conscience is neither right nor safe. Here I stand, I can do no other. God help me. Amen.

---

[8] One good example of the way historians differ on this question concerns the English Reformation. The former opinion was maintained in a classic work by A.G. Dickens, *The English Reformation* (Batsford: Fontana, 1964). Dicken's work was disputed by Eamon Duffy, *The Stripping of the Altars: Traditional Religion in England, 1400-1580* (New Haven: Yale University Press, 1992).

[9] To English speakers at least. In German, Worms is pronounced Vorms and is a German city in the Rhineland.

Or something like that.[10] Either way, the door to further disagreement was opened wide.

Luther had assumed that scripture was clear and that others would understand the scriptures in the same way he did. This was not to be the case. By 1529, Luther's call for reform had spread to Switzerland, where a reformer named Ulrich Zwingli had come to very different conclusions about what scripture said. Zwingli argued that when Jesus said "this is my body" at the Last Supper, he really meant "this signifies my body." The Eucharist, then, was just a symbol and the Catholic Eucharist an example of plain idolatry. Luther disagreed, holding that Christ really was present in the Eucharist. When the two met at Marburg in 1529, Luther took out his knife and carved the words "this is my body" on the table, challenging Zwingli to explain how Christ could have possibly meant 'signifies' when he said the word 'is.'[11] Zwingli's supporters responded that Christ could not have meant that the host actually became his body because Jesus' body was up in heaven; the rules of geometry simply wouldn't allow it. Luther retorted that God was beyond the rules of geometry, but his arguments did not convince Zwingli.[12]

Differences of opinion did not go away. In the 1540s, leadership of the Swiss reformation passed to a French reformer named John Calvin. In questions of theology and church government, Calvinists and Lutherans were nearly as divided from each other as they were from Catholicism. Calvin held a position on the Eucharist midway between Luther and Zwingli. He also believed in double predestination, the idea that God predestines souls to both heaven and hell. Calvinist churches were also typically less hierarchical than either Lutheran or Catholic churches, as Calvin rejected the idea that the bishop was a distinct office and instead entrusted church government to a group of elders. Calvin's theology and

---

[10] Bainton. Whether or not Luther actually said these famous words is a matter of dispute.

[11] "Estin" in Greek.

[12] Collinson, 77. In this case, it is important to note that Luther was arguing from a nominalist perspective, the late medieval philosophical school that held universal categories to be merely names that humans make up, a philosophical position that thereby torpedoes any efforts to make statements about the nature of God (or about the nature of anything for that matter).

form of Church government would eventually take hold in Switzerland, southern France, Scotland, the Netherlands, and colonial Massachusetts.[13]

The outlier in all of this controversy was England. England's reformation began with a crisis of conscience of a different form. In 1509, the English king, Henry VIII, married the widow of his dead brother, the Spanish princess Catherine of Aragon. To marry his brother's widow, Henry needed a papal dispensation, which the Pope granted. Though the marriage was not unhappy, Catherine repeatedly failed to produce a male heir, and by the 1520s, it had become fairly clear that she was never going to. The relatively devout Henry interpreted his wife's barren womb as a sign from God that the marriage was a terrible sin. As Henry's father had only ended a half century of civil war and disputed succession in 1485,[14] Henry was worried that the lack of a clear and legitimate heir would restart his country's civil war. To make matters worse, Henry was being seduced by the bewitching court lady, Anne Boleyn, whose conniving family was pressuring her into the king's bed—but only in exchange for a crown. Thus, Anne refused to simply become the king's mistress; she wasn't about to give Henry what he wanted until he divorced Catherine and married her. All of this presented a problem for both Henry and the Pope. Henry argued that the original dispensation had been invalid, and so the marriage should be annulled. The Pope determined it had been valid and thus, he could not separate what God had joined together. In the end, Henry decided to divorce Catherine, marry Anne, and get Parliament to name him head of the church in England by the Act of Supremacy (1534). The Pope, for his part, did not approve of any of this. In any case, Henry's marriage to Anne was a far sight more unhappy, as he would have her beheaded on trumped up charges of treason and incest in 1536.[15]

In his theology, Henry remained mainly Catholic, but he did take the opportunity to place an English-language Bible in every parish church, to dissolve England's monasteries, and to sell off the lands for a hefty

---

[13] Ibid., 87-122.

[14] The War of the Roses.

[15] J.J. Scarisbrick, *Henry VIII* (Berkeley: University of California Press, 1968).

profit.[16] Nor did Henry's death help to clarify England's religious situation. Henry was succeeded by his son, Edward, who was much more Protestant than his father; Edward was succeeded by his half-sister Mary, who was a devout Catholic. Mary was succeeded by her half-sister, Elizabeth, who was a Protestant. Thus, in the second half of the sixteenth century, England swung back and forth, now with Catholics in charge persecuting Protestants and now with Protestants in charge persecuting Catholics. A final settlement of the religious question was only reached during the reign of Elizabeth I, Henry's daughter with Anne Boleyn. Elizabeth's primary concern was the obedience of her subjects, but otherwise she chose not to "make windows into men's souls." Under Elizabeth, England settled in to a long period in which outward conformity to the Anglican Church hid a range of differing viewpoints; the Anglican Church was like a big tent under which a host of varying positions could find a home.[17] Many who could not or would not fit (like Puritans, Catholics, and Quakers) came to America to settle in Massachusetts, Maryland, and Pennsylvania, respectively. For the most part, however, the English avoided large-scale violence in the sixteenth century.

Meanwhile, European Catholics were trying to recover from the blow. By the 1540s, the Catholic Church had lost much of Europe. Two decades of negotiation had failed to produce agreement with the Protestants, and still, many of the abuses that had plagued the Catholic Church continued, which from the Catholic perspective only added fuel to the Protestant fire. In 1545, Catholic bishops from around Europe met in the Italian city of Trent at a general council. At Trent, the Catholic bishops responded to the Protestant challenge in dual ways: by reforming the church to clean up its abuses and by clarifying church teachings to distinguish them from the heresies of the Protestants.[18] From Trent on, the Catholic world would be militantly engaged and united.

---

[16] Richard Rex, *Henry VIII and the English Reformation* (London: Palgrave MacMillan, 2006), 83 and 45-54, respectively.

[17] Susan Doran, *Elizabeth I and Religion: 1558-1603* (London: Routledge, 1994).

[18] Ronnie Po-Chia Hsia, *The World of Catholic Renewal* (Cambridge: Cambridge University Press, 1999), 12.

The shock troops of militant Catholicism were undoubtedly the newly-formed Jesuit order, brainchild of the Spanish nobleman, Ignatius of Loyola. Like Luther, Loyola had not intended a religious profession. Rather, like most Spanish nobles, he had been destined for a career in the military. Fortunately for the Catholic Church, before his military career could really begin, he was struck by a cannonball that shattered one of his legs. While recovering, he asked to be brought the works of chivalry and knighthood that he had loved reading in his youth. No such luck. All that was available was *The Lives of the Saints*. Loyola read them instead and was inspired, setting out to outdo the saints by establishing an active religious order, who would preach the word of God amongst the Muslims in the Holy Land.[19] The Pope turned them against the Protestants in Europe instead. As a sort of training in Jesuit spirituality, Loyola wrote the *Spiritual Exercises*, a thirty day spiritual boot camp of solitude, silence, meditation, prayer, confession, and contrition. Following the lead of their founder, the Jesuits set their superior education, rigorous discipline, and intense spiritual training at the service of the Church, setting out to win souls for Catholicism in Europe and abroad. Jesuit schools sprang up all over Europe, and Jesuits made a point of offering the best education possible. They intentionally positioned their colleges to attract the children of European rulers, even the children of Protestant nobility. In addition to a top-notch education, these future rulers would get a healthy dose of Jesuit spiritual training.[20] Thus, within a few generations, the Jesuits had the ears of some of Europe's most powerful men.[21]

Catholic reform not only involved new orders, like the Jesuits, but also the reform of old orders, like the Carmelites. As Christendom drifted toward the Reformation, one of its biggest ailments was the growing cor-

---

[19] John W. O'Malley, *The First Jesuits* (Cambridge, MA: Harvard University Press, 1993), 23-27. It is worth noting the role that increased book production played in Loyola's story, for he would not have been able to read books in his recovery bed in an earlier time period.

[20] Marvin O'Connell, *The Counter-Reformation, 1560-1610* (New York: Harper, 1974), 214.

[21] Robert Bireley, *Religion and Politics in the Age of the Counterreformation: Emperor Ferdinand II, William Lamormaini, S.J. and the Formation of Imperial Policy* (Chapel Hill, N.C.: The University of North Carolina Press, 1981).

ruption in the monasteries, especially in convents. Much of this was due to the social position of women in early modern Europe, who had few options. Whereas poorer, unmarried women could work as prostitutes or spin yarn, only marriage or the convent was usually a suitable option for "honorable women." In the late fifteenth century, the marriage market exploded, and much like college tuition, the cost of dowries went through the roof.[22] As the price grew, families with more than one daughter grew increasingly likely to pool their dowry budget and bestow it all on the eldest, with the hopes that such a strategy would bring them a husband from the best possible family. This, however, left many younger daughters without many options. They couldn't get married, and they couldn't become prostitutes, so into the convent they went, whether they had a religious vocation or not. And thus, convents full of women who didn't particularly want to be there often became breeding grounds for all sorts of scandal.[23]

One such convent was home to one of the most remarkable women of the age: Saint Teresa of Avila. Though Teresa's convent was not particularly scandalous for the age, her life there was rather typical, meaning not very holy. Until the age of forty, Teresa enjoyed all the luxuries, recreations and social distinctions befitting her status as a child of the petty nobility, locked in the sort of general malaise and lack of spiritual fervor that marked most such convents. Around 1560, Teresa began having intense spiritual visions. Teresa herself was a mystic, a person who seeks a direct connection with God through the stages of purgation (ridding oneself of earthly desires); illumination (coming to knowledge of the divine through contemplation); and union (oneness with God).[24] Un-

---

[22] The dowry was a sum of money given to the bride by her family at the time of marriage. Though it technically remained the bride's property, it was under the control of her husband during the marriage. Also, like college tuition, families increasingly started saving up money for the dowry as soon as their daughters were born.

[23] Craig Monson, *Nuns Behaving Badly: Tales of Music, Magic, Art, and Arson in the Convents of Italy* (Chicago: University of Chicago Pres, 2010), 1-24.

[24] Arthur Devine, "State or Way," *The Catholic Encyclopedia*, vol 14 (New York: Appleton Company, 1912). Accessed June 5, 2014. www.newadvent.org/cathen/14254a.htm

nerved by her visions and dissatisfied with the ordinary convent life she was living, she attracted a small group of like-minded sisters to herself with the aim of returning the Carmelites to a strict observance of the ancient rule. As a sign of their devotion to God and to set them apart from more lax Carmelites, Teresa's sisters chose not to wear shoes, exchanging scandals for sandals and dedicating themselves to a life of prayer. Like almost all female monastics in the wake of Trent, the Carmelites were cloistered;[25] thus, whereas Ignatius of Loyola's Jesuits went to battle on the front lines of doctrinal controversy, Teresa's Carmelites did their battling within their walls, by praying for the salvation of souls.[26]

The most sinister aspect of Catholic reform was undoubtedly the dreaded Inquisition. Both the Papal Inquisition and Spanish Inquisition were courts entrusted with ensuring correct belief. Though they were not nearly as terrible as generations of bad press would suggest (even the Spanish Inquisition rarely ordered executions), they did engage in quite a lot of nasty behavior.[27] By forbidding certain books, utilizing torture, and infiltrating secret Protestant groups, the Inquisition kept Italy, Portugal and Spain Catholic, though at a tremendous cost to the culture of those countries, in which the rich, pre-reformation tradition of lay reading of the vernacular Bible was stamped out.[28] As a result, literacy rates in southern European countries took centuries to catch up to their Protestant neighbors.[29]

Though some Europeans were able to find a way to live with their religious differences, others could not, and before the Reformation was more than three decades old, the battle between Protestants and Catholics

---

[25] Cloistered normally meant that the nuns were not allowed to leave the convent.

[26] Jodi Bilinkoff, *The Avila of Saint Teresa* (Ithaca: Cornell University Press, 1989).

[27] Henry Kamen, *The Spanish Inquisition: An Historical Revision* 4th edition (New Haven, CT: Yale University Press, 2014), 254.

[28] Gigliola Fragnito, *Proibito Capire: La Chiesa e il volgare nella prima età moderna* (Bologna: Mulino, 2005).

[29] Keith Watson "Contrasting policies toward (mainly) Christian education in different contexts," in *Education and Religion: Global Pressures, Local Responses* ed. Keith Watson and William I. Ozane (London: Routledge, 2011), 42.

had already turned into a shooting match, which would break out in various forms until 1648, when Europe finally put an end to its most devastating religious conflict: The Thirty Years War (1618-1648). By that time, religious violence had touched almost every corner of the European West.

The idea of going to war over religion, especially amongst Christian religions whose founder told them to turn the other cheek, is difficult to understand. Historians are divided on why exactly Protestants and Catholics turned to violence. Some historians have suggested that religion was really a cover for political or economic disputes. Others have suggested that Europeans reacted violently towards rival Christian groups because they saw them as threatening to their own communities.[30] It is important to remember that for Catholics and Protestants alike, the beliefs of the other side were blasphemous. For strict Calvinists, the Eucharist and other Catholic doctrines, such as reverence for the saints, were idolatry, and risked provoking the wrath of God on the entire community. Thus, during the wars of religion, Calvinists provoked Catholics by pulling down the statues on Catholic churches and publically desecrating the consecrated host. For Catholics, who believed that the Eucharist was the body of Christ, this was the worst possible insult to God, nor did Catholics fail to commit atrocities of their own, for instance, by stuffing the crumbled-up pages of the Bible into the mouths of dead Protestants as a symbolic retort to the doctrine of *sola scriptura*.[31] In short, many early modern Christians overreacted to religious differences with fear and loathing and responded with a corresponding level of hysteria.

Yet, however much the Protestant and Catholic reformations differed, historians have recently begun to recognize how much they were alike as well.[32] In both cases, secular rulers gained new powers over local and national churches. In both cases, rulers used religious differences to cement political identities, a process that historians call confession-

---

[30] Mack Holt, "Putting Religion Back into the Wars of Religion," *French Historical Studies* 18 no. 2 (1993): 524-551.

[31] Natalie Zemon Davis, "The Rites of Violence: Religious Violence in Sixteenth-Century France," *Past and Present* 59 (1973): 53-91.

[32] Robert Bireley, *The Refashioning of Catholicism* (Washington D.C.: Catholic University of America Press, 1999).

alization. For instance, in the early modern period, Protestantism became part of the English national identity, and conversely Catholicism became part of what it meant to be Spanish or French. Finally, in both cases, secular rulers began to use religion to help them establish social discipline in areas which neither church nor state had been competent to exercise authority before.[33] Thus, Inquisition courts spent more time tracking down bigamists[34] than heretics, while Protestant church courts spent far more time as the referees of familial disputes than doctrinal ones. Perhaps the best symbol of social discipline is the work house, where people considered "undeserving poor" were taught the value of work ethic. In one such Dutch Calvinist version, the neer-do-well was locked in a room that contained nothing but a faucet and a pump. The work house authorities pumped in water through the faucet and began filling the room until the poor man found the work ethic to start cranking the pump. The lesson was obvious: learn to work or learn to swim. By turns cruel and effective, new institutions such as these helped to spark what one sociologist has called "a disciplinary revolution" in the European West.[35]

In summary, the Reformation began as a doctrinal dispute over indulgences but then expanded into a major disagreement about the nature of religious truth and the sources of religious authority. The ensuing controversies and religious violence led to a further splintering of opinions, generating a pluralism that remains with us today. The state benefitted from the controversy by submitting local and national churches to their own control and using them as agencies of social discipline.

---

[33] R. Po-Chia Hsia, *Social Disciplining in the Reformation: Central Europe, 1550-1750* (London: Routledge, 1989).

[34] Bigamists are people who had married more than once.

[35] Philip Gorski, *The Disciplinary Revolution: Calvinism and the Rise of the State in Early Modern Europe* (Chicago: University of Chicago Press, 2003).

Chapter Four:

The Scientific Revolution and The Birth of Modern Science

While the West was undergoing its religious revolutions, it was also creating the foundations of modern science. Here again, early modern peoples were looking back to their classical past, but in this case they were looking back to the past to fix a mistake, specifically Julius Caesar's mistake. Caesar's astronomers had made a slight error in calculation while reforming the calendar in 46 B.C. Before Caesar's reform, the Roman calendar had been a lunar calendar of 355 days, which could only be kept in phase with the solar year by the continuous tinkering of Roman priests, but as the priests were occasionally bribed to extend the year (and thus current office holders' terms in office) the calendar year drifted out of phase with the solar year. By 46 B.C., the Roman calendar was so wildly out of phase that the winter solstice was happening when the calendar said it was the middle of March.[1] Then, Caesar came to the rescue, using his dictatorial powers to establish a 365 day year with a leap

---

[1] William Dunstan, *Ancient Rome* (Plymouth: Rowman and Littlefield, 2011), 180.

day every four years, essentially the same calendar we use today.[2] This seemed to solve the problem, inasmuch as a priest could be bribed, but a calendar could not. Thus, Caesar had brought everything back into order—for a while, at least. Unfortunately, Caesar's astronomers had mistakenly calculated the solar year at exactly 365.25 days. It is actually more like 365.24 days. This means that to keep the calendar in phase with the solar year, three leap years need to be dropped every four hundred years. An error this small takes centuries to show up, so it wasn't until much later that people began to notice, but by the sixteenth century, the calendar was more than a week out-of-phase. Clearly, something needed to be done.

In 1514 Pope Leo X issued a call to European astronomers for help. One of the men who responded was a Polish astronomer, mathematician, and cathedral canon named Nicholas Copernicus.[3] Historians do not know exactly what Copernicus wrote back to the Pope, but before the end of his life, he would propose a wild idea about the cosmos. Greek astronomers knew that the planets were different than the rest of the stars; whereas most of the stars showed up in roughly the same place from night to night, the six planets seemed to wander all over the sky (planet from comes a Greek word that means wanderer). Aristotle had argued that the planets, including the sun and moon, were attached to crystal spheres that rotated around the earth in perfectly

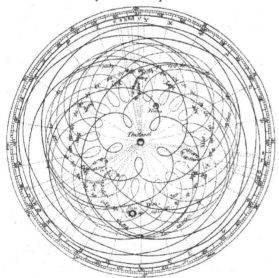

The Orbit of Venus with Epicycles, From "Astronomy," Encyclopedia Brittanica, 1777

---

[2] Suetonius, *The Twelve Caesars*, trans. Robert Graves (London: Penguin, 1979), 31.

[3] A canon is a priest in residence at a cathedral or a religious house.

circular orbits. Early astronomers, however, deduced that this model could not possibly make sense of where the planets actually showed up in their observations. The most authoritative astronomer of the ancient world, a man named Ptolemy, had begun to solve this problem. In the Ptolemaic system, the planets circled the earth but occasionally went on little detours called epicycles, in which they doubled back on their orbits (and sometimes even doubled back on the epicycle itself), adding little curly-cues to the orbits like the ones shown in the picture below. Aristotle's model was temporarily saved, but at the price of terrible complexity. Indeed, as the medieval Spanish King Alfonso sarcastically joked on the subject, "If God had asked me before he designed the universe, I would have recommended he try something simpler."[4]   Moreover, though Ptolemy's system worked tolerably well for many centuries, it was becoming ever more complex by the sixteenth century.[5] Copernicus thought that he could make everything simpler. By placing the sun at the center of the cosmos, he could do away with many of Ptolemy's epicycles, thereby drastically simplifying the picture of the universe.[6] This was thinking outside the box, and many European astronomers were sympathetic to the idea. However, Copernicus' big idea threatened many others.

No one was more frightened of the idea than rival Ptolemaic astronomers, who had spent their entire lives teaching the geocentric (earth-centered) view of the universe and were not about to let it go without a fight.[7] These people were not just being stubborn. Copernicus' theory was radical, and it took some time to adjust. In a manner of speaking, the heliocentric (sun-centered) view of the universe lifted the earth up into the heavens, where opponents of the Copernican system argued that it obviously did not belong. This was not the only objection. Whereas the earth was considered to be heavy, the stars were thought to be light. Whereas the earth was dark, the stars were bright. Whereas the earth was

[4] Jack Repchek, *Copernicus' Secret: How the Scientific Revolution Began* (New York: Simon and Schuster, 2007)15-16.

[5] Ibid., 15-16.

[6] Maria Boas, *The Scientific Renaissance*, (New York: Harper, 1962), 76-77.

[7] Stillman Drake, *Galileo* (New York: Oxford University Press, 1980), 38-52.

the realm of imperfect creatures, the heavens were the realm of perfection. How then could the earth be like the other celestial bodies? The
idea offended plain common sense.

The other attack was launched by biblical literalists, who claimed that
Copernicus' theory contradicted the Book of Joshua, where it is written:

> On the day the LORD gave the Amorites over to Israel, Joshua said to
> the LORD in the presence of Israel: 'Sun, stand still over Gibeon, and
> you, moon, over the Valley of Aijalon.' So the sun stood still, and the
> moon stopped, till the nation avenged itself on its enemies…The sun
> stopped in the middle of the sky and delayed going down about a full
> day. There has never been a day like it before or since, a day when the
> LORD listened to a human being. Surely the LORD was fighting for
> Israel![8]

Biblical literalists correctly saw that if the sun was the unmovable center
of the cosmos, it could not have stood still during the battle with the
Amorites. After lunch one day, Luther reportedly took the offensive, calling Copernicus a fool who wanted to turn the world upside down merely
for the sake of novelty. Luther proudly proclaimed, "Even in these things
that are thrown into disorder, I believe the Holy Scriptures, for Joshua
commanded the Sun to stand still and not the Earth."[9] Copernicus, then,
offended both common sense and *sola scriptura*. According to his critics,
either Copernicus was wrong, or the Bible was wrong.

One of the scientists of the next generation who thought that neither
the Bible nor Copernicus was wrong was an Italian named Galileo.
Galileo was unquestionably the finest scientific mind of his age, and in
addition to his genius, he had a trick up his sleeve to which Ptolemaic
astronomers had no answer: his telescope, which Galileo had built and
perfected himself around 1609. What Galileo saw through his telescope
would change our conception of the universe forever. One of the first
things he saw was a group of smaller stars that seemed to be orbiting the

---

[8] Joshua 10:12-14.

[9] Dava Sobel, *A More Perfect Heaven: How Copernicus Revolutionized the Cosmos*
(London: Bloomsbury, 2011), 178.

planet of Jupiter. Galileo called them the Medicean stars, after his patron, the Medici Grand Duke of Florence. These were the moons of Jupiter, which today we call Io, Europa, Ganymede, and Castillo. The discovery exposed a major flaw in Ptolemy's model, for Earth was clearly not the only center of rotation in the cosmos. Then Galileo turned his telescope on Venus and observed that Venus went through phases, much like our moon. The best explanation for this was that Venus was orbiting the sun. Here then, for the first time was evidence that suggested that the sun was the center of rotation. Finally, Galileo turned his telescope on the sun, and instead of finding the perfect celestial body that Aristotle had imagined, he found that the sun was full of spots. The sun, then, was not a perfect luminescent sphere, as Aristotle had thought. Galileo's telescope had proved Aristotle wrong.[10]

Though Galileo still could not prove the validity of the heliocentric model beyond a reasonable doubt, things were looking grim for Aristotle's vision of the universe. At stake, however, was more than just a vision of the universe; at stake was a battle for the future of scientific knowledge itself. Should scientists boldly reject the ancient Greek authorities to plumb the secrets of the universe themselves, aided only by mathematics and observation? Galileo said yes; others were not so sure, and to combat Galileo, they enlisted the help of his scriptural opponents. "Galileo," they charged, "is teaching outright heresy that flatly contradicts the plain sense of scripture." It was in response to such attacks that Galileo wrote to his patroness, Grand Duchess Christina of Tuscany in 1615, articulating why the Copernican theory did not necessarily contradict scripture. The pious Christina was apparently satisfied; Galileo's opponents in Rome were not.

In 1616, a panel of theologians condemned the heliocentric model of the universe as contrary to scripture. Galileo was warned not to uphold or defend Copernicus' theories. Faithful Catholic that he was, he fell silent on the issue for the next sixteen years. By 1632, however, he felt that he was in the clear. There was a different pope in Rome, Urban VIII, who was a friend to science and had publically stated that he did not

---

[10] Robin Briggs, *The Scientific Revolution of the Seventeeth Century* (New York: Harper and Row, 1969), 47-48.

support the decree of 1616. Moreover, Galileo thought he had new evidence for the Copernican theory from the motion of the tides. Thus, Galileo tried his hand at the Copernican theory again, this time in the form of a dialogue: a work that has subsequently come to be known as *A Dialogue Concerning the Two Chief World Systems*. Though Galileo would later argue that he was merely comparing the Copernican and Ptolemaic systems neutrally, the debater for the Copernican side clearly wins the argument against his Ptolemaic opponent, whom Galileo cheekily named *Simplicio*, Italian for idiot or fool.

Galileo probably would have gotten away even with this if it weren't for two things. First, he thought that he could propose Copernicus' theory as a theory, just so long as he wasn't defending it. He apparently thought making an argument in dialogue form would save him. "It wasn't me, it was just the characters in the dialogue," he could claim. However, someone had added a note into his Inquisition file that suggested that in 1616 Galileo had been told that he was not supposed to 'teach' Copernicanism at all. In other words, the Inquisition's files indicated that Galileo was supposed to remain completely silent about the whole business. Unfortunately, no one had bothered to tell him that.[11] Second, someone close to the papal court was whispering into the Pope's ear that Galileo had modeled the character Simplicio the fool on the Pope himself. The Pope, for obvious reasons, was furious.[12] In the end, the vote was 7-3; Galileo was found guilty of grave suspicion of heresy and sentenced to house arrest for the rest of his days. The Galileo Affair has become a touchstone for almost every other debate between science and religion to this day, which is exactly one of the things that Galileo had been attempting to avoid.[13]

However, the underlying debate between the Copernican and Aristotelian model of the universe concerned more than simply whether the sun went round the earth or the earth went round the sun: ancients and

---

[11] Drake, 66-68 and 73-79.

[12] James Reston Jr., *Galileo: A Life* (New York: Harper Collins, 2000), 274.

[13] Drake, 55-56. In 1992 St. John Paul II officially declared that Galileo was right. Modern papal writings (including *Humani Generis* by Pius XII [1950] and John Paul II's 1996 address to the Pontifical Academy of Sciences) have been careful to respect both the claims of faith and the claims of scientific reason.

moderns seemed to disagree about the very nature of the universe itself. Was the universe, as Aristotle seemed to suggest, like a living organism that propelled each of its parts towards some 'end' or *telos*? Or was the universe more like a machine, a divine cosmic clock that ticked away through eternity according to unchangeable laws? Should scientists probe the secrets of the universe as Galileo had done, by observation, experiment, and measurement, or should they take the word of Aristotle's own observations, which carried the weight of authority and custom on their side?

In the wake of Galileo's trial, one of his disciples, a man named Evangelista Torricelli, conducted a series of experiments with vacuum chambers that illustrated the stark differences of worldview. Ancient writers knew from their own observations that water would fill up a vacuum. Pump the air out of a tube, and water can rise into the empty space. This is, in essence, how every straw works. How, though, to explain why it happens? Aristotle had argued that the water filled the empty space because 'nature abhors a vacuum,' as if nature was a person with thoughts and feelings who could either like or abhor anything. Torricelli's experiments proved otherwise. He set out to understand why, pump as one might, water cannot be lifted higher than thirty-three feet. Hypothesizing that water in a suction pump was being pushed up the tube by the weight of the atmosphere, Torricelli surmised that water stopped rising in a vacuum when the weight of the water in the tube equaled the force of the atmosphere pressing down on it. To test his theory, he filled his tube with a denser liquid: mercury, which he knew was about 14 times as dense as water. If he was right, the weight of the atmosphere should hold the mercury approximately 1/14 as high as it held the water, or about two and half feet, which is exactly what it did. Almost by accident, Torricelli had invented the first barometer. (P.S. Don't play with mercury at home because it is highly poisonous). Thus, water did not rise in a vacuum chamber because 'nature abhors a vacuum,' but because it was being pressed upon by the weight of the atmosphere.[14] Indeed, the water was behaving according to mechanical

---

[14] Steve Shapin, *The Scientific Revolution* (Chicago: University of Chicago Press, 1996), 37-40.

laws, laws that could be proven by observation and then predicted and manipulated.

Another area in which scientific observation and experimentaton flourished in the seventeenth century was alchemy. Medieval scientists had practiced alchemy, but it grew in significance in the sixteenth and seventeenth centuries after renaissance humanists discovered the ancient texts of Hermes Trismegistus. Hermes' writings provided suggestions on how to exploit the hidden (and divine) powers of minerals, plants, planets, and other natural objects. In particular, alchemists searched for one magical substance, the philosopher's stone, which they believed transformed all less perfect substances into more perfect ones (e.g. base metals into gold) and potentially would heal all illnesses by creating the elixir of life. In laboratories, alchemists used furnaces, beakers, and tubes to run experiments that involved mixing and heating substances; simultaneously, their scientific work was infused with magical practices: reciting spells, incantations, prayers, and reading horoscopes. Although they may seem more like wizards than scientists to us, alchemists paved the way for modern chemistry and lab sciences, pioneering laboratory procedures and developing early theories of matter.

The final death blow was delivered to Aristotle's universe by a professor of mathematics at Cambridge University named Isaac Newton, whose wild unkempt hair and habit of muttering to himself at the lunch table made him the prototype of the kooky, genius academic. Newton was responsible for an almost embarrassing number of discoveries: he made important contributions to the science of optics, he improved upon Galileo's telescope, and he practically invented calculus from scratch.[15] On top of that, he was the greatest alchemist in Europe when such pursuits were still respectable, though practicing alchemy meant that Newton spent too much time playing with mercury, a habit that left him temporarily mad.

Nevertheless, his work in physics brought him immortality. Newton's great moment of insight came in a flash. While sitting in his garden one day, he saw an apple fall from a tree. He had been studying the

---

[15] Though Gottfried Leibniz invented calculus at almost the exact same time, and both men quarrelled bitterly about who had done it first.

motion of the moon, and in a moment, the idea came to him: what if the force that drew the apple to the ground was the same force that kept the moon in orbit around the earth? Here were the seeds of Newton's great discovery, which he called gravity. Newton would spend the next twenty years working out the mathematics behind gravity, although work on his greatest achievement, *Principia Mathematica*, only began in earnest in 1681, when he and his good friend Edmund Halley were stimulated by the appearance of a comet blazing in the night sky.

When Newton's *Principia* appeared in 1687, it was far more widely praised than read. Yet the scientific community immediately understood its importance; for Newton was able to describe the mathematical basis behind a whole range of observed motion. Why do objects accelerate towards earth? Gravity. Why do the planets orbit around the sun in an ellipse rather than a circle? Gravity. Why do the tides come in? Gravity. Why did Galileo's moons of Jupiter appear as they did? Gravity.[16] The theory, which in its barest essentials could be reduced to a simple mathematical formula, seemed to explain practically everything.

Newton had called his discoveries by the Latin word *lex*, or law. For Newton's discoveries, this made sense, since his laws were literally universal and uniform. As Newton showed, the universe behaved more like a clock, less like a person. So successful was Newton and so elegant and testable were Newton's theories that all the other sciences ended up with a bad case of "Newton envy." European philosophers of all kinds would try to formulate laws for everything: from the 'laws' that could guarantee moral behavior to universal 'laws' of human history. In some cases, the results were absurd. For instance, universal 'laws' were easy ways to justify racist and nationalist ideologies.[17] Still, in the hard sciences themselves, the results were spectacular. In the seventeenth-century Newton had gazed at the moon and wondered how it moved;

---

[16] James Gleick, *Isaac Newton* (New York: Vintage, 2003).

[17] Even when not utterly absurd, the language of the hard sciences crept into philosophy, politics, and literary criticism: keep this in mind when studying the Enlightenment. For instance, eighteenth-century literary critics often derided Shakespeare for not conforming his plays to the "laws" of tragedy and comedy.

before the millennium was out, science would use Newton's theories to land people on the moon itself.

In summary, the scientific revolution began because of problems with the calendar but eventually extended into a paradigm shift in the way that scientists conceived of the natural world, away from the conception of the cosmos as a divine animal and toward a mechanical view of the universe. The method scientists developed to study the natural world emphasized empirical observation, experiment, and mathematics. It is largely the same scientific method that we continue to use today.

Chapter Five:

Absolutism, Republicanism and State-Building

On a cold, January day in 1649, Charles Stuart, the one-time King of England and God's anointed monarch, climbed a scaffold in front of his own palace at Whitehall. He was wearing two shirts under his outer garments because he was worried that if he shivered from the cold, people would think that he was frightened.[1] On this day, it was more important than ever that he be seen as strong because by an act of the English Parliament, King Charles I of England was to die by beheading. To be fair, Charles had probably brought it on himself; he had spent most of the last decade locked in a bitter struggle for power with the English Parliament in a bloody civil war, and when he refused to acknowledge that he had obviously come out the loser, an exasperated Parliament finally sentenced him to die, charging him with the mildly ironic crime of treason. On that fateful day in January, Charles made a good show of bravery before the final blow was delivered—to the audible groans and gasps of spectators. Then, in reverence to the royal power, several of the onlookers rushed forward to dip their handkerchiefs in the royal blood.[2]

---

[1] Thomas Herbert, *Memoirs of the last years of the reign of King Charles I* (London: Nicol, 1815), 184-185.

[2] Graham Seel, *English Wars and Republic, 1637-1660* (Florence, KY: Routledge, 1999), 6064. Charles I was declared a saint by the Church of England

At issue in the contest was a central question of the early modern western world: who had authority in the state? Did the king alone have absolute power to live above the law and dictate the religion of an entire country, or was he limited by the consent of the people over whom he ruled? Before the executioner's axe severed head from body, Charles summed up the absolutist position aptly, "the liberty [of the people] consists in having government, those laws by which their life and their goods may be most their own. It is not for having a share in govern-ment...a subject and a sovereign are clean different things."[3] Parliament obviously disagreed and asked a related question instead: when a king's rule became tyrannical, did the people have the right to depose him? The English Civil War did not entirely solve the issue. After trying various forms of republicanism, the English restored the Stuart monarchy in 1660, but their tyranny and Catholic tendencies compelled the English Parlia-ment to chase them out again in 1688, in a revolt that was far less bloody and thus has come to be known as the Glorious Revolution. In 1688, the English settled on a mixed constitution, in which king and parliament cooperated in sharing power.

Out of the chaos of war and revolution emerged two of the most important political thinkers of the Modern West: Thomas Hobbes and John Locke. Hobbes had been born prematurely in 1588 as the Spanish Armada bore down on England, inaugurating a chaos that marked much of the rest of his life. Hobbes wisely chose to sit out the English Civil War, spending several years in self-exile in France while his countrymen back home hacked each other to pieces for lack of agreement on who held pol-itical sovereignty. His major political treatise, *Leviathan*, basically solved that problem by handing over absolute authority to the government. In theory, Hobbes preferred that this government be an absolute monarchy,

---

in 1662 and his feast was celebrated on January 30 of the Anglican Kalendar until 1859. Some members of the Anglican Communion (Episcopalians) still revere Charles I as a saint, calling him 'St. Charles, King and Martyr'.

[3] Cfr. C.V. Wedgewood, *A King Condemned: The Trial and Execution of Charles I* (London: Tauris Parke, 2011), 191.

but in practice, he was ready to swear allegiance to any *status quo*, so long as it prevented the chaos of civil war.[4]

Locke responded quite differently to the English Civil War. Though the king was beheaded just down the block from the young Locke's school, Locke consistently maintained a people's right to annul the contract made between king and subjects and depose their monarch. His *Second Treatise of Civil Government* is probably the most influential political work of the early modern period, as it describes the way in which people are naturally endowed with certain rights, such as life, liberty, and property, and how they maintain those natural rights when they enter into the contract of society. Locke's ideas echoed through the ages, most importantly into the American Revolution. Indeed, if Thomas Jefferson had drafted the Declaration of Independence for a political science class at the Mount, his professor probably would have turned him over to the dean for plagiarizing John Locke.

There was, however, more going on in these political debates than meets the eye. In some ways, early modern political thinkers, both republican and monarchist, had to respond to the major political development of the age: the rise of powerful governments and centralized nation-states. By the word state, historians are typically referring to rationalized and bureaucratic forms of governance with a monopoly on the use of violent coercion, as well as the power to tax, mint coins, make laws, and declare war. Governments that carried out these functions certainly existed before the seventeenth century, but they grew increasingly powerful and centralized in the early modern period. By the end of the eighteenth century, these powerful new states became linked to nations, by which historians generally mean a group of people who are bonded by a common identity centering on a shared sense of language, culture, and history. National communities were quite different than most premodern communities because unlike villages, for instance, they were composed mainly of people who had never met each other face-to-face;

---

[4] R.E.R. Bunce and John Meadowcroft, *Major Conservative and Libertarian Thinkers: Thomas Hobbes* (London: Continuum, 2009), 1-11.

because of this, social scientists call them "imagined communities."[5] Indeed, French national identity had to be practically invented in the French Revolution since only a third of the country even spoke French. Yet, so pervasive and normal has the nation-state become that regions where the nation and the state do not perfectly match up frequently become flashpoints for violence (think, for instance, of Israel and Palestine).

Centralizing governments were responding to two general crises of the seventeenth century: an increase in poverty due to climate change and the advent of gunpowder warfare. The first issue could hardly be helped, as it concerned a temporary lull in the radiation coming from the sun, and not even God's anointed monarchs could compel the sun to shine any brighter. Indeed, seventeenth-century astronomers looking through their telescopes noticed fewer and fewer of Galileo's sunspots, but what they could not have known was what the lack of sunspots meant for Earth's climate. Fewer sunspots mean less solar radiation; less radiation means lower seasonal temperatures (which tree-ring analysis has confirmed did occur in the seventeenth century). Lower temperatures cause shorter growing seasons and a reduction in the maximum altitude at which crops can be grown. All of this meant that in the seventeenth century, Europeans found it harder to grow enough food to feed the largest population the world had yet seen.[6]

The effects spawned several crises in the cities, where the swelling numbers of poor grew increasingly loud, organized, and militant. Little surprise, then, that the age was marked by frequent local revolts breaking out all over Europe. Meanwhile, crowded cities gave rise to Europe's first urban criminal networks.[7] While the poor clamored for relief, the wealthy grew increasingly worried. By this time, the state was really the only institution capable of restoring order, but first it had to rationalize and organize poor relief, separating out the truly needy from the able-bodied.

---

[5] Benedict Anderson, *Imagined Communities: Reflections on the Origins and Spread of Nationalism* (New York: Verso, 1997).

[6] Geoffrey Parker, *Europe in Crisis: 1598-1648* (Ithaca: Cornell University Press, 1979), 1-28.

[7] Parker, *Europe in Crisis*, 28-36.

This meant a total reformation in the way that European society took care of its poor. In the Middle Ages, beggars might be frequently seen sitting on the steps of the church door, begging for alms from passers-by. Pious churchgoers were encouraged to see the poor as an image of Christ, and to give them aid in order to win salvation by good works. However, in the early modern period, the rapid increase in poor made this system both dangerous and ineffective, so by the end of the seventeenth century, most states no longer allowed the poor to beg for their daily bread on the streets;[8] instead, the poor were increasingly confined in large, miserable, government-run institutions such as the orphanage, the work house, the hospital, the insane asylum, and the prison. All of this required funds, increasingly raised in the form of compulsory taxation. No longer were people encouraged to give money to the poor to earn salvation; they paid taxes instead. This also meant cities and states had to expand their capacities for organization and bureaucracy;[9] indeed, they had to invent many of the functions that we think of as central to governance.

The second challenge facing centralizing states was the rise of gunpowder warfare. Europeans had used gunpowder weapons on the battlefield since the fourteenth century; however, the earliest handheld weapons took several minutes to reload and used shot that bounced around like a knuckleball as soon as it exited the barrel.[10] No sane group of people were likely to face down a cavalry charge armed only with these early gunpowder weapons. However, in the sixteenth and seventeenth centuries, this began to change. The first development involved cannons. In the centuries-long competition between artillery and castle walls, castle walls had long had the upper hand. Throwing mechanisms such as catapults and trebuchets had long reloading times and were difficult to construct. Thus, military engineers built castle walls very tall, so as to prevent invading armies from using ladders to climb over them. However, for accurate cannons, tall walls were no more than a really nice

---

[8] Thomas Max Safley, *Reformation of Charity: The Secular and the Religious in Early Modern Poor Relief* (Leiden: Brill, 2003).

[9] Robert Jütte, *Poverty and Deviance in Early Modern Europe* (Cambridge: Cambridge University Press, 1994).

[10] Parker, *The Military Revolution*, 17.

target: cannons could reduce castle walls to rubble within a few hours. Thus, European states had to rethink castle defense. Military engineers began constructing star-shaped fortresses that were short and could withstand cannon fire. They added fortifications called bastions that jutted out from the corners of the fort. In the bastions, they placed their own gunpowder artillery; that way, if an invading army attempted to scale the walls, the artillery in the forward towers would have a perfect line of sight to pick them off. Of course, this meant that every castle in Europe needed to be rebuilt, which meant stunning increases in the cost of warfare.

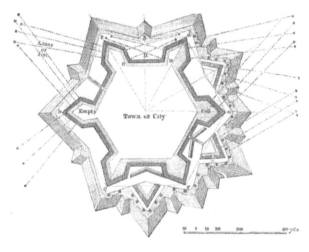

Star Style Fort
From John Hyde, *Elementary Principles of Fortfication*, 1860

The new fortresses had another effect on the cost of warfare. Because putting artillery in a fortress made it almost impossible to take by storm, the only way to take cities defended by the new style of fortress was by siege; armies either had to sit down and starve the population out or very slowly advance their trenches until they were close enough to bombard the fortress at close range.

Over the course of the seventeenth century, with wars raging in all corners of Europe, sieges got longer and longer. For instance, in the seventeenth century the siege of Oostende in the Netherlands lasted for almost three straight years! This also meant larger armies, which had to be kept in the field to defend and besiege cities; for instance, in 1629 alone, the Dutch army almost doubled, from roughly 70,000 men in arms to 128,000. All of this sent the cost of warfare through the roof.[11]

---

[11] Ibid., 1-14.

Moreover, by the middle of the seventeenth century, European generals had figured out how to use guns effectively on the battlefield. Rather than just order their musket men to shoot haphazardly into a cavalry charge, generals began deploying their gunpowder artillery with three tactical maneuvers: the *tercio* (in which groups of musket men were interspersed with pike men who could stave off a cavalry charge), the volley-fire (in which a group of musket men would fire in unison so as to keep up a constant discharge), and the countermarch (in which the first line of musket men would retreat to the back of their row and reload while new lines came to the front to volley fire into the cavalry charge). All of these had devastating effects on cavalry, but all of these were expensive. A group of musket men needed to function as a unit; they all needed the same type of weapons and equipment, and they needed time to practice and drill. All of this meant large, professional, costly standing armies.[12]

Between poor relief and gunpowder warfare, seventeenth-century governments had to meet challenges they had never faced before. In the first place, they needed revenue, which meant taxation. This was a big change from the Middle Ages, when kings possessed surprisingly limited abilities to tax their subjects. For instance, between 1497 and 1635, the tax revenues of the French crown increased from 3.5 million *livres* to 56 million *livres*: an increase of almost a thousand percent![13] How to raise these revenues? The seventeenth century saw the development of some of the Modern West's least popular institutions: the professional tax collector and the consolidated public debt.[14]

New taxes also meant new struggles for power. The winners of these power struggles differed from place to place. In the battle for control of taxation in England, the monarchy was the loser and parliament the winner. In Poland, for instance, the monarchy was a loser, but landed aristocrats the winner. In France, however, the opposite was true; the

---

[12] Ibid., 18-25.

[13] Richard Bonney, *The Dynastic States* (Oxford: Oxford University Press, 1991), 352-353.

[14] Ibid., 355-356.

monarchy won big, in the process creating the most absolute state that had yet existed in Europe.

The accomplishment of this was primarily due to the genius of one man: the French King Louis XIV. Indeed, in 1648, the year before King Charles I of England was beheaded, it almost looked as if France might go the way of England. Two of Louis' recent predecessors had been felled by assassins' daggers. France had just ended the expensive and disastrous Thirty Years War, and nobles and commoners alike were up in arms over taxation, which had nearly quadrupled in the previous decade.[15] Bands of armed men roamed Paris, slinging rocks into the windows of government officials and even breaking into Louis' bedchamber, where the twelve-year old king pretended to be asleep until the mob left him alone.[16] Louis spent the next few years as the plaything of various noble factions who cynically used this uprising, known as the *Fronde*, to jockey for political power. The whole experience left Louis deeply embarrassed and determined never to be so powerless again.[17]

When Louis took control of his own government in 1661, he took his vengeance by completely stripping the nobility of their traditional power. Louis denied that his own power was in anyway derived from the consent of the people or nobility; in Louis' France, the king's power came directly from God, and thus he had to answer to nobody but his conscience.[18] At least in theory, Louis did not share power, a feeling that he pithily summed up with his famous assertion that he was the state. "The state," he said, "I am the state (*L'état, c'est moi.*)" He ruled without the consent of France's representative body, the Estates General, and in pursuit of absolute power, he placed most of the real work of governance in the hands of people he trusted, men whom he had raised from the dust and who relied completely on him for their power.

---

[15] Roger Price, *A Concise History of France* (Cambridge: Cambridge University Press, 1993), 54.

[16] Walter Fitz-Patrick, *The Great Condé and the Period of the Fronde: An historical sketch,* vol. 2 (London: Newby, 1873), 122.

[17] J.H. Shennan, *Louis XIV* (London: Routledge, 2005), 11.

[18] Jacques-Bénigne Bossuet, *Politics Drawn from Holy Scripture*, ed. Patrick Riley (Cambridge: Cambridge University Press, 1990).

To keep the nobility under his thumb, he required their attendance at his luxurious palace at Versailles. He enticed them there with jobs and entertainment and surrounded them with luxury and with images of his own grandeur. The splendor of Versailles was legendary, as nobles attended a non-stop round of parties and festivities. These parties could last for days, as courtiers went from one entertainment to another: from Lully's ballets, to Moliere's plays, to games, parades, dinners, and fireworks.[19] All of this luxury was not without purpose. Louis knew that if his nobility was stuck attending parties at Versailles, they could not be out plotting another *Fronde*. Moreover, at Versailles, he could set them against each other and make them all compete for his favor. To that end, Louis made it an honor for nobles to be selected to do everything from putting on his shirt to holding his chamber pot. If a noble was exceptionally lucky, he might be allowed to watch the king eat or to wear a hat at court.[20] Louis invented thousands of petty rules and thousands of ridiculous honors for which he made nobles compete. As the nobility conformed to life at Versailles, they learned absolute obedience. In this way, Louis kept his nobles powerless; for himself, he held a power that he imagined to be absolute, and was probably closer to it than any king had ever had.

In summation. The seventeenth century was a period of general crisis marked by poor weather, increased poverty, and continuous warfare, which was made more expensive because of gunpowder weapons. Emerging nation-states responded by centralizing authority and increasing their taxing and governing competencies. In France, this meant the emergence of an absolute monarchy; in other places, like England, it led to constitutionalism and expanded powers for representative institutions like Parliament.

---

[19] Georgia Cowart, *The Triumph of Pleasures: Louis XIV and the Politics of Spectacle* (Chicago: University of Chicago Press, 2014), 166-167.

[20] Edward Muir, *Ritual in Early Modern Europe*, (Cambridge: Cambridge University Press, 1997), 256-257.

Chapter Six:

Reason and Authority in the Enlightenment

Like the Renaissance, the eighteenth-century philosophical movement known as the Enlightenment profits from really excellent branding, much better than say, the Middle Ages, or even worse, the Dark Ages. But what is Enlightenment? That is a question that was asked before the age was even over and answered most famously by the German philosopher Immanuel Kant: "Enlightenment," he claimed, "is man's emancipation from his own self-imposed intellectual immaturity. Intellectual immaturity is the inability to follow your own reason without the guidance of another…Have the courage to use your own reason! That is the motto of the Enlightenment."[1]

Reason may have been the motto of the Enlightenment, but it is unfair to suggest that the Enlightenment suddenly discovered reason where nothing but ignorance and stupidity existed before. It was the Greeks, after all, who had discovered philosophy in the first place, and it is the Middle Ages, not the Enlightenment, that invented the university. Thus, it was really the other half of Kant's statement that marked the Enlightenment as something new: the separation of reason from the guidance of authority. Hitherto, it had been assumed that individuals produced knowledge within a community, a community that quite democratically included the opinions of the dead; even Newton said that

---

[1] Immanuel Kant, "*Was ist Aufklarung*," Accessed, May 5, 2014, http://www.unipotsdam.de/u/philosophie/texte/kant/aufklaer.html, translation mine.

he only saw farther because he had stood on the shoulders of giants. Enlightenment thinkers of the eighteenth century were far more likely to think of reason as a practice that was set against authority, and in this they found a new sense of freedom.

Why, then, did this rejection of authority occur in the eighteenth century? Part of the answer is to be found in a fundamental shift in Western Europe's underlying social structure, like massive tectonic plates shifting deep and unseen beneath the earth but making the surface quake and rumble. In brief, the Enlightenment was linked to the growth of cities and the appearance of a new, literate, urban-dwelling class: the bourgeoisie. Unlike their peasant predecessors, the bourgeoisie read avidly, talked science and politics, and rejected much of the status quo, including the division of society into the three traditional medieval orders (those who fought, those who prayed, and those who worked). These men (and sometimes women) formed the Republic of Letters, an international community that exchanged their ideas formally and informally through letters, manuscripts, books, and literary productions. Membership for this republic was the use of reason, not social class or national identity, and its citizens participated in a public sphere of debate and discussion that often contested the more elite and closed culture of monarchy.[2] In many ways, then, the Enlightenment is the story of a new middle class, who grew along with cities, but whose ideas were shared internationally.

Though the story of the Enlightenment may end in the city, it does not begin there. Cities, after all, can only house as many people as society can feed. Thus, like all periods of urbanization, the Enlightenment began on the land, with the agricultural revolution of the late seventeenth and early eighteenth centuries. Between 1700 and 1800, greater agricultural productivity led to an almost twenty-five percent increase in population. In some places, notably France and England, this meant many more people moving to cities, which grew apace as hubs of global trade and

---

[2] See Dena Goodman, *The Republic of Letters: A Cultural History of the French Enlightenment* (Ithaca: Cornell University Press, 1994).

administrative centers for nation-states. In brief, cities like London and Paris got really, really big.[3]

But this increasingly urban population could only survive because it was fed a steady diet of newfangled crops like rice, tomatoes, and especially potatoes, all of which had technically crossed the pond from America or Asia a century earlier but which Europeans had only finally gotten around to growing in the late seventeenth century.[4] The delay was caused by a number of things, from picky palates (Europeans initially thought potatoes were sticky and disgusting) to silly prejudices (they also refused to eat potatoes because they thought potatoes caused excessive farting). Nevertheless, beggars cannot be choosers; eventually, even the pickiest eaters ended up choosing potatoes over starvation. Once that leap had been made, Europeans discovered that they had stumbled upon some tremendously useful crops. Potatoes, for instance, could feed twice as many people as wheat, and though marauding armies could trample a field of wheat to oblivion, the same army would leave a field of potatoes (which grow underground) relatively untouched.[5] In many ways, the potato was the food of Enlightenment.

As potatoes fed the growth of cities, new social classes came to the fore. Whereas the economic structure of the Middle Ages encouraged warfare, the great movements of the Early Modern Age (state-building, urbanization, global trade, and industrialization) increasingly rewarded those who could think: doctors, lawyers, teachers, bureaucrats, engineers, merchants and business people. This was a new breed of people; unlike peasants, the bourgeoisie could read and had both the leisure time and extra money to spend on learning. For the first time in history then, large groups of people were reading newspapers, journals, political pamphlets, and philosophical works. And they read differently than people had in the past. The literate men and women of an earlier age often read the same book, usually the Bible, over and over again—slowly, carefully,

---

[3] Vincent Milliot, "City: Urbanization," *Encyclopedia of the Enlightenment*, ed. Michael Delon (New York: Routledge, 2013).

[4] Gérar Béaur, "Agriculture: Agronomy," *Encyclopedia of the Enlightenment*, ed. Michael Delon (New York: Routledge, 2013).

[5] Fernand Braudel, *Civilization and Capitalism: The Structures of Everyday Life, 15th-18th Century* (New York: Harper and Row, 1979), 163-172.

and aloud to an audience. Access to cheaper, mechanically-produced print books and the development of the lending library meant that the bourgeoisie could read a much wider range of literature. They read more, they read more quickly, and they read silently to themselves, absorbing their knowledge as individuals rather than as part of a community. Above all else, they read novels, which replaced religious literature as the most popular genre, a status that the novel has never lost. Little wonder then, that many Enlightenment philosophers spun their philosophical ideas and social satires into fictional narratives,[6] like the international bestseller *Candide* by the Frenchman Voltaire. Indeed, the reading culture that developed during the Enlightenment is the reading culture that largely still exists today.

This new intellectual culture centered on new, more egalitarian spaces of sociability, such as the coffee house, the salon, and the Masonic lodge. Coffee was one of those consumer goods (Europe had only gotten it from the Turks in the 1600s) that Europeans began drinking in the eighteenth century as if it were a drug, even though contemporaries often complained that it tasted like excrement or soot.[7] Nevertheless, by 1714, there were five hundred coffee houses in London alone. For just a penny, a man could get his caffeine fix, read a newspaper, discuss the local news, get tips on the latest stocks, and engage in spirited debate with fellow coffee-drinkers about politics, science, or literature.[8] According to one observer, the coffee house was "the seat of English liberty."[9] In France, the coffee house found its counterpart in salons, in which wealthy aristocratic women gathered poets, playwrights and intellectuals around themselves to share Enlightenment ideas.[10] The urban middle class could also join one of Europe's many new Masonic lodges, which were sprouting up like dandelions all over European cities in the eighteenth century.

---

[6] Dorinda Outram, *The Enlightenment* (Cambridge: Cambridge University Press, 1997), 18-21.

[7] Brian William Cowan, *Social Life of Coffee: The Emergence of the British Coffeehouse* (New Haven, CT: Yale University Press, 2005), 5 and 131.

[8] Roy Porter, *London: A Social History* (Cambridge, MA: Harvard University Press, 2001), 170-171.

[9] Cfr. Ibid., 171.

[10] Outram, 91-93.

Though deeply secretive, Masonic societies were relatively egalitarian clubs, dedicated to the enlightenment principles of equality, liberty, and brotherhood, though by equality and brotherhood, they meant equality for brothers only since very few Masonic lodges were open to women.[11] In Freemasonry then, the breakdown of the old medieval orders was already foreshadowed, and the group numbered among its members many of the age's most revolutionary minds, like Voltaire, Jean-Jacques Rousseau, Alexander Pope, Jonathan Swift, James Watt, Mozart, Beethoven, Benjamin Franklin, and George Washington.

In the coffee house, the salon, and the Masonic lodge, Enlightenment thinkers discovered a new self-confidence, a belief in the power of reason liberated from authority. Of course, with everyone using their own reason, there was plenty of disagreement, and there is very little, if anything, that all enlightenment thinkers agreed upon. This can be seen in the great *Encyclopédie* project undertaken by Denis Diderot and Jean Le Rond d'Alembert, which collected 60,000 articles and 2,885 illustrations by 140 authors, across 28 volumes, in an attempt to compile, organize, and classify all human knowledge. The *Encyclopédie* billed itself as a universal source of academic learning for the good of all humanity — and indeed, it sold copies far across Europe and even to Thomas Jefferson and Benjamin Franklin in America; yet, its 60,000 articles were riddled with disagreement over the very definition of humanity, gender, philosophy, and politics. For example, Jaucourt's article on wives (*femme*) argued that natural reason supported the equality of the sexes in marriage, for he described women as equal and potentially even superior to men in intellect and judgment; Desmahis' article on the same topic, however,

---

[11] James Melton Van Horn, *The Rise of the Public in Enlightenment Europe* (Cambridge: Cambridge University Press, 2001), 252-264. While Masonic mythology places their founding in ancient Egypt, with King Solomon and the Knights Templar as Masonic successors to esoteric knowledge, they are actually a modern institution, far less mystical than Hollywood would have us believe. The fact that the Freemasons co-opted pre-modern symbolism (either from Antiquity or the Middle Ages), however, is quite telling: in the eighteenth century, even new organizations had to invent ancient histories for themselves. Reason was not quite freed from authority yet.

argued vehemently that women were incapable of equality with male partners due to natural female vices, weaknesses, and inferior minds.

No odd couple represent the pluralism of the Enlightenment, in temperament and philosophy, more than Voltaire and Rousseau. A suave, witty, and cultured man, Voltaire had been born to a middle-class family and eventually achieved fame as a popular playwright, philosopher, and author of the international bestseller *Candide*. Although he was chased out of several countries for his biting pen and unorthodox political views, he still managed to hobnob with kings and princes. By comparison with other enlightenment thinkers, Voltaire was politically conservative; for instance, he did not hesitate to offer his pen to the King of Prussia in exchange for safety and a stipend. On religious matters, though, the Jesuit-educated Voltaire was fanatically anti-Christian, adopting deism as a substitute religion, embracing hedonism as a substitute life plan, and finding God in "a fine bottle of wine and the kiss of a pretty girl." His targets were many, but he spent most of his biting wit in a series of devastating critiques of religion.[12]

On the other end of the political spectrum was the younger Rousseau. Having run away from his middle-class Genevan life at the age of 15, an aimless young Rousseau had been taken in by an aristocratic cougar named Madame de Warens, who had a habit of converting young Protestants to Catholicism and then seducing them into her bed. With the help of her Jesuit accomplices, under whose influence Rousseau fell, the impressionable Genevan runaway took the bait, converting for a time to Catholicism and falling obsessively in love with Warens, whom he somewhat disgustingly referred to as Mama. Unlike Voltaire, Rousseau was shy and awkward. He quarreled with almost all his friends, whom he constantly thought were plotting to get him.[13] Nevertheless, he was a brilliant author. His *Discourse on Inequality* was a stinging indictment of social inequality, which Rousseau thought had appeared with civilization and property. In this work, Rousseau argued that human nature is essentially good but becomes corrupted by entering into a society

---

[12] Wayne Andrews, *Voltaire* (New York: New Directions, 1981).

[13] Leo Damrosch, *Jean-Jacques Rousseau: Restless Genius* (New York: Mariners, 2007).

marked by property relations.[14] Like his near contemporary Thomas Jefferson, he was also a man of deep contradictions. In 1762, Rousseau wrote a long book describing the ideal raising of a child; yet his own mistress gave birth to five children, each of whom he deposited in the orphanage.[15]

Rousseau and Voltaire both agreed that they hated Catholicism and Catholic priests, but beyond that, they agreed on little else and so quarreled bitterly. For instance, the wealthy Voltaire had very little patience for Rousseau's attacks on private property. When Rousseau sent Voltaire a copy of his *Discourse on Inequality*, Voltaire wise-cracked, "I have received your new book against the human race, and thank you for it. Never was such a cleverness used in the design of making us all stupid. One longs, in reading your book, to walk on all fours. But as I have lost that habit for more than sixty years, I feel unhappily the impossibility of resuming it."[16] On the publication of Rousseau's deeply republican work *The Social Contract*, the monarchist Voltaire wrote, "They have burned his book here in Geneva. Burning it must have been almost as boring as reading it."[17] For his part, the less witty and more emotional Rousseau shot back to Voltaire, "I don't like you at all…You have done me all the harm that could hurt me the most. You have gotten me chased out of Geneva…and you have alienated my fellow citizens from me. Finally, I hate you."[18]

Enlightenment debates were more than just personal, however. Individual reason often meant endless disagreement. Though most Enlightenment thinkers admired the new science, resented the privilege of the nobility, and hated Christianity, the rest was up for grabs. Though the Italian reformer Cesare Beccaria argued against the death penalty;[19] the French revolutionary Maximillian Robespierre sent thousands to the

---

[14] Jean-Jacques Rousseau, *Discourse on Inequality*, trans. Maurice Cranston (London: Penguin, 1984).

[15] Damrosch, 191-193. On the other hand, Rousseau's parenting advice guide, *Emile*, did inspire the first kindergartens.

[16] Cfr. Andrews, 74.

[17] Ibid., 89.

[18] Ibid., 102.

[19] Cesare Beccaria, *On Crimes and Punishments*, ed. Adolph Caso (Boston, MA: International Pocket Library), 62-70.

guillotine. While the Marquis de Condorcet believed that in time, even the most difficult scientific concepts would be made easy for anyone to understand;[20] the Scotsman David Hume argued that nobody could ever really be sure of the causes of anything at all.[21] The corpuscularians located existence in tiny indivisible material elements; immaterialists believed that matter did not even really exist.[22] And so it went. Some Enlightenment thinkers were deists, others pantheists.[23] Some were abolitionists; others were slave-owners. Some were republicans; others, like Joseph II, were actually monarchs themselves. The disagreements never ended.

Enlightenment thinkers couldn't really even agree on what they meant by the word reason. For Descartes, who deeply mistrusted his senses (on the off chance that some evil genius was tricking him into thinking that he actually had a body), the only sure way to acquire knowledge was the use of pure, abstract reasoning, relying as little as possible on sense experience, a doctrine that came to be known as rationalism.[24] For John Locke, however, Descartes' ideas were utter nonsense. He argued that reason was entirely dependent on sense experience; there was simply no escaping it. In his 1690 *Essay Concerning Human Understanding*, Locke argued that at birth people were a blank slate, a *tabula rasa* without any innate ideas. As babies, we start with nothing but sensations: hot, cold, pain, light. All of our ideas and our knowledge are only gradually produced by these sense experiences (a doctrine which came to be known as empiricism). From this, we progress to developing lang-

---

[20] Marquis de Condorcet, *The Future Progress of the Human Mind*. http://www.fordham.edu/halsall/mod/condorcet-progress.asp accessed May 6, 2014.

[21] David Hume, *On Human Nature and the Understanding*, ed. Anthony Flew (New York: Collier, 1962), 47-91.

[22] Jasper Reid, "Immaterialism," in *The Routledge Companion to Eighteenth-Century Philosophy*, ed. Aaron Garrett (London: Routledge, 2014), 120-125.

[23] Pantheism is, very simply speaking, the idea that God and nature are the same thing.

[24] Rene Descartes, "Meditations on First Philosophy," in *The Essential Descartes*, eds. Margaret D. Wilson and Robert Paul Wolff, trans. Elizabeth S. Haldane and T.R.T. Ross (New York: Meridian, 1993), 169-170.

uage and from there, ideas about morality and nature.[25] Thus, Locke and Descartes profoundly disagreed over what the use of reason should entail. How then do we know what we know? Do we really even know what we know? Who knows? Modern philosophers are still divided over these issues.

Nevertheless, none of these disagreements seemed to temper the Enlightenment's enthusiasm for reason. As Voltaire wrote:

> Wretched human beings, whether you wear green robes, turbans, black robes or surplices…never seek to use authority where it is only a question of reason. You have been spoken to a hundred times of the insolent absurdity with which you condemned Galileo, and I will speak to you for the hundred and first…Would that there might be engraved on the door of the Inquisition, "Here seven cardinals had the finest thinker of Italy thrown into prison at the age of seventy… because they were ignorant."[26]

Voltaire's attack was not so much on the wearing of many-colored robes as it was on the authorities who wore them. For Voltaire then, enlightenment really did mean reason against authority.

In summary, the Enlightenment was a philosophical movement that stressed the use of individual reason over and against institutional authorities. In this, it gave rise to thousands of disagreements and helped create the pluralistic society in which we live today. It was primarily an urban movement, stimulated by urbanization and the ensuing literate, intellectual, bourgeois culture of city life.

---

[25] John Locke, *An Essay Concerning Human Understanding* (London: Tegg, 1836).

[26] Voltaire, "Philosophical Dictionary," in *The Essential Voltaire* (London: Penguin, 1977), 77.

Chapter Seven:

The French Revolution and Napoleon

In 1754, a young British lieutenant named George Washington marched a Virginia militia into the forests of what is now Western Pennsylvania, an area which at that time lay in French North American territory. After a brief skirmish between the Virginians and the French, in which prisoners were taken, one of Washington's native allies took the initiative to punish the French on his own, bashing an unlucky Frenchman's skull in with a tomahawk and bathing his hands in the dead man's brains.[1] It could not have been clear to Washington at the time, but these actions in the remote forests of North America would not only set off a global war between the French and the British, but also set in motion an economic crisis in France that would eventually help to bring about the French Revolution, a movement that swept away the French monarchy and much of the old order with it.

The ensuing war, known in America as the French and Indian War, was waged on a truly global scale, and though the French sunk a load of treasure into the conflict, they eventually lost. Between this war and their intervention in the American Revolution, the French ran up a debt that was more than the French taxation system could bear, especially since the whole rickety structure was a highly regressive system, whereby the poor

---

[1] Fred Anderson, *Crucible of War: The Seven Years War and the Fate of Empire in British North America* (New York: Vintage, 2001), 55-57.

(who could least afford to pay) contributed the most, while the nobility (who could most afford to pay) contributed very little.[2]

By 1787, it was clear that the French government could no longer pay its bills and that King Louis XVI had no choice but to reform the government and raise new taxes. But when Louis tried to force the *parlement* of Paris into registering a new set of taxes, he so offended its members that they flatly refused, insisting that the king get the permission of the Estates General, a representative body that the absolutist French kings had not bothered calling for over a hundred years. In the intervening century, French society had changed. For one thing, the French Enlightenment had made many people more mistrustful of traditional authorities than they had ever been. Moreover, gunpowder and absolutism had turned the traditional nobility into a largely useless, vampire class, living absurdly lavish lives while they sucked the lifeblood from the body politic. Perhaps the most important change occurred in the Third Estate (those who worked). Urbanization, trade, and professionalization had made fortunes for more than a million new bourgeoisie in the eighteenth century; thus, as a group the bourgeoisie had come to exercise considerable social and economic power, and now they wanted political power to match. Meanwhile, as rich bourgeoisie got richer, the poorer members of the Third Estate just got poorer.[3] Thus, by 1789, France was a roiling, boiling stew of social tensions; the calling of the Estates General threatened to blow the lid off the whole thing.

The issue that caused those tensions to boil over was the question of how the Estates General would vote. It had traditionally met in three bodies, divided according to the three medieval orders. The votes were tallied in bloc, so the nobility and clergy could essentially overrule the Third Estate by a count of two to one. Almost all the nobility and a majority of the clergy thought that the Estates General should vote as it always had. Most members of the Third Estate did not agree. Before the meeting, the king's government proposed that the representation of the Third

---

[2] Sylvia Neely, *A Concise History of the French Revolution* (Lanham: Rowman and Littlefield, 2008), 7-12 and 29-50.

[3] William Doyle, *The Oxford History of the French Revolution*, 2nd ed. (Oxford: Oxford University Press, 2002), 22-26.

Estate be doubled, but by the time the body met in May, it was not clear if the Estates would vote as one body and thus give the Third Estate an equal voice or if the clergy and nobility would continue to meet separately, and thus continue to veto any new taxes for which they would have to contribute their fair share. While the government debated the matter early in 1789, a pamphlet war erupted over the issue. The most compelling and famous pamphlet was written by a frustrated clergyman named Abbé Sieyes, the son of a bourgeois government official, whose advancement in the church had been blocked by the privileges of his noble rivals at every turn. In his pamphlet, "What is the Third Estate?" Sieyes wondered aloud why the Third Estate should merely ask for equal representation when it comprised the majority of the population and did all the useful work. The idea, argued Sieyes, offended simple arithmetic.[4]

By June it seemed clear to the members of the Third Estate that neither the king, the clergy, nor the nobility was likely to give them the equal representation they wanted, so the members of the delegation simply walked out, moving to a nearby tennis court (the famous Tennis Court Oath) and declaring themselves a National Assembly. In response, the king offered a compromise, but it was too little too late. For the next two weeks, king and assembly stared each other down in a game of chicken, with the king too paralyzed to either recognize the National Assembly or to disperse it by force. Finally on June 27th, the king blinked, ordering the first two estates to join the third in the new National Assembly.[5] The Third Estate had won; the revolution had begun.

At this moment, it was still possible for moderation to win out, but it was precisely at this moment that the Parisian mob threw its weight into the balance of history, urged on by the poor weather of the previous summer. Indeed, hail had destroyed much of the harvest of 1788, which caused food shortages in the summer of 1789 (the price of bread almost doubled in a matter of months).[6] Unsurprisingly, this upset the Parisian mob. Convinced that the king was moving troops into Paris to quash the

---

[4] Neely, 56-58.

[5] Ibid., 66-68.

[6] Crane Brinton, *A Decade of Revolution* (New York: Harper and Row, 1963), 29.

National Assembly and believing that they alone could save the revolution from the treachery of the king, the mob stormed the Parisian prison known as the Bastille. When the king's guards denied them entry, the mob attacked, freeing the seven prisoners they found there, murdering the governor of the prison, and then parading his head around the city on a pike.[7] Obviously, the time for moderation had passed.

Working-class members of the Parisian mob continued rioting, eventually forming the *sans-culottes*, a militant and revolutionary band of citizens who distinguished themselves from the aristocracy by wearing long trousers and red liberty caps rather than the fashionable knee breeches (*culottes*) of the upper-classes. Although their political involvement was controversial, women participated directly in the politics and violence of the revolution, most famously in the October Days of 1789 when 20,000 women marched to Versailles with cannons and weapons, demanding that the king defend the revolution and lower the price of bread. After successfully forcing the royal family to accompany them back to Paris, the women chanted that they had captured "the baker, the baker's wife, and the baker's boy!" In the summer of 1789, the panic also spread beyond Paris and Versailles to the countryside, where peasants attacked the shockingly ill-defended manors that dotted the countryside and destroyed any records of their manorial obligations,[8] a stake through the heart of the blood-sucking aristocracy.

Meanwhile, the assembly tried to get on with the work of fixing France's broken government, but it was an uphill battle. In August, the assembly ended feudalism in France and adopted the Declaration of the Rights of Man and Citizen.[9] The Declaration made sweeping claims about individual and collective rights and inspired advocates of democracy, equality, and liberty across Europe and America. Its application, however, disappointed many who hoped this new French nation would allow for the political participation and enfranchisement of all people regardless of gender, class, or wealth. By the time the National Assembly finished writing the Constitution of 1791, supposedly based

---

[7] Doyle, 67-69 and Neely, 75.

[8] Brinton, 34-37.

[9] Neely, 85-86.

upon the principles of the Declaration of Rights, they had distinguished between "active" and "passive" citizens. Only "active citizens" – citizens who were male and had enough wealth to pay taxes equal to three days of an unskilled laborer's wages – could vote; only men of more substantial wealth could run for office. Those who fell into the inferior class of "passive" citizens, and who could not vote or run for office, included a third of the male population and all of the female population. As a result, many progressivists who had been excited by the broad claims of the Declaration of Rights became highly disappointed in its application, and progressive writers such as Mary Wollstonecraft responded by arguing for the political rights of women, the poor, and the enslaved.

The Declaration of Rights likewise proved to be a rather hard promise to keep due to financial burdens. When the assembly took over, some people thought it meant the end of taxes forever. But a bankrupt treasury is a bankrupt treasury, no matter who is in charge, and France's new leaders had few easy solutions since they refused to repudiate the debt or confiscate property, which they had just declared a sacred right. However, there was one possible solution: confiscate the property of the French Catholic Church, which was not guaranteed the same rights as a person. This was accomplished by a series of measures that culminated in 1790/1791 with the Civil Constitution of the Clergy, a law that limited papal authority in France and authorized the government to make Catholic priests salaried employees of the revolutionary state. The Pope was not pleased. He condemned the law and forbade Catholics to follow it. Catholic priests were thus faced with an Antigone-like dilemma: follow their consciences and the law of God or swear allegiance to the state. Some fled, like the twenty-six year old John Dubois, who landed in the Catholic haven of Emmitsburg, MD, where he did a few things that may be of interest to the reader.[10] Back in France, the split with the

---

[10] John Dubois (1764-1842) was the third Bishop of New York (1826-1842), and, to this date, the only Bishop of New York without Irish ancestry. In 1808, he also founded a beautiful little college and seminary in Emmitsburg, Maryland named Mount St. Mary's and assisted St. Elizabeth Ann Seton in founding St. Joseph's College for women the following year

Catholic Church provoked a civil war. The king tried to flee, but the flight was thwarted when a post-master recognized him from his image on French money. This severed the last thread of trust between the king and the assembly. After that, it was only a matter of time before the king's neck would end up under a guillotine blade.[11]

The moment that turned the Revolution radical occurred in 1792 when the National Assembly pushed through a declaration of war on Austria, attempting to beat its most dangerous enemy on its own soil[12] before the Austrian Empire could strike back. War, however, did not go well. With France losing on several fronts and Louis failing to support the new government, the Parisian mob stormed the Tuileries and imprisoned the royal family, forcing the king at swordpoint to don the cap of liberty. Several weeks later, the mob struck again, deposing the king and dissolving the assembly. In its place, the French took a cue from America, electing a kingless convention endowed with full powers to write a new constitution. However, unlike in America, the convention did not go home; rather, it exercised emergency wartime powers for several years. Urged on by radical Masonic parties like the Jacobins, the new convention began a thorough purge of the old regime, starting with the old calendar, which they scrapped by declaring 1792 as Year I. Next on the chopping block was the king, whom they claimed "must die so that the nation might live."[13] By a rather thin margin, the Convention sentenced King Louis XVI to death in January of 1793 and sent him to the guillotine the next week. His Austrian wife, Marie Antoinette, would follow him there in October of the same year.

So began the most radical phase of the French Revolution and so began one of its great ironies. A movement that had begun as a quest for liberty, equality, and fraternity passed into the hands of a brutal and paranoid dictatorship: the infamous Committee of Public Safety, which ruthlessly hunted down and executed 'enemies' of the revolution, in-

---

[11] Brinton, 47-53.

[12] In this period, Austria held a piece of land known as the Austrian Netherlands, which is today Belgium. Thus, Austria was a major threat because they had territories right next door to France; moreover, many royalist exiles had landed in the Austrian Netherlands.

[13] Neely, 155-170.

cluding priests, nuns, royalists, political opponents, and other largely innocent bystanders. Utilizing some mind-bending double-think, the spokesman of the terror, the incorruptible Maximillian Robespierre, argued that in revolutionary times, liberty must be preserved with terror. What he meant by liberty was unclear, since he suspended almost all the basic rights of due process. What he meant by terror, however, was abundantly clear, as thousands went to the guillotine with little more than a show trial, in what has come to be known as the Reign of Terror.[14]

To win the foreign war, which by 1793 was being waged against the combined forces of almost all the other European powers, the Convention instituted a general conscription, the *levée en masse*, mobilizing all the resources of France to create an enormous army. The *levée en masse* was one of the few things the revolutionary government did that actually worked; by the end of 1793, the army was winning on all fronts, although Robespierre fell victim to the army's success since without a military emergency, there was little reason to keep chopping off heads at such a steady clip. In 1794, the moderates seized power, ending the Reign of Terror and sending Robespierre to the same guillotine to which he had condemned so many others.[15] Revolutionary France then established yet another constitution: the Directory.

In its quest for liberty, the French Revolution rather ironically ended with the rise of Napoleon, a man who wielded near absolute power after taking control of France's government. Napoleon was an undeniably magnetic little general from the island of Corsica, an outsider with a chip on his soldier and something to prove, who would have lived a life of frustrated ambition were it not for the revolution. When in 1795 a royalist mob took to the streets to try to overthrow the government, Napoleon, legend has it, met the crowd with cannons and did the unthinkable; in a move worthy of Machiavelli, he ordered his men to pack the cannon with grapeshot (a combination of nails, rocks, and other loose particles) and

[14] Ibid., 197-215.
[15] Brinton, 128-130.

fire it from point-blank range at the Parisian crowd. The mob was decimated; Napoleon got a promotion.[16]

After this so called "Whiff of Grapeshot" incident, Napoleon's star was on the rise, and he made the most of his opportunity, winning a series of stunning victories in Italy and heading a major military campaign in Egypt. By 1799 it had become clear that the corrupt Directory was not going to last much longer on its own, so Napoleon abandoned his army in Egypt and returned to France: either to save the Directory and take a place on it, or to destroy it altogether. As events moved forward, he decided for the latter option, but when he entered the representative council to win support for his coup, he was met with cries of "down with dictators," and "death to Caesar." Napoleon was so shaken up, he nearly fainted, but later that day, he pulled himself together, marched his soldiers back to the same council, bullied his way in and dissolved it by force of arms: the first military coup of the modern age.[17]

Most historians see Napoleon's coup as the end of the revolution and the beginning of the French empire. However, Napoleon's relationship to the revolution was complicated. All along, he claimed to be acting to save the revolution, not destroy it. This was obviously a lie, but not a total lie. For instance, in 1804, many revolutionary principles were reflected in the law code that Napoleon compiled, the famous *Code Napoléon*, which standardized the legal code in France and which became the basis for most modern European law systems.[18] Nevertheless, he increasingly acted and behaved like a king. In 1804, he invited Pope Pius VII to France to crown him as emperor. As the Pope was about to retrieve the crown, Napoleon snatched it away and placed it on his own head. Just like the absolutist kings before him, Napoleon did not share power.

Meanwhile, an unbroken string of military successes between 1799 and 1808 allowed Napoleon to bring revolutionary principles to the rest

---

[16] The literature on Napoleon is vast. For an authoritative account of Napoleon's rise to power, see Philip Dwyer, *Napoleon: The Path to Power* (New Haven: Yale University Press, 2008); for a short readable biography, see Paul Johnson, *Napoleon: A Life* (New York: Penguin, 2002). For an interesting documentary, see *Napoleon*, directed by David Grubin (Arlington, VA: PBS, 2000).

[17] Dwyer, 480-501.

[18] Johnson, 105-106.

of Europe, along with untold misery, war, and bloodshed.[19] In the early stages of his career, he simply could not lose, utilizing his penchant for speed and surprise, the almost inexhaustible manpower of France, and an utter disregard for human life to defeat all comers, whether that be Austria, Spain, or Prussia.[20] By 1812, all that remained was to slay the Russian bear. Here, however, Napoleon overshot the mark. When Tsar Alexander of Russia broke the anti-British military alliance that Napoleon had forced on him, Napoleon put together a massive army of more than half a million soldiers to march into Russia. The army was so big that from its front to its end, it took eight days to pass a given spot. In the face of such a juggernaut, the Russian military wisely retreated, scorching the land and slowly drawing Napoleon's army deep into Russian territory. The Russians fought Napoleon's army to a draw just outside of Moscow at the Battle of Borodino; meanwhile, the Russians burned Moscow to the ground to prevent it from falling into French hands. In the evacuation, the Russians had taken the food but left the vodka, so Napoleon's army celebrated its draw at Borodino by slaughtering its horses for food and getting rippingly drunk in the charred ruins of Moscow. With no food at hand and the Russian winter coming, all Napoleon could do was slink back out of Russia. It was, however, a long way out of Russia, especially in winter, and much of Napoleon's army did not make it. Napoleon fled to Paris to secure his political position, leaving his army straggling behind.[21] Napoleon's lucky star had failed him, as it would continue to do for the next three years, when he lost several more battles, and was even exiled for a time to the Mediterranean island of Elba. The little emperor would fight his last battle at Waterloo in 1815, when he was beaten in the field for the last time and the combined powers of Europe sent him packing to the small island of Saint Helena, where he could do

---

[19] The United States of America profited handsomely from Napoleon's military campaigns; in 1803, Napoleon sold the Louisiana territory to the U.S. to help finance his wars, vastly increasing the size of the country and giving Americans at least parts of Montana, North Dakota, South Dakota, Wyoming, Minnesota (Go Vikings!), Iowa, Nebraska, Colorado, Kansas, Missouri, Oklahoma, Texas, Arkansas, and Louisiana.

[20] Johnson, 49-51.

[21] Johnson, 128-132.

no more damage.[22]   The revolution was over, but the west would be changed forever.

Perhaps the most important change to come out of the French Revolution was the introduction of revolutionary ideology to the western tradition. Political revolts had, of course, happened throughout western history (think back to the overthrow of the Tarquins and the formation of a new Roman constitution in Livy); what differed in the French Revolution was that it was motivated not by traditional moral or political philosophy, but by modern ideology. "Ideology" is one of those words that is easy to throw around but is hard to define.[23] Usually it is simply used as a synonym for "worldview" or "philosophy", but it is, more technically, a system of thought that claims to definitively answer all of the questions of human existence. One telling way of understanding ideology is as a kind of secular religion that "immanentizes the eschaton;" simply put, modern ideology attempts to make heaven on earth, usually through science, economics, and technology.[24]   Ideological systems are content to ignore or do away with previous traditions or social structures, and they comfortably recreate, from the ground up, systems of knowledge and government. Revolutionary French thought and Marxist Communism can be seen clearly as ideologies; others, such as classical liberalism/libertarianism can be as strongly ideological as Marxism, even if they may initially appear to be less so to many 21st-century Americans. Ideologies ultimately function like early gnostic religions: once you are initiated into the *gnosis* (the secret knowledge) of the cult, you have the "correct" answers for any question, answers that

---

[22] Ibid., 169-187.

[23] The Oxford English Dictionary (which you can access for free via the Phillips Library!) notes that the French word/concept *idéologie* (the origin of our English term) grew directly out of the French Revolution. The first witness comes in 1796, in which the term is used to describe French Revolutionary philosophy of the mind. Napoleon himself is the first person to use the term to refer to "abstract speculation", and by 1842 the word's meaning had become solidified into the political and epistemological sense in which we are treating it in this section.

[24] See Eric Voegelin, *Science, Politics, and Gnosticism* (Wilmington, DE: ISI Books, 2007 [1968]).

serve to indoctrinate you and others into a kind of group-think.[25] Whereas traditional philosophy encourages questioning (particularly *self-questioning*), ideology discourages hard questions, questions which might undermine the principles of faith on which the ideology rests.[26]

In summary. The French Revolution was a period of dramatic political upheaval caused by social, economic, and political factors. At first, it was a moderate political movement in which the Third Estate demanded a political voice under the watchwords liberty, equality, and fraternity, but it eventually overturned the old regime and gave way to the Reign of Terror and the advent of Napoleon, whose military victories allowed him to spread revolutionary ideology to the rest of Europe.

----

[25] You should notice that ideologies have unusual relationships with authority. Revolutionaries will disavow any previous authority, yet insist that *their* system of thought is the only one that is *truly* authoritative, thus functioning as a kind of secular religion that seeks salvation here on earth. When Marx and Engels give a reinterpretation of the history of Western Civilization in *The Communist Manifesto*, they are essentially arguing that their ideology is the authoritative interpretive key to explain correctly everything that came before them. Those of you who have studied Freud will recognize his psychology to be highly ideological: once you realize that all problems stem from repressed memories of infant sexuality, you have the *gnosis* to explain (or explain away) all culture and civilization.[25] As we go forward into the 19th and 20th centuries, consider this shift in Western thought from competing philosophies in dialogue with the past tradition and each other to competing ideologies that purport to answer all questions about reality, even while resting on principles that are unquestionable articles of faith. What ideologies might be at work in 21st-century America? What "philosophies" are treated more like *gnosis*-based religions in their level of zealotry and discomfort with questioning first principles or authorities? The answers might be grim.

[26] Are Fox News and MSNBC interested in authentic, rational debate? If they are not, they function as popular mouthpieces of nothing more than political ideologies, which are secular religions.

Chapter Eight:

The Romantic Reaction

The French Revolution invented the very concept of revolution: a strict break with the past that overturns all the old order in its wake. By comparison, the American War for Independence was tame. Whereas many Americans were actually fighting to preserve their rights as Englishmen (many of which stretched back to the Middle Ages), the French Revolutionaries set out to create an entirely new order, though most of them did not anticipate that the new order would involve so much bloodshed. The next century would be left to deal with the aftermath.

For a short time, that aftermath would be dominated by a group of artists and thinkers known as Romantics, so-called because they drew inspiration from the fantastical and heroic elements of the narratives (*romances*) of medieval literature. The Romantics had a complicated relationship to the Enlightenment, to the French Revolution, and to Napoleon. Many Romantics shared certain enlightenment ideals, such as equality and emancipation; some of them, such as Percy Shelley and Lord Byron, would remain revolutionaries to their dying days. Byron even practiced what he preached, by raising a personal army to liberate Greece from the Ottoman Turks. Others, such as William Wordsworth, would grow gradually more conservative.[1] Either way, they were almost all disappointed with the way the French Revolution had played out. For instance, Wordsworth wrote of his initial reactions to the revolution thus:

---

[1] Our current notions of 'conservative' and 'liberal' began to be developed in this period, with adherents to the former term skeptical or opposed to revolution and reinvention of society, and adherents to the latter term supporters of revolutionary movements.

"Bliss was it in that dawn to be alive; But to be young was very heaven!--Oh! Times, In which the meagre, stale, forbidding ways of custom, law, and statute, took at once the attraction of a country in romance!"[2] Wordsworth, however, had misread the revolution, for as heads began to roll off the guillotine, the revolution began to read less like a romance and more like a tragedy. For his part, Wordsworth turned away in disgust, looking to a different model—a German literary movement known as *Sturm und Drang* (storm and thunder or stress). In this German literature, which cared very little for reason, order, or harmony, the Romantics would find the exaltation of a very different part of man's nature: the passions.[3]

No one indicted the French Revolution more bitterly than the Romantic conservative Edmund Burke, who wrote:

It is now sixteen or seventeen years since I saw the Queen of France…at Versailles; and surely never lighted on this orb, which she hardly seemed to touch, a more delightful vision…little did I dream that I should have lived to see such disasters fallen upon her in a nation of gallant men, in a nation of men of honour and of cavaliers. I thought ten thousand swords must have leaped from their scabbards to avenge even a look that threatened her with insult. —But the age of chivalry is gone. —That of sophisters, economists, and calculators, has succeeded; and the glory of Europe is extinguished forever.[4]

---

[2] William Wordsworth, *The Prelude, Or, Growth of a Poet's Mind* (London: Moxon, 1850), 299.

[3] On the relationship between German *Sturm und Drang* writers and the English Romantics see Paul Davies, "German Romanticism," *Encyclopedia of Romanticism*, ed. Laura Dabundo (London: Routledge, 2010), 226-231. The most prominent member of German Romanticism was Goethe, whose *Sorrows of Young Werther* is one of the three texts that Frankenstein's monster reads and whose *Faust* is a classic of Western literature.

[4] Edmund Burke, *Reflections on the Revolution in France* (London: Sharpe, 1819-1820), 105-106.

According to Burke, the problem with the Enlightenment was that it put too much faith in individual reason as the solution to all humankind's problems, for Burke, as the passage above demonstrates, was not convinced that the cold reason of economists would be the salvation of humankind. In place of reason, the Romantics would attempt to restore beauty, chivalry and passion to their proper place. The sublime, Burke would claim, did not consist in perfect order and proportion but in mystery, imagination, wonder, awe, and the infinite.[5]

For poets and artists, this meant returning their art to the wellsprings of nature. Poets wrote about mountains, flowers, ruins, beauty, and love. Artists painted landscapes in which the enormity of nature dwarfed the human forms and in which nude and semi-nude bodies tangled together in masses and heaps of motion and energy. From a technical point of view, "[Romantic painters] avoided clarity, straight lines, and sharp edges... Romantic artists wanted to get rid of passivity or subordinate it to their power, swap geometry for dynamism, give up the precision that satisfies only the mind and instead, resort to the senses and the soul."[6]

In music, composers wrote operas and symphonies designed to touch deep emotional chords in their listeners. The most famous example probably comes from the fourth movement of Beethoven's *Ninth Symphony*, which set its music to a poem: Schiller's "Ode to Joy."

All creatures drink joy
At nature's breast;
All the good, all the bad
Follow her rose-bedecked trail.
She gave us kisses and grapevines,
And a friend true unto death;
Pleasure is given even to the worm,
And the cherub stands before God.

---

[5] Edmund Burke, "A Philosophical Inquiry into the Sublime and the Beautiful," in *The Portable Edmund Burke*, ed. Isaac Kramnick (London: Penguin, 1999).

[6] Léon Rosenthal, *Art of Century: Romanticism* (New York: Park Stone, 2012), 52-55.

Beethoven's music builds from its pleasantly cheerful first three verses to the great crescendo at the end of this, the fourth verse, with an explosive repetition of the word God [*Gott*] at a volume, pitch, and length that seems to exceed the limits of the human voice. Beethoven then immediately slows the tempo and turns the volume down, instructing the chorus to sing these later lines devoutly, like a prayer:

> Do you bow down, millions?
> Dost thou fear the creator of the world?
> Seek him above the canopy of stars.
> He must dwell above the stars.[7]

So much for Galileo's telescope; the Romantics were far more concerned with what was beyond its reach.

Romantic thought also tended to stir up national pride. For many in Europe, Romanticism meant a recovery of the folklore and mythologies that had supposedly sprung from the genius of their respective peoples and formed the core of their national identities. This often meant a return to the enchanted worlds of myth and legend. It was in this period, for instance, that the Grimm Brothers began collecting German fairy tales like "Hansel and Gretel."

Romantic national pride produced great works of art, but it also had a dark side. Just as the Grimm brothers had mined German folklore, so nineteenth-century composers like Schubert, Chopin and Liszt would mine the rhythms and harmonies of native folk songs to give life to national schools of music. Perhaps no Romantic composer was more fervently nationalist than Richard Wagner, who drew on the enchanted world of Norse mythology (think Odin and Loki) for his *Nibelungen* cycle, a story about a struggle over a magic ring that gives the bearer the power to rule the world.[8] In the series of four operas, the blond, Germanic hero

---

[7] Harvey Sachs, *The Ninth: Beethoven and the World in 1824* (New York: Random House, 2012), 155-161.

[8] Norman Davies, *Europe: A History* (Oxford: Oxford University Press, 1996), 812-821.

Siegfried battles valiantly against giants and money-grubbing dwarves, which the virulently anti-Semitic Wagner obviously meant as a proxy for Jews. As non-Christians of ultimately Middle Eastern origin, the Jewish people were often regarded with suspicion by nationalists like Wagner: the Jews were religiously and racially not part of the 'folk.' Wagner even called for the expulsion of all Jews from Europe, which he called 'The Final Solution." No wonder Wagner was Hitler's favorite composer.

The importance of Romanticism as a reaction against, and product of, the Enlightenment and French Revolution should not be understated. While it championed the individual (particularly the individual artistic genius), it situated the individual within a national culture, tied to particular language, custom, tradition, and mythology. While it rejected rationalism, its fascination with spirit (*Geist*) and mystery point to realities *beyond* scientific, empirical reason. While it called for revolution, Romantic authors eventually settled on revolutions within the arts and human consciousness as the vehicles of progress, rather than on violent political revolution.[9] If you feel national pride in the symbols of America, if you appreciate folk culture and history, if you enjoy fantasy literature, if you like emotion-filled music, if you believe in social progress through education and art . . . you are an heir to the Romantics.

In summary, Romanticism was an artistic and philosophical reaction to the Enlightenment that stressed passion, emotion, and creativity over reason, order, and harmony. It was primarily marked by an exaltation of nature and a focus on individual genius.

---

[9] See M.H. Abrams, *Natural Supernaturalism: Tradition and Revolution in Romantic Literature* (New York and London: W.W. Norton & Co.), 1971.)

Chapter Nine:

Progress and Misery in the Industrial Revolution

If one takes a very long view of human history, it might seem as if humankind only has three real accomplishments: the Agricultural Revolution, when we first learned how to grow our food rather than gather or hunt it; the Information Revolution, when we connected the globe with wires and computers; and the Industrial Revolution, which is the subject of this chapter. Indeed, it is incredibly difficult to overstate the importance of the Industrial Revolution. To the extent that it is possible to measure such things, it can be reasonably estimated that between the age of Pericles' Athens and the beginning of the Industrial Revolution, per capita GDP in the West hovered around 500 modern U.S. dollars per year, sometimes a little more and sometimes a little less, but always far below what we would consider the most wretched form of poverty for the vast majority of people.[1] By contrast, per capita GDP in Western European countries ranged between $30,000 and $50,000 dollars in 2013.[2] A tremendous change, but why? The answer is mainly due to the fact that in the intervening years, we figured out how to make machines do our work for us. Let's look at this another way. In the late Roman age, it took a typical weaver three hours of work to earn enough to purchase a loaf of

---

[1] William Rosen, *The Most Powerful Idea in the World* (New York: Random House, 2010), xvi-xvi.

[2] According to the CIA World Factbook.

bread; by 1800, a weaver could do it in two. By 1900, the time had decreased to fifteen minutes, and today a weaver working a mechanized loom can do it in five.[3] Simply put, never in human history has productive capacity increased so rapidly, and probably never in human history will it increase so rapidly again.

But why did it happen in Western Europe and why in the eighteenth and nineteenth centuries? There is no simple answer to this question: such a complex development cannot be attributed to a single factor alone. Rather, the Industrial Revolution required just the right cocktail of factors; remove one ingredient and most of us would still be living on farms, consuming only as much as we could make ourselves. In the first place, industrialization required access to the raw materials of industry: iron to build machines and railroads, coal to fire the steam engines, and raw materials like wool (and later cotton) to produce the finished goods. Industrialization also required excess manpower to work in the factories.[4] In a sense, then, potatoes were the food of industry as well as enlightenment. However, the main ingredient was technological advancement, the result of thousands of individual inventions in hundreds of different technologies made by thousands of different inventors. This required access to capital and an educated risk-taking class who could "drive innovation." The patent system was crucial as well, since the protection of intellectual property gave inventors the motivation to innovate, create, and market their inventions in the hope of becoming wealthy.[5] With the exception of cotton, all the ingredients of this industrial cocktail could only be found in one time and one place: eighteenth and nineteenth-century England.

Nowhere was the cumulative process of developing technology more clear than in the ingenious new ways the English devised to make cloth. Making cloth involves three interrelated processes: preparing the raw material, spinning that into yarn, and then weaving the spun yarn into fabric. Before the Industrial Revolution, the weaving was done by skilled

---

[3] Rosen, xviii.

[4] Peter Stearns, *The Industrial Revolution in World History* (Boulder, CO: Westview Press, 2013), 42.

[5] Rosen, 52.

weavers working relatively small hand looms. The spinning was 'put out' to rural women, often unmarried 'spinsters' who turned wool into yarn on their own spinning wheels. All that changed in the eighteenth century.

Around 1733 the Englishman John Kay invented the flying shuttle. This was a device that allowed the weaver to send the shuttle and weft yarn through the warp with a quick twist of the wrist, rather than running it through by hand. This dramatically increased the speed with which cloth could be woven and the size of the finished product, which could now be larger than a mere human wing span. However, the efficiencies of the flying shuttle generated other problems; with so much cloth being woven, the spinners could not keep up with the weavers. An advance in one technology had led to a shortfall in another area, and another inventor responded. In 1764, James Hargreaves patented the spinning jenny. The idea was simple; rather than twist a single spindle (like the one you are probably familiar with from Sleeping Beauty) the spinning jenny operated eight spindles at one time. Yarn could now be produced eight times as fast. Yet, even this did not solve all the problems. The yarn the spinning jenny produced was strong enough to be used for the weft but not for the warp; thus five years later, Richard Arkwright patented the water frame, which rolled the yarn out tightly as it spun so that it was much stronger and could be used for both warp and weft. Several years later, Samuel Crompton patented the spinning mule, which essentially combined the power of Arkwright's water frame with the productive capacity of the spinning jenny. Now plenty of high quality yarn could be churned out at once. Yet this led to another problem. Spinning machines now produced so much yarn that the weavers could not keep up. Thus, in 1784, Edward Cartwright designed the first power loom: a fully mechanized loom that produced massive quantities of fabric. Thus, by the start of the nineteenth century, technological innovation had set the stage for almost fully automated production.[6]

Textile mills also needed a reliable source of non-human power to get cranking. Enter the steam engine, whose earliest incarnations grew out of an age-old problem: how to get water out of mines. Traditionally,

---

[6] Rosen, 222-239.

water had been drawn out of the mines by muscle power, usually by horses turning a crank (thus, the undying metric of horsepower). This was slow and cumbersome, and the horses had to be fed and cared for, so the whole business was slow, costly, and messy. Over the course of the eighteenth century, enterprising engineers had developed a number of solutions to the problem, including trying to suck the water out with a vacuum. Vacuum pumps, however, had one major problem: they couldn't draw water higher than thirty-three feet (remember Torricelli's experiments with the barometer).

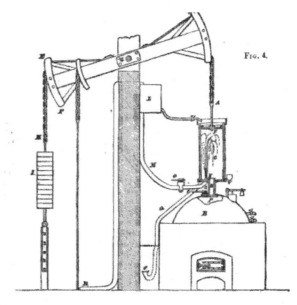

Newcomen Steam Engine from Thomas Tredgold's *The Steam Engine*. 1897.

This obviously created a major problem when the goal was to remove water from mines that were deep below the surface. In 1712, an inventor named Thomas Newcomen hit upon an ingenious solution. In his design, he combined the vacuum principle with a mechanical pump. He raised some capital investment and got to work. The resulting product, the Newcomen Steam Engine, would not only revolutionize mining but almost every field of industry. The design was elegant, yet brilliant. At the top of the engine sat a beam, one end of which was attached to a plunger that drove a mechanical pump; the other end was connected to a piston that sat above an empty cylinder. Below the cylinder sat a heating chamber, where water was boiled into steam. As the water expanded, it filled the cylinder, driving the piston on one side up and the pump plunger on the other side down. When the piston reached its maximum height, a valve injected cold water on the steam. The steam condensed, leaving a vacuum in the cylinder.[7] When that happened, atmospheric

---

[7] Ibid., 32-35.

pressure pushed the piston down and the pump plunger up. The whole process then repeated itself again, driving the pump up and down. Thus, the discoveries of the Scientific Revolution began to bear fruit; the secrets of nature could now be put to useful work.

By the end of the nineteenth century, steam engines had grown so efficient that they could be used to run the gears in factory systems, power the wheels of locomotives, and push the paddles of steamboats. It is hard to overstate the importance of steam. For all prior human history, humans had relied only on muscle power, water power, and wind power—but usually muscle power. Steam changed all that. It drained the mines that produced the coal used to power the steam engines themselves. It then transported that coal in steam locomotives to factories that were also powered by steam engines. Those factories produced goods whose raw materials had been delivered to them by steam engines and whose finished products would return to market on steam engines.[8] Thus, in many ways, the Industrial Revolution was an age of steam.

Technology thus created a true revolution, the consequences of which almost no one could escape. Machinery increased the amount of goods that an average person could consume. As one historian put it, "For the first time, the common man could afford underwear…Personal hygiene changed drastically, so that commoners of the late nineteenth and early twentieth century often lived cleaner than the kings and queens of a century earlier."[9] Over the course of the Industrial Revolution, the real purchasing power of every group of workers increased (perhaps even doubled).[10] Moreover, except in the very large industrial cities like Manchester, life expectancy improved almost everywhere.[11] The Scottish father of modern economic thought, Adam Smith, called it universal opu-

---

[8] Ibid., xxi-xxii.

[9] David S. Landes, *The Wealth and Poverty of Nations: Why Some are so Rich and Some So Poor* (New York: W.W. Norton, 1999), xvii.

[10] Peter H. Lindert and Jeffrey G. Williamson "English Workers' Living Standards During the Industrial Revolution: A New Look," *The Economics of the Industrial Revolution*, ed. Joel Mokyr (New York: Rowman and Littlefield, 1985), 187.

[11] Ibid., 196.

lence, and though historians debate just how much the quality of life improved, it certainly did improve for most people.

On the other hand, industrialization exacted a steep human cost as well. In the first place, the machines put a lot of weavers and spinners out of business. When the highly skilled labor of weaving could be done by a fully automated machine, society had little use for the weaver or his skills. Some weavers responded violently. Known as Luddites, these weavers mobilized into small militias and unleashed their pent-up frustrations against the new machines by marching on factories and smashing them to bits. In response, Parliament made the breaking of the new machines a capital offense in 1812.[12]

The new modes of economic production made for other social transformations as well. No longer was it economically feasible to spin yarn at thousands of individual spinning wheels in thousands of individual households. The new machines were far too big to fit in a house and too expensive for individual purchase. By 1780 a British textile mill already required 150 times more capital investment than a good hand loom. Only a very wealthy investor, or even more likely, a corporation of wealthy investors, could afford to buy them. Rather than sending raw materials out to be worked by individuals, eighteenth-century entrepreneurs concentrated the machines, the materials, and the peoples in one place: the factory system of production was born.[13]

As Adam Smith pointed out, factory production and the division of labor made for much cheaper goods. On the other hand, the factory invented new miseries. A factory can only move as fast as its slowest part, and this meant a revolution in the way people worked. If a businessman had invested capital in factory machines, he wanted the factory to be producing goods as fast as possible for as many hours in the day as possible; thus, the worst factory owners kept their employees at their machines for sixteen hours a day, and grew tremendously wealthy off the profits. Thus, for thousands of factory workers, work life took on a dreary and regimented form, every minute regulated by the tyranny of

---

[12] John Archer, *Social Unrest and Popular Protest in England, 1780-1840* (Cambridge: Cambridge University Press, 2000), 52.

[13] Stearns, 32.

the clock. No more stopping work when the sun went down. No more working to the gentle, agricultural rhythms of planting, harvest, and fallow period. No more seasons of play for children. Factories hummed on relentlessly through the hours, through the seasons, and through the years. Worse yet, because factory workers had become merely wage laborers, they could be fired at any time. Old, injured, or sick employees who could no longer keep up were simply discarded. Perhaps most distressingly, the small hands of children as young as five were set to work doing the most dangerous tasks of factory life.[14] As the communist Karl Marx would argue, labor lost much of its charm, and the individual worker was reduced to single, mindless, and repetitive steps. He became, in the words of Marx, "a mere appendage of the machine."[15] Who, then, was the servant of whom: the man or the machine?

In northern England, where many of the new steam-powered factories were located, poor workers flooded into the ugly, sprawling, and massively growing cities like Liverpool and Manchester. It was hard for the infrastructure to keep up, which led to all sorts of social problems. Cramped, dirty, choked by factory smog, and lacking basic sanitation, the slums of the industrial cities were a damning rebuttal to the champions of progress. Consider Frederick Engel's description of industrial Manchester:

In dry weather, a long string of the most disgusting, blackish-green, slime pools are left standing on the bank [of the River], from the depths of which bubbles of miasmatic gas constantly arise and give forth a stench unendurable even on the bridge forty or fifty feet above the surface of the stream. But besides this, the stream itself is checked every few paces by high weirs, behind which slime and refuse accumulate and rot in thick masses. Above the bridge are tanneries, bone mills, and gasworks, from which all drains and refuse find their way into the Irk, which receives further the contents of all the neigh-

[14] Ibid., 32-36.

[15] Karl Marx and Friedrich Engels, *"The Communist Manifesto"* http://www.gutenberg.org/files/61/61.txt. Accessed June 5, 2014. You might note that our word robot comes from the Slavic word for slave/worker.

boring sewers and privies. It may be easily imagined, therefore, what sort of residue the stream deposits. Below the bridge you look upon the piles of debris, the refuse, filth, and offal from the courts on the steep left bank; here each house is packed close behind its neighbour and a piece of each is visible, all black, smoky, crumbling, ancient, with broken panes and window frames. The background is furnished by old barrack-like factory buildings. On the lower right bank stands a long row of houses and mills; the second house being a ruin without a roof, piled with debris; the third stands so low that the lowest floor is uninhabitable, and therefore without windows or doors. Here the background embraces the pauper burial-ground, the station of the Liverpool and Leeds railway, and, in the rear of this, the Workhouse, the "Poor-Law Bastille" of Manchester, which, like a citadel, looks threateningly down from behind its high walls and parapets on the hilltop, upon the working-people's quarter below… If any one wishes to see in how little space a human being can move, how little air and *such* air! he can breathe, how little of civilisation he may share and yet live, it is only necessary to travel hither. True, this is the *Old* Town, and the people of Manchester emphasise the fact whenever any one mentions to them the frightful condition of this Hell upon Earth; but what does that prove? Everything which here arouses horror and indignation is of recent origin, belongs to the *industrial epoch*.[16]

Engels was speaking about nineteenth-century Manchester, but he might as well have been talking about twenty-first century Beijing. Indeed, this context set the tone for a debate about politics, economy, and environment that remains with us today. On one side of the economic debate were an assortment of groups who lamented the fact that industrialization drastically widened the gap between the haves and have-nots and who called for various mixes of government intervention, organization of labor, redistribution of wealth, or violent revolution to restore the balance. On the other side were the classical free-market liberals (though it should be noted that in an economic sense, liberalism today means the

---

[16] Friedrich Engels, "Industrial Manchester," *Modern History Sourcebook.* Accessed May 21, 2014.

opposite of what it did in the nineteenth century. Today we would call the liberals of the nineteenth century by a different name: Republicans). These thinkers argued that a rising tide lifted all boats; that is, though a free-market economy would benefit some more than others, everyone would benefit nonetheless. The ideological positions staked out in the Industrial Revolution would play out in political battles, the struggles of organized labor, and the realm of international conflict well into the twentieth century. Indeed, with some variations, they are essentially the same battles that continue to divide Democrats and Republicans today.

To meet the problems of the Industrial Revolution, popes from the nineteenth century to the present day have written so-called "social encyclicals," which have clarified the dignity of workers alongside rights to private property. The social encyclicals do not fit easily into either Democratic or Republican ideologies; rather, they seek to propose principles for social change drawn from the Gospels and traditional Catholic moral theology.[17]

In summary, the Industrial Revolution was an age of technological innovation, centered in England, in which machinery, the division of labor, and steam power allowed Western Europe to produce massive quantities of goods far more cheaply and efficiently. This also led to various social problems associated with industrial cities and factories and a widening gap between the rich and poor.

---

[17] Leo XIII's *Rerum Novarum* (1891), St. John Paul II's *Centesimus Annus* (1991), Benedict XVI's *Caritas in Veritate* (2009), and Pope Francis' *Lumen Fidei* (2013) and Laudato Si' (2015) are perhaps the most significant social encyclicals.

Chapter Ten:

Imperialism, Nationalism, and The Great War

In June of 1914, a nineteen-year old Serbian nationalist named Gavrilo Princip secretly stewed in a Sarajevo café. His plot to kill the Archduke Franz Ferdinand of Austria, symbol of the hated Austrian aggression in the Balkan Peninsula, had failed miserably. The plotters had placed seven potential assassins on the archduke's route to city hall, but as the procession reached the third conspirator, he threw a bomb that bounced off the car and exploded behind it. Badly shaken, the remaining conspirators lost their nerve, and the archduke made it safely to city hall. After the festivities, he wisely chose to change his route out of town, but no one told the driver, who went the wrong way and had to stop on a side street to turn around. As luck would have it, he had stopped right in front of the very café in which Princip had been sitting. Fate had given Princip another chance, and he seized it. The young assassin took out his pistol, strode to the car, and fired two shots. The first one hit the Archduchess Sophie in the stomach; the second hit the archduke near the heart.[1] Princip was immediately arrested, but it hardly mattered; he had hit his mark, thereby lighting a deadly fuse, a fuse that would set Europe ablaze. By August, all the major European powers were at war.

How then did Europe go from the age of machines to the age of machine warfare? This is the final topic of this book. At least part of the answer

---

[1] Mike Sharp, Ian Westwell, John Westwood, *History of World War I* (New York: Marhsall Cavendish, 2002), 70-71. Or as some sources have it, in his neck.

lies in imperialism. Indeed, the technological advancements of the machine age permitted Europeans to force their way into all the corners of the globe that they had previously been unwilling or unable to conquer. Railroads tied continents together, while canals and steamships made water transport faster and safer. Coincidentally, the last spike was hammered into the North American transcontinental railroad in 1869, the same year that half way around the world, French engineers finished digging out the last part of the Suez Canal, which linked the Mediterranean to the Red Sea and spared ships the unpleasantness of sailing around Africa to get to Asia. The development of medicines such as tonic water (quinine), which protects against malaria, allowed Europeans to live in tropical climates like Africa without simply dropping dead in the first few years. Englishmen, who could not stand the taste of tonic alone, mixed it with their favorite alcohol: gin. Thus, the birth of the gin and tonic. Indeed, quinine is a perfect example of the way in which the world had grown smaller. Here was a medicine derived from the bark of a tree that had originally grown on the slopes of the Andes in South America, which the English then transplanted, grew, and harvested in their colonial dominions in India, so that they could protect colonial administrators working in Africa, who then turned it into the English national drink.[2] It's a small world, after all.

Above all, Europeans were able to colonize much of the world at the end of the nineteenth century because of the machine gun. Against the hundreds of bullets that Gatling and Maxim guns could fire every minute, native warriors stood little chance. In a satirical poem, Hilaire Belloc painted the scene of an imaginary rebellion of natives put down by an English captain, aptly named Blood. He writes:

> I never shall forget the way
> That Blood upon this awful day
> Preserved us all from death.
> He stood upon a little mound,
> Cast his lethargic eyes around,

---

[2] Daniel R. Headrick, *The Tools of Empire: Technology and European Imperialism in the Nineteenth Century* (Oxford: Oxford University Press, 1981).

And said beneath his breath:

"Whatever happens we have got
The Maxim Gun, and they have not.[3]

Indeed, when westerners had the Maxim Gun and the rest of the world did not, it was almost never a fair fight.

Technological advancement made European domination of the world possible, but it was also technology that made it necessary. The great machines of the industrial age were producing massive quantities of finished goods, yet to produce these goods, they needed to be fed ever more massive quantities of raw materials, which Europeans often needed to seek elsewhere on the globe. As Karl Marx wrote in *The Communist Manifesto*, the industrial bourgeoisie's search for new markets and new products "chases the bourgeoisie over the entire surface of the globe. It must nestle everywhere, settle everywhere, establish connections every-where."[4] Like an infestation of rats, from Marx's point of view.

There were perhaps no more vicious rats than the cotton planters of the American south, who made their fortunes supplying raw materials to European and Yankee industry. In 1794, Eli Whitney developed a cotton gin that could separate usable cotton fibers from the plant more efficiently; American planters took advantage, moving cotton plantations into the west and the deep south. As technology fueled demand, more cotton needed to be planted and picked, backbreaking labor that elite white American southerners were not about to do themselves when they could simply purchase African slaves to do it for them. They justified this enslavement with racist ideologies that declared whites racially sup-erior.[5] This time the horrors that went into producing their cotton clothes eventually did prick the consciences of some Westerners. Under pressure from Evangelical Christians like William Wilberforce, England outlawed

---

[3] Hillaire Belloc, *The Modern Traveller* (London: Edward Arnold, 1898), 41.

[4] Karl Marx and Fredrich Engels, *Manifesto of the Communist Party* (Chicago: Kerr, 1906), 17.

[5] Christopher Childers, "Slaves," *The Industrial Revolution: People and Perspectives*, ed. Hennifer L. Goloboy (Santa Barbara, CA: ACB-Clio, 2008), 36-39.

the slave trade in 1807 and slavery itself in 1834; on the other side of the Atlantic, it took the efforts of abolitionists such as Frederick Douglass, the unlikely election of an abolitionist president, and a bloody civil war for the United States to outlaw it in 1865.

Nevertheless, the West's appetite for markets and materials remained. In the first half of the century, the British annexed South Africa, opened China up to trade, and submitted India to direct control. In mid-century, American gunboats opened Japan up to trade, the French invaded Indochina, and the Austrians and the Russians snatched up territories in Eastern Europe and Central Asia from the dying Ottoman Empire. Late-comers like Germany, which was not united until 1871, feared they had lost out and scrambled to catch up in the game of colonial empire-building; in the 1880s the Germans snatched up several territories in Africa, setting off a frenzy for colonies known as the Scramble for Africa. In the coming years, Europeans would divvy up all the rest of the continent between them. Other up-and-coming powers got into the game as well. For instance, in 1898 the United States took Cuba, Puerto Rico, and the Philippines from the Spanish Empire and annexed Hawaii. By the outbreak of war, Europeans controlled eighty-four percent of the world's territory.[6]

This colonial competition intensified nationalistic antagonisms. France and Germany were already at each others' throats over the fate of Alsace-Lorraine, a small multi-national region that lay between the two countries and in which French and German speakers lived side by side. Thus, Alsace-Lorraine was one of those regions in which nation and state did not perfectly align, and this made it a flashpoint for tension. The French had held Alsace-Lorraine until 1871, when the Germanic Prussians took some of it from them in the Franco-Prussian War. The French, however, spent much of the latter half of the nineteenth century seething over this defeat and making plans to take their territory back.

Meanwhile, the Germans were locked in a naval arms race with the British. If Germany was going to compete in the game of colonial expansion with the British, they needed naval parity, so the upstart Germans

---

[6] William Kelleher Storey, *The First World War: A Concise Global History* (London: Rowman and Littlefield, 2010), 8.

began a naval building program, aiming to challenge British supremacy on the high seas, a supremacy the British had held since at least the Napoleonic Wars. The British responded by sinking money into ever more costly and intimidating vessels called dreadnoughts. In response, the Germans built dreadnoughts of their own. In response to that, the British built more.[7] Europe was drifting towards war; everyone knew it, but no one seemed to have the will to stop it.

As everyone knew that war was coming, they all hurried to make partnerships, hoping to be on the more powerful side when the guns started firing. These fears were given expression by a series of defensive alliances made between the European powers in the latter half of the nineteenth and early part of the twentieth centuries. By the time war finally came in 1914, Europe had been divided into two camps, with Germany, Austria-Hungary, and Italy on one side and Britain, France and Russia on the other.

This was the powder keg that exploded when Gavrilo Princip assassinated the Austrian Archduke in 1914, but it was events in the Balkan Peninsula that ignited the fuse. In 1914, the major power in the Balkans was Austria-Hungary, a multi-ethnic empire in which German speakers lived next to Hungarians who lived next to Slavs who lived next to Muslims. In an age of rampant nationalism, many of these ethnic min-orities began calling for political independence. This situation only worsened as the Austrians and Russians took more and more of the multi-ethnic territory that had belonged to the Ottoman Empire, the so called sick man of Europe, who could not keep up in the game of gun-powder warfare. In 1878, the Austro-Hungarian Empire occupied Bosnia. This was a slap in the face to Serbian nationalists, who considered Bosnia a Slavic land that had no business in the hands of Austrians. Thus, when the heir to the Austrian throne, the Archduke Franz Ferdinand, visited the Bosnian capital of Sarajevo in June of 1914, Gavrilo Princip, burning with nationalist zeal, seized the opportunity to strike at the Austrians.

The aftermath of the assassination involved one of the costliest failures of diplomacy in human history, for there was little in the Balkans that inherently interested Germany, France, or Great Britain. The dispute

---

[7] Storey, 27-28.

was really between Austria and Serbia alone. However, when the Austrians declared war on Serbia, their allies in Germany backed their play. Russia, however, would not sit idly by while the Austrians intimidated their fellow Slavs, so they mobilized. Germany then declared war on Russia in order to honor its commitment to its Austrian ally; however, all its guns were pointed towards Russia's ally, the French, so the Germans declared war on France too, planning to deliver them a knock-out blow early in the war and then turn around to deal with Russia. To do so, however, the Germans had to march through Belgium, to whom Great Britain was allied. The British thus entered the war on the side of the French in order to honor their treaty with the Belgians.[8] Thus, all sides entered into an ill-advised war over a political dispute that most of them had little direct interest in. War, it seems, had come for no good reason at all.

Nevertheless, the idea of war was remarkably popular in a Europe in which colonial conflict and arms race had keyed up national rivalries. Europeans on all sides expected a quick victory. What actually happened came as a bitter shock. The age of machine warfare reaped its bitter and bloody harvest in the trenches on the Franco-German front. Hopes of an easy victory faded quickly as the German offensive ground to a halt, and both sides settled into a stalemate of trench warfare, in which unimaginative generals flung a whole generation of their nation's youth into no-man's land,[9] where they became bloody fodder for artillery and machine guns.[10]

Though schoolboys had ridden off to war dreaming of glory, most of them found only horror: the damp and disease infested trenches; the constant barrage of artillery shells; and worst of all, the mustard gas, inarguably the most ghastly achievement of modern chemistry. Wilfrid Owen's poem *"Dulce et decorum est,"* satirically playing on a line from the Roman poet Horace, captured the horror of a mustard gas attack most aptly:

---

[8] J.M. Roberts, *The Penguin History of the World*, (London: Penguin, 1995), 859-860.

[9] The term used to describe the area between opposing trenches.

[10] Storey, 35-43.

Bent double, like old beggars under sacks,
Knock-kneed, coughing like hags, we cursed through sludge,
Till on the haunting flares we turned our backs
And towards our distant rest began to trudge.
Men marched asleep. Many had lost their boots
But limped on, blood-shod. All went lame; all blind;
Drunk with fatigue; deaf even to the hoots
Of tired, outstripped Five-Nines that dropped behind.[11]
Gas! Gas! Quick, boys! – An ecstasy of fumbling,
Fitting the clumsy helmets just in time;
But someone still was yelling out and stumbling,
And flound'ring like a man in fire or lime . . .
Dim, through the misty panes and thick green light,
As under a green sea, I saw him drowning.
In all my dreams, before my helpless sight,
He plunges at me, guttering, choking, drowning.
If in some smothering dreams you too could pace
Behind the wagon that we flung him in,
And watch the white eyes writhing in his face,
His hanging face, like a devil's sick of sin;
If you could hear, at every jolt, the blood
Come gargling from the froth-corrupted lungs,
Obscene as cancer, bitter as the cud
Of vile, incurable sores on innocent tongues,
My friend, you would not tell with such high zest
To children ardent for some desperate glory,
The old Lie; Dulce et Decorum est
Pro patria mori.[12]

At the turn of the twentieth century, Europe had been brimming with confidence and unbounded hope in its glorious technological future. For obvious reasons, much of that hope died in the trenches of World War I.

---

[11] 5.9" artillery shells used by the Germans in World War I.

[12] "sweet and fitting is it to die for one's homeland."

In summary, the end of the nineteenth and beginning of the twentieth centuries were periods in which Western European powers expanded their colonial dominions and engaged in increasingly hostile nationalistic rivalries. This eventually led to The Great War, the first industrial war, which was a shockingly traumatic experience that cost millions of lives and shook Europeans' faith in the idea of unlimited progress.

Epilogue

World War I spelled the beginning of the end for Western dominance in the world. To defeat each other, European powers mobilized their colonial populations, who naturally returned to their respective countries expecting the freedoms that they had been promised.[1] No longer could native peoples buy into the myth of white moral superiority. In the poem "White Man's Burden," Rudyard Kipling had argued that Europeans had a duty to bring civilization to the rest of the world; World War I had brought only barbarism.

Indeed, the human, cultural, and political costs of World War I are hard for us to imagine. The Treaty of Versailles put an end to the fighting, but it humiliated the Germans and paved the way for the rise of the Nazis, the devastation of World War II, and the horrors of the Holocaust. Before the Great War was even over, the Russian Tsar had been murdered by Marxist Bolsheviks, ushering in the era of Soviet Russia and the horrors of Stalin's brutal dictatorship. The United States of America, relatively untouched by a war that had killed nearly an entire generation of Europeans, emerged as a global power. This put Western Civilization's two most precocious offspring, Russia and the United States, on a collision course that would come terrifyingly close to annihilating humankind altogether.

In the wake of such a tragedy, it began to seem to many that perhaps Nietzsche had been right when he had predicted the imminent collapse of civilization. To a Europe reeling from the devastation of the twentieth century, even Nietzsche's more wild assertions began to sound plausible.

---

[1] Melvin Page, "Black Men in a White Man's War," in *Africa and the First World War* (New York: Saint Martin's Press, 1987).

99

Perhaps morality was a big lie. Perhaps reason and faith were meaning-less. Perhaps truth itself was nothing more than a pathetic delusion. In the age of machine warfare and nationalistic genocide, perhaps God was dead after all. Even with its cities, its global power, its technology, its pluralism, and its nation-states, the West faced a profound crisis of iden-tity, a crisis that arguably remains with us to this day. If authority and truth are nothing more than the arbitrary will of stronger, more powerful people, if political and personal liberty is an illusion in the technocratic bureaucracy, if the primary long-term consequence of universal opulence is the devastation of the natural environment, is there anything in this civilization worth saving? Has the past 500 years of modern 'Progress' ultimately been a lie? We need to consider these questions and their implications carefully as heirs of the Modern West.

And yet despite all that, the West could still sound a hopeful note, for 1918 also saw the posthumous publication of the works of the Jesuit poet Gerard Manley Hopkins. In "God's Grandeur," this spiritual descendant of Ignatius of Loyola had reminded the West that:

> ...nature is never spent;
>   There lives the dearest freshness deep down things;
> And though the last lights off the black West went
>   Oh, morning, at the brown brink eastward, springs —
> Because the Holy Ghost over the bent
>   World broods with warm breast and with ah! bright wings

On Duties, II.19-43

Marcus Tullius Cicero, 43 B.C.

In a moment I will discuss the best methods for winning and keeping friends, but first let me say this: in both good times and bad, the power of fortune is tremendous. When she gives us a favorable wind, we arrive at greatness; when she blows against us, we are ruined. Some misfortunes are rare, especially those caused by non-living things like storms, tempests, shipwrecks, and fires. Even more infrequently, we suffer misfortunes from animals, who beat, bite, and attack. But what about [misfortune caused by other men], like the destruction of armies? We have just seen this happen three times. We have also seen the downfall of a great and remarkable man who held the Roman *imperium*.[1] Moreover, the envy of the mob frequently leads to the exile or expulsion of a city's most worthy citizens. Nevertheless, though fortune is partly responsible for honor, power, and victory, no one could achieve them without the help of others. So, I will now tell you how to cultivate the goodwill of men for your own utility. If you find this passage long, simply consider its usefulness, and you will probably rethink your opinion.

Whenever one man benefits another or bestows some dignity on him, he does it for one of five reasons: love and good will (*benivolentia*); admiration (if the giver thinks the receiver's virtue makes him worthy of greater

---

[1] Cicero is likely talking about Pompey here, who had just been defeated by his one-time collaborator turned rival, Julius Caesar. Pompey had been granted "imperium," the Roman term for command of an army.

fortune); trust (in which case he often is acting out of self-interest as well); fear; or hope of gain (like when kings give gifts to their people or when someone takes a bribe, which is a most dirty and wicked practice).

It is a bad thing to buy loyalty, which should be won by virtue; however, sometimes this is necessary, so after I speak of virtue, I will show how money can be used to win allies. In summary then, men submit themselves to the power of another for a variety of reasons: good will, favors, the greatness of the other's dignity, hope of future gains, fear that they will be compelled to obey by force, and hope of reward or gifts, which as we see in our own republic, often take the forms of bribes.

There is nothing more useful for keeping power than to be loved, and nothing more harmful than to be feared. Thus Ennius says, "people will hate whomever they fear, and whomever they hate cannot last long." No one is able to hold onto power if the people hate him; if this was not recognized before, it certainly is now. This lesson is not only true of this one man, who used force to oppress his country (which obeys him even after his death),[2] but also true of similar tyrants, few of whom have escaped the same fate.

Men who oppress and enslave others by force must use cruelty to hold on to their power, but it is crazy to try to make oneself feared in a free city. Although a tyrant might overturn the laws and stifle the people's freedom, some men will find a way to express their liberty in the choice of whom to bestow honor on, for liberty that has been lost is more acutely felt than liberty that is simply maintained. Thus, it is far better to rely on love, not only for keeping yourself safe, but for maintaining power and influence. The man who is loved has a much easier time getting what he wants, in both his public and private affairs.

If a man wants to inspire fear, he must himself fear those very people he hopes to instill fear in. What should we think of the elder Dionysus? How much was this tyrant tortured by fear? He singed his hair off with burning hot coals because he feared the barber's blade. What should we think of Alexander the Pherean? We read that he loved his Theban wife, yet whenever he came into her bedchamber, he ordered a barbarian…to

---

[2] Cicero is referring here to the assassination of Julius Caesar, which had occurred only a few months before he wrote this.

go in first with his sword drawn. He also ordered his guards to rummage through his wife's drawers to make sure that she had not hidden some sort of weapon amongst her clothes. O miserable man, who trusts a barbarian more than his own wife...

Phalaris is another example of great cruelty. He was neither killed by a plot, like Alexander, nor at hands of a few conspirators, like our own tyrant.[3] Rather, he was killed by the all the citizens of Agrigento. Did not the Macedonians betray Demetrius and defect to Pyhrrus? When the Spartans ruled unjustly, did they not lose all of their allies, who watched them suffer defeat at the Battle of Leuctra without trying to help them?

I am using foreign examples because it pains me to reflect on Roman examples. When the Roman people held their power by doing good to others rather than by injuring them, the wars that we waged were only fought to protect our allies or our empire. At the ends of those wars, the Romans were merciful, except when it was necessary to be unmerciful. Our senate was the refuge of kings, peoples and nations, and our magistrates and generals sought just one thing: to be praised for defending our provinces and allies and treating them with justice and honesty.

When this was the case, we were more like the patrons than the rulers of the world. Over time, however, we gradually lost the habit of doing good to others, and after the reign of Sulla,[4] we stopped doing good altogether. When there was such cruelty in the heart of Rome itself, we cared little if cruelty was also committed against our allies. For instance, Sulla went to war for a good and just (*honesta*) cause, but he did not have a good and just victory. For he held a public auction and dared to say he was simply selling his own booty, when in fact he was selling the fortunes of good men, even the goods of citizens. He was followed by Marius,[5] who had an impious reason for war and an even more immoral victory, and thus not only sold away the goods of a single city, but brought calamity on entire provinces and regions.

---

[3] Julius Caesar again.

[4] Roman dictator (138 B.C.-78 B.C), whose cruelty and ambition launched Rome into a half-century of civil war.

[5] Roman dictator (157 B.C.-86 B.C.); Julius Caesar's uncle through marriage.

During this period, we saw foreign nations being harassed and destroyed. For example, we saw Marseilles lose its power and forced to take part in one of our own general's triumphs,[6] even though without their help, we never would have had any victories beyond the Alps worthy of a triumph. I could recite a list of other evils we had committed against our allies, though it is not necessary because this one is surely the worst. It is right that we be punished for these crimes, for if the evils of the multitude had been properly punished in the first place, we would have never given so much license to one single man, who bequeathed his possessions to his relatives but his greed to many.

This taste for plunder always plants the seeds of civil war. Indeed, Sulla's kinsman put all that ill-gotten booty on sale, and then held another sale thirty-six years later... From this, we must learn that the civil war will never be over as long as the hope of unjust gain remains. Already, our republican form of government is lost; only the walls of our city remain standing, though these await even more depraved wickedness. Coming back to my point, we have brought this disaster on ourselves because we have thought it better to be feared than loved. If such was the case when the Romans exercised their dominion unjustly, what might individuals expect?

Since it is clear that the power of benevolence is so great and the power of fear so weak, I still need to speak about how we might easily attain our desires by the means of admiration, trust, and good will (*honor, fides, caritas*). However, we do not all have the same needs in this regard, and a man should accommodate his desires to his lot in life. Some people need a lot of influence, and others need only a little, yet all men need the love and trust of friends; this is something that is equally necessary for great men and small men alike and can be accomplished by both in the same way.

---

[6] A triumph was a Roman celebration held to honor generals who had won great battles or wars. It frequently involved the public humiliation of the conquered peoples. During Caesar's war with Pompey, Marseilles had sided with Pompey, and thus Caesar conquered it and forced it to participate in his triumph in Rome in 46 B.C.

However, not everyone has the same need for honor, glory, and the good will of fellow citizens. Men who do need them will find them just as useful as friendship. I have written about friendship in a book called Laelius,[7] so now I will speak about glory (though I have already written two books on glory as well). Let us talk about how glory relates to governance. The highest and most perfect glory consists in three things: the good-will, trust, and admiration of the people. Briefly put, the same things that win friends and influence individual people give us influence over the many…

Let us first deal with capturing the good will of the many. The best way to do this is by benefitting others, the second is the desire to benefit others, even if we lack the ability to do so; the third is a reputation for liberality, beneficence, justice, trustworthiness, and all of those virtues which pertain to a life of restraint. These qualities are called good and fitting because they are pleasing in and of themselves, and they shine through those virtues that I have mentioned. We are compelled to love any man who shows these virtues, though there are also less serious ways to win the love of others.

The people's trust can be won in two ways: namely, with justice and prudence. We trust people whom we think are more intelligent than we are, who better gauge the future, and who know the best course of action to take when difficult business is at hand. All men consider this type of wisdom to be useful and truly prudent. We also place our trust in good men, whom we do not suspect will injure or deceive us, and we rightly think it wise to entrust such men with our health, fortune and families.

Between the two, justice is more useful for winning trust than prudence. Imprudent men are often given authority, but prudence alone can never win someone trust. The multitude will never trust in the honesty of a man who seems to be crafty and cunning; rather, these qualities will cause him to be suspected and hated. For this reason, intelligence must be joined to justice in order to inspire trust, for justice without prudence is able to do much, but prudence without justice is useless.

---

[7] Remember *De Amicitia (On Friendship)* in the Veritas Symposium!

The reader may wonder how this is possible, since all philosophers agree with me that whoever has one of the virtues possesses all of the virtues. How can I say, then, that a man can be prudent but not just? When I call a man prudent here, I am not using the term in its philosophical sense, but rather in its popular sense. I am accommodating my speech to the common man. Thus, when we call something strong, good, and prudent in the common tongue, it means something different than when we speak philosophically. We should use the popular sense when we speak about popular opinion, which Panetius did often. But let us return to the subject at hand.

Of the three items that pertain to glory, the third consists in winning admiration from one's fellow man. The multitude usually admires anything that surpasses their understanding and anyone whom they think possesses unexpectedly good qualities (*nec opinata quaedam bona*). Thus, the multitude praise men they consider great and extraordinarily virtuous, while they despise and condemn those who do not seem to possess virtue, spirit, and courage. This does not mean the multitude condemns any person that seems to be bad, since they by no means condemn dishonest, slanderous, fraudulent, or injurious men. Rather, men are generally despised for laziness and lack of industry, the type of man who takes no care for either himself or for others.

Men can win admiration by excelling others in virtue and avoiding dishonor and those vices that the multitude find difficult to resist. Now, pleasure, which is a charming mistress, turns most souls away from virtue, and fear of pain and misfortune terrify most men. Life, death, riches, and poverty are all powerful motivators. Whoever despises life, death, riches and poverty in pursuit of some other honest goal will show that he has a lofty soul. Will such a man not win admiration, for who does not admire the splendor and beauty of virtue?

This indifference to death or poverty excites the admiration of the multitude. It also produces justice, the virtue that makes a man worthy to be called good. As a result, he will seem wonderful to the multitude, who will not fear any injury from him. No man can be just if he fears death, pain, exile, or poverty or places any of these things ahead of equity. The multitude especially admires a man who is not moved by greed, for such a man appears to be tried by fire.

Thus, of those three things that lead to glory, all of them are accomplished by justice: the good will, trust, and admiration of the multitude can be won by justice because justice seeks the good of the many and spurns and neglects those things that usually excite greed.

In my opinion, all of life's plans and arrangements require the help of other men. In the first place, a man needs to have familiars with whom he can speak; this is difficult unless he has a reputation for goodness. Even a solitary man living in the countryside needs a reputation for justice since his reputation is his only defense and protection against the many dangers of such a life.

Justice is quite necessary for merchants when they buy, sell, or do business; indeed, its power is so great that even those who live by crime must have some small particle of justice in order to survive. Even a thief practices a form of justice, for the head thief is either killed by his compatriots or overthrown if he does not distribute the booty equally. Thus, even thieves have laws that they obey and observe. By this equitable sharing of booty, Bardyllis the Illyrian, whom Theopompus mentions, piled up a great fortune. Viriatus Lusitanus had an even bigger fortune, though he was eventually defeated by our army and captains… Given that the power of justice is so great it can even win riches for thieves, how much greater must it be when it is constituted by law in a well-ordered republic (*in constituta re publica*)?

Like the Persians that we read about in Herodotus, our own ancestors first made kings in order to enjoy the fruits of justice. Because the multitude was oppressed by the wealthy, they sought protection from a man of extraordinary virtue, who maintained equal justice by preventing the strong from injuring the weak and by preserving equality between the highest and the lowest class of citizens.

Our ancestors instituted laws for the same reasons, as everyone always desires an equality of rights, for without it there can be no rights at all. When one man alone was able to provide justice, the people were content; when this could no longer be done, the people invented laws, which were equal for all men and stable throughout time. Thus, it is clear that men were usually chosen to rule due to their reputation for justness. If they also happened to be prudent, men thought that there was nothing they could not accomplish under such authority. For all these reasons, justice is to be prized and practiced, as much for its own sake (since otherwise it would not be justice) as on account of increasing honor and glory. As there is a method not only for seeking money, but even for piling it up for necessary and extra expenses, so there must be a method for seeking and piling up glory.

Socrates has pointed out the way to this glory in a wonderful, little saying: "if you want glory, be what you want others to think you are." If anyone thinks he can win eternal glory with deceit (*simulatio*), empty boasting (*ostentatio*), and the dishonest fashioning (*fictus*) of his words and appearance, he is seriously mistaken. True glory plants deep roots and spreads far and wide, falsehood quickly fades away like a pretty little flower, for deceit cannot last long... Thus, whoever wants to obtain true glory will fulfill the demands of justice.

Letter to Francesco Vettori

Niccolò Machiavelli, 1513

Magnificient ambassador. Divine graces never come late. I say this because it seemed to me that I had not only lost your favor but that it had completely vanished, since it had been a long time since you wrote me, and I was not sure why. I dismissed everything that came into my head, except when I wondered if you had not written me because someone told you that I had not taken good care of your letters, though I knew that except for Filippo and Pagolo, only I had seen them. I have received your last letter; I have been most happy to see how ordered and peacefully you are exercising your public office, and I urge you to continue to do so, for whoever loses his own comforts for the sake of another may not get anything in return. Since fortune wants to do everything, she wants you to let things be, and to let things be without causing trouble. Wait for the right time to try to help me. For now, it will be good for you to do your work industriously, to keep an eye on things, and to leave me here on my villa to say, "Here I am." I will be happy to tell you what my life is like here, and if you decide that you would like to exchange mine for yours, I would be happy to do so.

I am here at my villa; since my recent problems began, I have not stayed more than twenty days in Florence. Up to now, I have been setting little bird traps with my own hands. Every day I get up, making the lime and trudging out with a bundle of cages on my back, just like Geta when he came back from port with Amphitryon's books.[1]   And this is what I

---

[1] This is a reference to Plautus' comedy *Amphitryon* and/or its medieval adaptation, *Geta*.

have been doing with my September. Since then, I have had to give up this strange little hobby, to my displeasure, and I will tell what my life has been like since then.

I get up every morning with the sun and go to my little timber cutting operation in a wood I own, and there I stay for two hours to inspect the previous day's work and to pass the time with the woodcutters, who always have some misadventures at hand either amongst themselves or with the neighbors. I could tell you a thousand great tales that have happened to me while managing these woods, particularly with Frosino da Panzano and others who want this timber. For instance, Frosino sent for some of my wood without telling me about it, and when I asked for payment, he demanded I knock off ten *lire* that he said I had owed him from a game of *cricca* at the house of Antonio Guicciardini four years ago.[2] I began to swear and curse at him and accused the driver that had fetched the wood of being a thief. Finally, Giovanni Machiavelli intervened, and we made peace. Batista Guicciardini, Filippo Ginori, and Tommaso del Bene each bought some firewood from me when the cold wind started to blow. I promised it to all of them and sent one to Tommaso; when it got there, he, his wife, his servants, and his sons all stacked it up very neatly, so it ended up measuring half as much as what we had thought to send… Then, when I saw who was getting the better deal, I said to the others that I didn't have any more wood; and they all made a big fuss about it, especially Batista, who acted like it was some sort of crime…

When I leave from my wood, I go to a spring, and from there to where I set my bird traps. I bring a book with me, either Dante or Petrarch, or one of the minors poets, like Tibullus, Ovid, or something like that.[3] I read of their amorous passions, and their loves remind me of my own. I enjoy a little bit of time in these reveries. Then I walk towards the inn; I speak with those who pass by and ask them news from their parts. I hear all sorts of things, and I take note of the different tastes and imaginations

---

[2] Cricca is a game of chance that is a precursor to our game of poker.

[3] Dante Alighieri is a major Italian poet and author of *The Divine Comedy*; Franceso Petrarcha is a major Italian poet and author of *Canzoniere* (songs; he invented the sonnet). Tibullus is a minor Latin elegiac poet, and Ovid is a Latin poet famous for the *Metamorphoses* and *The Art of Love*.

of different kinds of men. Then comes lunchtime and with my family and servants, I eat the type of food that a poor villa and small inheritance can provide. Once I have eaten, I go back to the inn; there I play a game of *cricca* and *tric-trac* with the butcher, the miller, and two bakers.[4] This always gives rise to a thousand disagreements and harsh words. Most of the time we are fighting over a tiny amount of money, but you can probably hear us from San Casciano. All this helps me keep my mind off my bad luck, for I let lady luck ride roughshod over me when I gamble to see if eventually she will be ashamed of herself for treating me so.

When evening comes, I return to my house and enter into my study; before I go in, I take off my work clothes, full of muck and dirt, and I dress myself with royal and curial garb; thus decently dressed, I enter into the courts of the ancients, and they receive me as their friend.[5] They feed me with the food that is mine alone and for which I was born; I am not ashamed to speak with them and probe the reasons for their actions. In their humaneness, they answer me. For four hours I feel no boredom, and I forget all my troubles, for I fear neither poverty nor death. And I give myself completely over to them.

And because Dante says that no one really learns anything unless he remembers what he has learned, I have made many notes, and composed a little tract called *The Prince*, where I delve as deeply as I am able into some thoughts on this subject, discussing what a monarchy is, what types there are, how they are acquired, how they are kept, and why they are lost. And if you have ever liked any of my little whimsies, this one is sure to please, and perhaps will be received well by a prince, and especially a new prince, so I am going to dedicate it to his Magnificence Giuliano [de Medici]. Filippo Casavecchia has seen it. It sums up many conversations that I have had with him, though I have added some things and polished others.

You would like, magnificent ambassador, that I leave this life and come to see you. I would love to do this, but I am restrained by certain business that I will have to do in about a month or so. What worries me

---

[4] Tric-trac is a little like backgammon.

[5] These "courts of ancients" are, of course, Machiavelli's collection of great books.

is that [if I come visit you in Rome] I will have to go visit some people who were on Soderini's side [against the Medici], so when I return home, I will probably go right to prison because although this [Medici] state has most wonderful foundations and great security, it is still a new state, so the government is suspicious. Moreover, there are a bunch of know-it-alls like Pagolo Bertini, who would buy lunch for others, and leave me to pick up the tab. Clear me of this fear, and I will come to you immediately

I have spoken to Filippo [Guicciardini] about this little book of mine and whether or not I should give it [to Giuliano dei Medici], and if I should give it, should I bring it to Giuliano myself or send it to you. He made me doubt whether Giuliano or anyone else would even read it. I am also worried that Ardinghelli would take credit for it. But necessity and poverty will probably force me to give it to them, because I cannot live like this much longer without being shamed for my poverty. More-over, I want these Medici lords to make some use of me, even if they should begin by making me roll a stone. If I could not win them over then, I would only have myself to blame. Moreover, when they read my little book, they will see that I have not spent my fifteen years in politics asleep or playing games, and each of them should consider themselves lucky to be served by someone with so much experience. And they should not doubt that they can trust me because I have always kept faith, and I should not learn how to break it now, for a man who has been good and faithful for forty-three years, as I have, can not change his nature at my age. My poverty is a witness to my goodness. Please write me with your opinions on the matter... Be happy.

Niccolò Machiavelli.

The Prince

Niccolò Machiavelli, 1513-1519

DEDICATION

To the Magnificent Lorenzo Di Piero De' Medici:[1]

Whoever wishes to garner favor with a prince normally gives him whatever he happens to like the most; thus, princes are usually given horses, weapons, golden brocades, precious stones and other ornaments worthy of their greatness. I, on the other hand, have nothing more valuable to offer than my knowledge of the actions of great men, which I have learned from long experience in modern political affairs and continuous reading of ancient ones. Thus, I am sending you this little book as a token of my devotion. In it, I have condensed all my knowledge into a few chapters. Though I do not consider the book a worthy gift, I hope that you will find it acceptable, knowing that I can offer nothing better than the lessons of my experience...

Because I wanted to speak the truth plainly and show the gravity and seriousness of the subject matter, I have not written in fancy prose. Nor do I want others to think me too bold for daring to venture above my station in discussing the affairs of princes. If you want to paint a mount-

---

[1] Lorenzo Di Piero De'Medici was Duke of Urbino and ruled Florence from 1513-1519; his uncle was Pope Leo X, who excommunicated Martin Luther in 1521. Machiavelli had originally planned to dedicate the work to the Pope's brother Giuliano, who had briefly ruled in Florence as well, but Giuliano died in 1516, so Machiavelli dedicated it to Lorenzo instead.

ain, you need to descend to the valley and look up; so it is in describing the heights of princely rule. Receive then, your Magnificence, this little gift with the same spirit with which I send it. Once you read it, you will realize how much I desire your fortune and success. And if your Magnificence will look down from the heights from time to time, you will realize how undeserved is the misfortune that I now suffer.

CHAPTER I — HOW MANY KINDS OF MONARCHIES THERE ARE, AND BY WHAT MEANS THEY ARE ACQUIRED

All states and dominions that have power over men are either republics or monarchies. Monarchies that have been in the same family for a while are called hereditary monarchies; otherwise, they are new monarchies. New monarchies are either completely new...or added to existing reigns... People in acquired territories are either accustomed to living under a prince, or they are used to being free. Acquired territories are either acquired with a prince's own armies or with another's, and either by fortune or by *virtù*.

CHAPTER II: ON HEREDITARY PRINCES

I will not speak of republics because I have written about them elsewhere at length.[2] Rather, I will direct my attention to monarchies, following the order that I have set out in the last chapter and describing how monarchies should be governed and maintained.

Hereditary states that have been in the same family for a while are usually easier to hold than newly-acquired states because a ruler can simply follow the example of his predecessors and deal prudently with situations as they arise. If such a prince is at all diligent, he will easily maintain his position...and even if he is overthrown, he will easily win his state back when the first bit of bad luck befalls the usurper.

In Italy, we have the example of the Duke of Ferrara, who was not overthrown when attacked by the Venetians in 1484 nor when attacked by Pope Julius II in 1510. He survived for no other reason than that he was an hereditary monarch. A natural, hereditary prince has less need

---

[2] In the *Discourses on Titus Livy*.

to harm his subjects, and for that reason, he is more beloved. Unless he has some particularly evil vice, his subjects will naturally love him...

CHAPTER III: MIXED MONARCHIES[3]

When a prince adds a new territory to his old territory, he faces a problem common to all new monarchies, a problem that makes new monarchies the most difficult to hold; that is, men happily take up arms to change one lord for another, hoping to better their condition, but they soon discover that they are worse off because a new prince must always aggrieve and injure his new subjects. Thus, new princes make enemies of those they have harmed and tend to lose their allies as well. Indeed, a new prince can neither satisfy his allies' desires nor act firmly with them since he will need their help in integrating the new territory, regardless of his other strengths. For instance, King Louis XII was able to take Milan quite quickly, and then he lost it just as quickly, as soon as the old ruler's troops returned. The people who had opened the gates of Milan to King Louis XII found him to be much worse than they had expected, and he quickly grew intolerable to them...Thus, the question arises: how can a prince keep his position better than Louis did?

When a prince adds a new state to his territories, the new state is either in the same region and speaks the same language, or it is not. When it is in the same region, it is very easy to hold, especially if the inhabitants are not used to being free. To possess it, all one has to do is kill its rulers. Since the people will not have to change their laws, they will live peacefully. We see an example of this in France, which acquired the regions of Burgundy, Brittany, Gascony, and Normandy. Although the men of these regions did not speak French, they did have French customs; thus, these regions were easy for the French kings to hold. When a prince takes such a territory, he really only has to do two things: completely eliminate the old ruling family and avoid changing the laws or imposing new taxes. In a short time, the new and the old territories will be like one body.

---

[3] Note that Machiavelli's use of the term mixed is unusual here. He does not mean a mixed constitution in which power is shared between the one, the few, and the many. He means a mixture of old states and newly-acquired states.

Difficulties arise when a prince acquires territory with different language, customs, and laws. A prince will need great diligence and fortune to hold it. One of the best things a prince can do to secure a conquered land is to live in it. This is exactly what the Sultan of Turkey did when he conquered the Byzantines; if he had not, it would have been impossible for him to keep his Byzantine conquests. If a prince lives in a territory, he can respond to problems as they arise. If he does not live in the conquered territory, he will not realize when problems have gotten out of hand, and he will not be able to respond to them. Moreover, if a prince lives in the conquered territory, he can ensure that his officials will not plunder it, and the subjects will be able to appeal directly to him. Good men will then have more reason to love him and evil men to fear him. Finally, potential invaders will be more cautious in attacking since they know it will be hard to wrest control of such a territory from a prince who lives there.

The other way to hold a new state is to establish a couple military colonies in it. Colonies do not cost much, so a prince can maintain them at little expense. Colonies harm only a few people, whose lands and houses must be taken away to give to the new inhabitants. The dispossessed subjects remain scattered and poor and thus unable to avenge themselves on the prince. Everyone else lives peacefully, terrified of being dispossessed like their neighbors if they get out of line. I conclude that colonies are inexpensive, more faithful, and harm only a few people...Let us make a general note then: a prince either has to coddle his subjects or crush them. If you hit a man, hit him so hard that he cannot get back up and take his revenge.

On the other hand, if you occupy a territory, you use up all the taxes of the state in maintaining the garrison. Everyone has to pay taxes, and thus everyone becomes your enemy, but these enemies remain in their houses and on their estates. This is why a full occupation is a bad idea, and colonization is a good idea.

When a prince conquers a territory that differs in customs from his own, he needs to make himself the leader and defender of his less powerful neighbors, weaken his more powerful neighbors, and make sure that no foreign powers intervene, which is always a danger in places filled with unhappy, ambitious, or fearful people...When a foreign power enters a region, all the little powers usually flock to it because of their jealousy towards the major powers. Thus, minor powers can easily be won over. Just don't let them grow too powerful...and you will easily become master of the whole region. Follow these rules, and you will keep your power; otherwise, you will encounter a thousand problems.

The Romans observed all these rules in the territories that they seized. They set up colonies, became protectors of less powerful states... weakened the powerful states, and never let other powerful foreign states gain a foothold. We only need to look at what the Romans did in Greece, for instance. They supported the Achaeans and Aetolians (though they never let them grow any more powerful than they already were), they weakened the Macedonians, and they expelled the powerful King of Syria from the region...

Machiavelli continues with a discussion of how the Romans always brought a fight to their enemies rather than waiting for it to come to them. He then discourses on the failure of King Louis XII of France in his invasion of Italy and seizure of Milan. Louis, Machiavelli argues, did everything wrong in not follow- ing the principles that Machiavelli has just finished laying out. Louis supported the power of the papacy rather than the weaker Italian powers, and he invited the King of Spain to share power with him in Southern Italy.

It is perfectly natural and ordinary to want to acquire, and everyone praises the man who takes what he can. However, when a man desires to conquer more than he can on his own, he deserves criticism. If France could have assaulted Naples on its own, they should have done it on their own; if they could not have conquered Naples on their own, they should not have shared control with the Spaniards...Thus, Louis made the following five errors. He weakened the minor Italian powers. He made the major powers more powerful. He invited a very powerful foreign prince into Italy. He did not live in Italy. And he did not establish French colonies in Italy....

Thus, King Louis of France lost Lombardy and Milan because he did not follow the example of other successful rulers. There is nothing sur- prising about this at all. Indeed, I spoke about all of this to the Cardinal of Rouen, when Cesare Borgia, son of Pope Alexander VI, was occupying the Romagna.[4] The cardinal told me that Italians did not understand war, and I responded that the French did not understand matters of state, because if they did, they would never have let the Papal States remain so powerful. Experience taught us that the French themselves brought about the power of the Papal States and Spain in Italy and in turn brought about their own ruin. From this example, we can deduce a general rule: whoever supports another's rise to power paves the way to his own ruin; the same qualities that he uses to help his partner will eventually give the partner cause for suspicion.

CHAPTER IV: WHY THE PERSIAN REALMS DID NOT REBEL AGAINST THE MACEDONIANS AFTER THE DEATH OF ALEXANDER THE GREAT

If you consider the difficulty involved in holding a newly-acquired territory, you might marvel at the story of Alexander the Great. Alexander the Great became lord of almost all of Asia in a few short years, having taken it from the Persian Empire. After having occupied it for barely more than a few years, he died. Though we might suspect that all of Asia would have immediately rebelled against the Macedonians, Alexander's successors held it easily and would have continued to hold it easily if not for the disagreements that arose amongst themselves.

How do we make sense of this? First, it is important to distinguish between two types of monarchies. In the first type, there is one prince and everyone else is a servant who only helps to govern the realm on the prince's say-so. In the second type, the barons who help the prince to govern the realm possess their own authority and do not rely on him. These barons have their own lands and their own subjects, who recognize them as their lords and thus have a natural affection for them. Princely authority is greater in the first type because no one thinks himself superior to the prince, and when the subjects obey the prince's officials, they do it because they respect the prince, not because they respect the officials.

---

[4] A region in central Italy.

In our own times, we have two perfect examples of these two kinds of monarchy: Turkey and France. Turkey has one monarch, the sultan; everyone else is his slave. Dividing his country into various regions, he sends out different officials and replaces them at his pleasure. But the King of France must share his authority with many other lords, whose families have held their lands for a long time. These other lords are recognized and beloved by their own subjects. They are preeminent in their own states, and it would be dangerous for the French king to deprive them of their power.

Given this, it is clear that conquering a state like Turkey would be very difficult; however, once it had been conquered, it would be fairly easy to keep. It would be difficult to conquer because the sultan's officials would not ally with you nor could you count on inciting a rebellion. Because all the governors are the sultan's slaves, it would be hard to corrupt them, which would not be much help anyway since they do not command the loyalty of the people. Thus, whoever attacks the Turk should expect to find a united enemy and would thus need to make sure of his own strength. However, once the Turkish armies were crushed, an invader would only have to worry about the royal family. Once he had executed all of them, there would be no one left to fear, since none of the other officials would have the loyalty of the people. Thus, before the victory, one would have nothing to gain from the Turkish officials; after the victory, one would have nothing to fear from them.

France, however, is just the opposite. It would be easy to invade France because there is always some unhappy French baron who might help you to victory. But you would find France difficult to keep, both because of the barons you defeated and because of the barons who helped you to power. It would not be enough simply to kill the royal family because other powerful lords would remain. Since you could neither keep them all happy nor wipe them all out, you would lose your state the first time anything went wrong.

Now, if we look at the Persian realm that Alexander conquered, we will see that it was similar to Turkey. Thus, the first thing Alexander needed to do was to defeat the Persians in battle; after that (as the Persian king was dead) Alexander was perfectly secure, and if his successors had remained united, they would have been able to enjoy that security in

119

comfort. Indeed, the only tumults that happened in Persia were caused by Alexander's successors themselves. On the other hand, states that are constituted like France are nearly impossible to hold so peacefully. Thus, we see frequent uprisings in France...

Consider all these things, and you will understand why Alexander's successors held Asia so easily and why others...have such problems. The difference is not in the *virtù* of the conqueror; it is in the type of state that is conquered.

CHAPTER V: HOW ONE SHOULD GOVERN CITIES OR MONARCHIES THAT LIVED BY THEIR OWN LAW BEFORE BEING CONQUERED

There are three ways to hold newly-acquired states that are used to living as free men under their own laws: one, destroy them; two, live there personally; three, let them live according to their own laws, take a little tribute from them, and create an oligarchy who will be loyal to you. Inasmuch as the oligarchs know that they owe their authority to you alone and cannot survive without you, they will do all they can to maintain your authority. Indeed, the best way to hold a city that is accustomed to freedom is to get its own citizens to work for you, assuming that you do not want to destroy it instead.

The Spartans and Romans are good examples of this. The Spartans took Athens and Thebes and established oligarchies there, though they later lost them both. The Romans, on the other hand, completely demolished Capua, Carthage, and Numantia and never lost them. The Romans had wanted to hold Greece as the Spartans had, leaving it free and letting each city-state keep its old laws. This was not a successful policy, and after it failed, the Romans were forced to demolish many city-states in order to keep them.

My point is that the only way to hold on to a free republic is to destroy it. Whoever conquers a free republic without destroying it is only setting himself up to be destroyed by it. When it rebels, it will always remember its former freedoms. To be on the safe side then, a conqueror must destroy the city and scatter its inhabitants. Otherwise, its patriots will never forget the name of liberty...

However, when a city is used to living under a prince, the conqueror has nothing to fear, provided he kills the old prince. People who are used to living in a monarchy are accustomed to obedience; moreover, they do not know how to elect a new ruler and they do not know how to live free, so they are slow in taking up arms when their old prince is dead. Thus, a conqueror can easily overwhelm them. On the other hand, in republics there is more vigor, more hatred, and more desire for vengeance; the memory of past liberty will never die. Thus, the more secure way to rule a republic is to destroy it or live there personally.

CHAPTER VI: ABOUT NEW MONARCHIES THAT ARE ACQUIRED WITH ONE'S OWN ARMIES AND WITH VIRTÙ

...A private person becomes a prince either by *virtù* or fortune; thus, he needs either *virtù* or fortune to keep his power. Of the two, it is safer to rely on *virtù*...Thus, let us consider men who gained power with their own *virtù* rather than those who gained power by fortune; of these, the most excellent are Moses, Cyrus, Romulus, Theseus and others like them. Though we should probably not include Moses here because he was merely following God's orders, we can admire him for the grace that made him worthy to speak with God. Moreover, Moses' actions were not much different than those other admirable men, even though he had such a great teacher in God. In any case, none of these men had particularly great fortune; they just had an opportunity, and they seized it...Without that chance, their *virtù* would have been good for nothing; but without their *virtù*, their chance would have been wasted.

Machiavelli then proceeds to a discussion of how each of his exemplars seized an opportunity to acquire or found a state and describes how difficult it is for someone to set themselves up as the leader of a new government. He points out that the new ruler is always in danger.

It is necessary to distinguish between new rulers who have their own forces and new rulers who rely on the forces of others...Rulers who rely on the forces of others never come to a good end, but those who have their own forces are rarely in grave danger. From this follows the rule:

armed prophets conquer, while disarmed prophets fall. This is because human nature is fickle; it is easy to persuade people of something but hard to keep them persuaded. When the people no longer believe you, they will no longer follow you. Moses, Cyrus, Theseus, and Romulus would not have been obeyed for long if they had been disarmed prophets, like Girolamo Savonarola in our time.[5] Savonarola's laws were overturned as soon as the mob stopped believing in him, and Savonarola had no way to keep the believers in check or to make the unbelievers obey.

Thus, new rulers have many obstacles in their path to power, and only *virtù* can overcome them. However, after the obstacles are overcome and a prince has wiped out anyone who might be jealous of his power, the people will start respecting him, and he will be powerful, secure, honored, and happy....

CHAPTER VII: ON MONARCHIES THAT ARE ACQUIRED WITH THE ARMS AND FORTUNE OF ANOTHER

Those who become princes merely on account of fortune have an easy time rising to the throne, but a hard time keeping it. They sail through difficulties on their way to power but are beset by problems when they achieve it...This is because dependence on someone else's fortune or goodwill is not a stable basis for political power. Unless such a prince is a very clever man with great *virtù*, he is not likely to keep his position... Thus, a state that is easily acquired is also easily lost...unless the prince has so much *virtù* that he knows how to keep what luck has thrown in his lap...

I want to cite two modern examples of men who acquired their states, respectively, by *virtù* and fortune: Francesco Sforza and Cesare Borgia, son of Pope Alexander VI. Francesco Sforza was a private citizen who overcame a thousand setbacks to become the Duke of Milan. It was very difficult for him to acquire his state, but then he held it very easily. On

---

[5] Savonarola (1452-1498) was a Dominican friar who preached in Florence. He denounced worldly wealth, art, and culture, and prophesied that a great cataclysm was immanent if people did not repent. He was excommunicated by Alexander VI and publically executed in 1498.

the other hand, Cesare Borgia acquired his state because of the fortune of his father, the Pope, and when his father's luck ended, Borgia lost his state, even though he did everything a prudent prince in such a situation should do. Whoever does not lay good foundations before building their state may be able to do it later, but only with grave danger to himself and to the state itself. If, then, you will observe the actions of Cesare Borgia, you will see that he did lay strong foundations. Thus, I do not think it a waste of time to examine his career because a new prince can do nothing better than to imitate his actions. Even though Borgia failed, it was not really his fault; his failure was the result of some really bad luck...

I would like to include one thing that Borgia did because I think it was an act worthy of imitation. When Borgia conquered the Romagna, he found that its leaders were weak and would rather rob their subjects than rule them. Indeed, the leaders of the Romagna were better at causing violence than promoting unity, so the land was full of robbers, wars, and other types of insolent behavior. Thus, Borgia thought he needed to make the people obedient to his authority in order to give the Romagna good government. To do this, he handed power over to a man named Remiro d'Orco, who was known for his cruelty and swift judgments. In a short time, d'Orco's cruelty made the Romagna peaceful and united, but after that had been accomplished, Borgia thought such a heavy hand was no longer necessary, and he was afraid the people would grow to hate him. So, he set up a court of judgment in the middle of the Romagna; each of the cities was allowed to keep an advocate there, and Borgia assigned an excellent administrator to run it. However, he knew that the people hated d'Orco's harsh government, and he wanted to fool them into thinking that he was not responsible for d'Orco's cruelty. Thus, one morning he had d'Orco's body chopped in half and publically displayed in the town square of Cesena, with a butcher's chopping block on one side and a bloody knife on the other. The ferocity of this spectacle satisfied and stupefied the people...

In order to secure his position, Borgia had to make sure none of his family's enemies were elected to succeed his father as Pope. Thus, he took four steps. First, he exterminated the families of all the lords whose lands he had taken...Second, he won over the important families of Rome, who might help him to control the new pope. Third, as far as he was able, he stacked the College of Cardinals with his own supporters. Fourth, he tried to acquire enough military power before his father died to defend himself. By the time his father died, Borgia had accomplished three of these things and had almost accomplished the fourth. He had killed many of the lords whose lands he had taken, he had won over the great Roman families, and he had won the support of many cardinals. He had already taken Perugia and Piombino. The French were no longer powerful in Italy, so he pounced on Pisa, took Siena and Lucca…and had designs on Florence. If he had been able to acquire that much power, he would have been able to rely on his own strength rather than depending on the fortune and strength of others.

Unfortunately for Borgia, his father died too soon, when only the Romagna had been secured; all the rest was in flux. Moreover, when his father died, he was surrounded by two powerful enemies and so sick that he was nearly on his own deathbed. Nevertheless, Borgia was a man of such ferocity, *virtù*, and clear-sightedness that he certainly would have been victorious had it not been for his bad luck. The foundations that he laid were certainly good…

When I recall all the actions of Cesare Borgia, I cannot think of anything to criticize; rather, it seems to me that he should be imitated by all those who come to power by fortune. Borgia was a man who had greatness of soul and lofty intentions, and he should not have done anything differently…Thus, there is no better person to imitate than him.

CHAPTER VIII: THOSE WHO COME TO POWER BY WICKED MEANS

There are two other ways a private citizen may become a prince, neither of which can entirely be attributed to fortune or *virtù*…First, a prince might come to power by doing wicked deeds. Second, a prince might come to power by the support of his fellow citizens. I will show an example of the first without discussing its merits. It is enough to know what to do in this situation if necessary.

Agathocles the Sicilian was born a poor wretch, but had risen through the military ranks to achieve political authority in Syracuse; nevertheless, he wanted to be its prince. So one morning, Agathocles convened the people and the senate of Syracuse, pretending that they needed to discuss some political business. At a prearranged signal, he had his soldiers massacre all of the senators and richest citizens. After that, he held the city without any problems, even when defeated by the Carthaginians...

Agathocles wasn't particularly lucky. He didn't rise in the world because of someone else's favor; he did it through military prowess. Only by overcoming a thousand difficulties did he finally become a prince, and he only held on to his throne in the face of hostile opposition. Nonetheless, we should not call it *virtù* to kill one's fellow citizens, to betray one's friends, and to be without faith, without piety, and without religion. In these ways, a man can acquire power, but he cannot win glory. If we consider Agathocles' fortitude, his ability to get out of danger, and his unbeatable spirit in adversity, he seems to be one of the greatest military captains who ever lived. Nevertheless, his beastly cruelty, inhumanity, and infinite wickedness prevent us from praising him as one of history's most excellent men. His rise, then, was due neither to fortune nor to *virtù*.

Machiavelli then proceeds to a modern example, Oliverotto da Fermo, which essentially makes the same point: if you come to power by wicked means, you better be ready to massacre a lot of citizens.

One may wonder how Agathocles and other rulers like him could live so long and defend their homelands against enemies even after committing so many betrayals and crimes. Why didn't their subjects overthrow them? Many other cruel rulers have not even been able to hold onto their positions in peacetime, much less in war. First, we must differentiate between cruelty poorly used and cruelty well used. Well-used cruelty (if it is licit to speak well of evil) is done all at once and only when necessary to keep oneself secure. Otherwise, a prince should only use cruelty when it benefits his subjects. Cruelty is poorly used if (even if it is small in the beginning) it gets worse as time goes on. Those who use cruelty well, like Agathocles, might have some relief (*rimedio*) for their state from God and man...

When seizing a state, the occupier needs to commit all of his offenses at once, so that he doesn't have to keep committing crimes all the time... Whoever does otherwise, either because of timidity or bad advice, will always need to keep a knife in his hand. He will never be able to trust his subjects…because he will be injuring them constantly. Rather, do your injuries to your subjects all at once, so that you will offend them less, but dole out benefits little by little, so that they will be more grateful…

CHAPTER IX: ON CIVIL MONARCHIES

…When a private citizen is made prince by the favor of other citizens, rather than by some wickedness or violence, we call this a civil monarchy. Civil monarchs are neither entirely dependent on fortune nor *virtù*; rather, they are both fortunate and cunning. One can become a civil monarch either by the favor of the common people or the favor of the nobles because in every city there are two competing desires: the nobles want to oppress the common people, and the common people do not want to be oppressed. This tension gives rise to one of three things: a monarchy, civil liberty, or anarchy.

Civil monarchies are created by either the nobles or the common people. When the nobles see that they are less powerful than the commoners, they begin to build up the reputation of one of their own, so as to make him a prince and satisfy their appetite for oppression under his protection. On the other hand, when the common people find themselves less powerful than the nobles, they build up the reputation of one person and make him a prince, in order to be defended by his authority. Those who become princes with the help of the nobles have more difficulty keeping their position than those who become princes with the help of the common people because a prince who is made by the nobility finds himself surrounded by people who think they are his equal and who are difficult to command. However, those who are brought to their throne by the favor of the common people find themselves all alone, and almost everyone around them is ready to obey them. Moreover, the only way to satisfy the desires of the nobles is to harm others, but the common people only want to avoid oppression. Also, if the common people hate you, it is impossible to keep your position because there are so many of them. On the other hand, you can keep yourself safe from the nobles even if they hate you because there are so few of them. The worst thing that the common people can do to a prince is to refuse to support him; the nobles will not only refuse their support, but also conspire against him. As they are cleverer, they will always change sides just in time and seek to win favor with whomever they think is going to come out on top. Also, a prince must always deal with the same common people, but he can change the nobles at his own whim.

To clarify this point, I want to distinguish between two types of nobles: those who bind themselves to their prince and those who do not. A prince should love and honor a noble who binds his fortune to theirs, as long as he does not rob the subjects. However, some nobles will not bind their fortune to the prince; before a prince judges them, he should consider whether their behavior is caused by cowardice or not. If such a man is merely a coward but otherwise gives good advice, a prince should use him…since a prince has nothing to fear from a coward. But if the man is either cunning or ambitious, this is a sign that he cares more about himself than the prince. A prince should treat someone like this as a future enemy because when the chips are down, this type of man will help to bring about the prince's ruin.

Anyone who is made a prince by the common people should try to keep them happy. This is easy because they only want to avoid oppression. Even those princes who are made by the nobles should try to win over the people at all costs….

CHAPTER X: HOW ONE SHOULD MEASURE THE STRENGTH OF A PRINCE

In this chapter, Machiavelli extols the benefits of a prince being able to defend himself by his own force of arms, without relying on others; this includes having enough money to raise an army or to fortify his towns, keeping a stock of provisions, and utilizing a sufficiently abundant and well-trained militia.

CHAPTER XI: ON THE PAPAL STATES

The last type of monarchy is an ecclesiastical monarchy, like the Papal States of Rome…These are acquired either by *virtù* or fortune, but they can be held without either. This is because their constitution rests on religion, which is so powerful that the Pope's subjects will not rebel against him no matter what he does. Among all princes, only the Pope has lands that he does not defend and subjects whom he does not govern, and though his lands are undefended, no one takes them from him, and although his subjects are ungoverned, they do not dream of rebellion. Thus, the Papal States remain prosperous and safe...but the Papal States are exalted and maintained by God, so it would be rash of me to speak about them.

Machiavelli then discusses the way in which the power of the Papal States had grown in the first two decades of the sixteenth century.

CHAPTER XII: ON MILITIA AND MERCENARY FORCES

Having written about all the different types of monarchies, considered the reasons of their success or failure, and shown the way many have sought to hold and acquire them, I will now show their offensive and defensive capabilities. We have already stated that a prince must build on solid foundations; otherwise, he will fail. The most important foundations for any state are good laws and a strong military. There cannot be good laws without a good military, and where there is a strong military, there will inevitably be good laws. Thus, I will leave aside the discussion of laws and speak of the military instead.

A prince can defend his state with his own forces, with mercenaries, or with allies. Mercenaries and allies are not useful; on the contrary, they are quite dangerous. A state defended by mercenaries will never be secure because mercenaries are disunited, ambitious, undisciplined, unfaithful, and cowardly in the face of enemies. Mercenaries neither fear God nor keep their word with men; they run away as soon as they are attacked. They will rob a prince during peace time and let him be robbed by his enemies in war. Nothing keeps a mercenary in the field except his pay, which is not enough to make him want to die for you. They love to be your soldier as long as you do not need to make war, but as soon as war comes, they flee. Indeed, mercenaries have been the cause of Italy's ruin. As long as they were fighting against each other, they seemed strong, but as soon as a foreign power came to Italy, they showed their cowardice. A few years ago, King Charles of France seized Italy easily, and Savonarola told us that Charles was a punishment for our sins. Savonarola was right, but he was mistaken about which sins we were being punished for…[6]

I want to speak a little more about mercenaries. There are two types of mercenary captain: competent and incompetent. Competent captains cannot be trusted; they will aspire to greatness and either overthrow you or escape your control. Incompetent captains cannot win battles for you. It might be objected that this is to be feared from any general, so let me be clear about how princes and republics need to conduct warfare: a prince needs to conduct his wars in person and to be his own general; a republic needs to send its own citizens. Republics need to fire their incompetent generals and restrain their good generals with good laws. Experience teaches us that only princes and armed republics can accomplish great things and that mercenaries only bring harm.

Moreover, it is much more difficult to establish a monarchy when the citizens are armed than in a country that relies on mercenaries. For many years, both Rome and Sparta were armed and free. The Swiss are armed to the teeth, and they are the freest people in Europe. On the other hand, Carthage had its own generals but relied on mercenary soldiers, and in the end, they lost their liberty.

After the death of Epaminodes, the Thebans made Philip of Macedon their captain, and after his victory, he took their liberty away. After the death of Duke Filippo, the Milanese employed Francesco Sforza to fight against the Venetians, and after he had conquered their enemies at Caravaggio, he joined with those enemies to oppress Milan itself…And although the Venetians and Florentines increased their power with the help of mercenaries who did not make themselves kings of those cities, the Florentines were very lucky because among the skillful captains that the Florentines might have feared, some did not win battles, some had opposition, and some directed their ambition elsewhere. If Giovanni Acuto had won battles, he would not have kept faith with the Florentines, but everyone realizes that if he had won battles, he would have tried to

---

[6] Machiavelli is being a little sarcastic here. The invasion of the French was not, as Savonarola had claimed, God's punishment on Italians' sodomy and blasphemy, but rather a result of their reliance on mercenary soldiers.

take over Florence. The ambition of Sforza was always checked by the Bracceschi, so Francesco Sforza directed his ambition to Lombardy and Milan, and Braccio directed his ambitions against the Papal States and Naples. But let us speak of examples that are closer to our own time period.

The Floretines made Paolo Vitelli their captain; he was a most prudent man, who had a private fortune and a great reputation. If he had wiped out Pisa, the Floretines would have been stuck with him because they could not have risked his going over to their enemies. Let us consider the Venetians, who did great things and made great conquests when they armed their nobles and plebs, fought their own wars, and demonstrated *virtù*. But when they switched from naval to land warfare, they lost this *virtù* and began to imitate the other powers of Italy. When they began to construct their empire on land, their power was not great, and they had nothing to fear from their mercenary captains; however, as it grew under Carmignola, they discovered their mistake. Carmignola was a most capable general, who even beat the Duke of Milan. Knowing that he was a stone cold killer, they recognized that they could not conquer more territory with him without running the risk that he would take for himself that which he had acquired for them, so they had to kill him instead.

The Venetians then employed captains such as Bartolommeo de Bergamo, Robert da San Severino, the Count of Pitigliano, and others like them, who were incompetent. Thus in the course of a single day, the Venetians lost all the territories that had taken eighty years to acquire. With weak generals, it takes a long time to acquire territory, but one can lose it all in an instant.

Since I have been talking about Italy in particular, which has used mercenaries for many years, I want to speak a little about the origin of mercenary soldiers so that we can better correct the situation. You have to understand that as soon as the Holy Roman Empire was destroyed in Italy and the Pope acquired more temporal power, Italy was divided into more states, because in many of the large cities, the citizens took up arms against their nobles, who had oppressed them when the Holy Roman Empire was powerful in Italy. In turn, the papacy supported the common people. In many other cities, some citizens became princes. Because of this, Italy fell into the hands of the Church and republics. The church lands were ruled by priests and the republics ruled by citizens who were not skilled in bearing arms; thus, they began to hire mercenary soldiers...

After many years of mercenary soldiers, the result has been that these cities have been defeated by the French kings, humiliated by Spanish kings, and wiped out by the Swiss. In order to win reputation for themselves, the mercenary captains (who fight on horseback) have gutted the infantry. They do this because they do not possess states of their own and having just a few infantry will not help them develop a great reputation, so they raise a small cavalry, which they are able to maintain. Things have come to such a pass that in an army of two-thousand soldiers, one can barely find two hundred infantry. Moreover, mercenaries do everything they can to make sure that their soldiers never have to fight too hard. They never kill each other; they just take each other prisoner. They never attack at night, they never make a proper camp, and they don't fight during the winter. All of this is to avoid danger and hard work, and all of this has given Italy over to slavery.

CHAPTER XIII: ON ONE'S OWN AND ALLIED SOLDIERS

Allied soldiers, which are also useless, are soldiers that a prince requests from his allies...These might be good troops, but they are almost always dangerous because if they lose, the prince is ruined, but if they win, the prince is their prisoner. And even though antiquity is full of examples, I would like to discuss the recent case of Pope Julius II, whose bad example we cannot fail to consider. Julius desired to take the city of Ferrara and in so doing, he delivered himself entirely into the hands of a foreign power: Spain. However, his good fortune saved him, so that he did not have to reap the fruits of his terrible decision. His Spanish troops were beaten at Ravenna by the French, but then to everyone's surprise, the French victors were destroyed by the Swiss. Thus, he was neither ruined by his enemies (because they had fled) nor a prisoner to his allies (because they had lost)...

Never rely on allies because they are even more dangerous than mercenaries. Indeed, allied troops will surely ruin you because they are united, but they are obedient to someone else. On the other hand, mercenaries are not united, so they need the right opportunity to harm you, and mercenary generals rarely have enough authority to lead a rebellion. Thus, mercenaries are dangerous because of their weakness, allied troops because of their strength.

Wise princes do not use allied troops; they use their own. They would rather lose with their own troops than win with someone else's, thinking that they have not won a real victory unless they have won it with their own army. Cesare Borgia is a perfect example. He began by taking the Romagna with allied French troops, but since he did not feel secure, he switched to mercenaries…Because he found these mercenaries unfaithful and dangerous, he fired them and raised his own troops. As he changed from allied soldiers to mercenary soldiers to his own troops, his reputation correspondingly improved. Indeed, he was never more esteemed than when led his own army.

If a prince does not recognize dangers at their beginning, he is not truly wise, which few are. The first cause of Rome's downfall was when they begin to hire the Goths as mercenaries, for this took away their own fighting spirit, and all the *virtù* that had belonged to the Romans passed over to the Goths.

To conclude then, no monarchy is secure unless it be armed. An unarmed prince must depend entirely on luck, since he will have no force (*virtù*) to defend himself in adversity. For it has always been the opinion of wise men that nothing is more weak and unstable than a reputation for power that is not built on strength. Good armies are made up of citizens, subjects or servants; all others are mercenaries or allies…

CHAPTER XIV: ON WAR

A prince should think of nothing else but preparing for war and making war. This is the only skill that a leader really needs, for war not only keeps a prince in power but can even win him a kingdom. On the contrary, when a prince thinks more about comfort than arms, he will lose his state…Being unarmed brings many problems, but the worst is that it causes others to despise you…

There is no comparison between an armed and an unarmed prince. No one who is armed will ever voluntarily obey someone who is not.

And the unarmed man will never be secure if his servants are armed... Moreover, a prince who does not understand the art of war will never be respected by his soldiers...

Even in peacetime, a prince should never stop preparing for war and thinking about war...In addition to keeping his army in good order, he should go on frequent hunting trips. This will keep his body accustomed to hardship and teach him the geography of his land, which is useful for understanding how it can be defended and how one can attack similar lands. Failing to learn geography means failure in one's first duty as a captain. Knowledge of geography teaches the captain to find the enemy, set up camp, lead an army, prepare for battle, and use the land to his own advantage...

Machiavelli recommends that a prince read about past wars and the deeds of great generals in order to prepare himself.

CHAPTER XV: ON THOSE THINGS FOR WHICH PRINCES ARE USUALLY PRAISED OR CRITICIZED

All that remains now is to discuss how a prince should govern his subjects and allies. I do not want anyone to think me presumptuous; I know that many have written about these things and that my advice is going to be quite different from theirs. However, since I intend to write only useful things for intelligent people, it seems better that I should speak only the truth rather than write about some imaginary world. Many have written about imaginary republics and monarchies that have never existed in real life. However, the way that people actually live is so different from the way that they should live that whoever neglects what needs to be done for what ought to be done paves the way to his own ruin. A man that desires to be morally good at all times will certainly come to a bad end because he must live amongst so many who do not share his moral scruples. Thus, if a prince wants to keep his position, he must learn how to do bad things when necessary.

Let's forget about the imaginary republics, then, and talk about the way things really are. All men, but especially princes, are known for some qualities that either win them praise or earn them criticism. Some princes are generous, others cheap...Princes can be cruel or merciful, treacherous or faithful, effeminate or ferocious, weak or strong, humane or prideful, lustful or chaste...etc. Surely, it would be great if a prince could have only the good qualities, but unfortunately no prince can be entirely good; the human condition will not allow it. A prince must be clever enough to avoid a reputation for vice if such a reputation might cause him to lose his state, and he should avoid vice whenever he can; but if necessary, he should do whatever it takes to maintain his state, even if others criticize him for it. If we consider the matter closely, we will find that some things that seem like virtue will actually lead to a prince's ruin and other things that seem like vice will make a prince secure.

CHAPTER XVI: GENEROSITY AND CHEAPNESS

...Some princes are considered generous; nevertheless, you might spend a lot of money and still not gain a reputation for generosity. Thus, if you want to be sure that others think you are generous, you will have to spend money constantly, and you will quickly use up all your funds. Then, if you want to keep your reputation for generosity, you will eventually need to raise taxes...This will make your subjects hate you and will make others despise your poverty; thus, your generosity will benefit a few but will harm many...

Since a prince cannot gain a reputation for generosity without harm to himself, he should not worry about being thought generous at all. In time, people will see that his generosity consists in living within his means, as well as defending the realm and undertaking projects without taxing his subjects too heavily. In this way, he benefits many but only harms a few...

As long as he is not weak, rapacious, or poor, a prince should not care if others think him cheap. It might be objected that Julius Caesar, as well as many others, achieved their power by generosity. I would distinguish between those who are trying to become princes and those who already are princes. Generosity is harmful for the latter but not necessarily for the former. Caesar was generous when he was trying to become the prince of Rome, but if he had survived and not cut down on his expenses, he would have lost his power...

Above all, a prince needs to ensure that he is not hated. Generosity will lead to hatred, so it is wiser to be thought cheap...

CHAPTER XVII: ON CRUELTY AND CLEMENCY AND WHETHER IT IS BETTER TO BE LOVED OR FEARED

All princes should desire to be thought clement rather than cruel. Nonetheless, a prince must use his clemency wisely. Cesare Borgia was considered cruel; nevertheless, his cruelty restored, united, and pacified the Romagna and made its subjects loyal. If we consider his example wisely, we will see that Cesare Borgia was much more clement to the Romagna than the Florentine Republic was to Pistoia. In order to avoid the charge of cruelty, the Florentines let Pistoia tear itself apart. Thus, a prince should not worry if people think him cruel, as long as he keeps his subjects united and peaceful.

A prince can benefit his subjects by making an example out of a few people. If he is too merciful, the whole realm will fall into disorder, and his country will be full of murderers and robbers. This harms everyone, but an execution or two only harms individuals. Moreover, because a newly-acquired state is full of danger, it is almost impossible for a new prince to avoid a reputation for cruelty. As Virgil puts in the mouth of Dido:

Severe conditions and the kingdom's youth constrain me to [harsh] measures, to protect our long frontiers with guards.[7]

Nevertheless, a prince should be slow to act, and he should not show fear. He should try to appear temperate and humane. He should neither let overconfidence make him incautious nor too much suspicion make him intolerable.

From all this arises a question: is it better to be loved or feared? I say that it is best to be both loved and feared, but because this is difficult, it

---

[7] English translation from Virgil, *The Aeneid*, trans. Robert Fitzgerald (New York: Vintage Classics, 1990), 23 (I.764-66 [original: I.563-64]). Remember Origins!

is much safer to be feared than loved, if one must do without one or the other. This is because human nature is typically ungrateful, inconstant, deceptive, cowardly, and greedy. As long as you benefit others and don't actually need anything from them, they are totally dedicated to you; they will offer you their blood, their goods, and the lives of their children. But when you need them, they will abandon you. Any prince that relies only on the promises of his subjects will be ruined; in time of need, a prince will not be able to rely on friendships that he has bought. Men are more willing to harm someone whom they love than someone whom they fear. Love ties men together by bonds of obligation, but because people are wicked, they will break this bond at any opportunity. Fear, however, is a consistent motivator.

If a prince cannot win his subjects' love, he should make them fear him, but he should avoid their hatred. This is easily done so long as he keeps his hands off their goods and off their women. If he needs to execute anyone, he should make sure that he has a good excuse. Most importantly though, he needs to keep his hands off his subjects' goods because a man will sooner forgot the death of his father than the loss of his inheritance...

A prince certainly cannot worry about a reputation for cruelty when he is leading his army because without cruelty, he will never keep his army united and obedient. For instance, despite waging war in a foreign land with a huge, multinational army, the Carthaginian general Hannibal never had to face mutiny, neither in good fortune nor bad. The reason for this must have been his inhumane cruelty, which together with his many skills (*virtù*) made his terrified soldiers respect him...Writers often praise Hannibal's feats, but they fail to recognize the reason for them.

On the other hand, we can consider Scipio. Though he was just as skilled as Hannibal, his army rebelled against him in Spain. This was because he was too clement, which gave the soldiers more license than is suitable for military discipline. For this, Scipio was reprimanded by the Roman Senate and called the corrupter of the Roman military...His apologists in the Senate said that he was better at avoiding error himself than keeping others from it. If he had been a prince, this would have been his undoing, but because he lived in a republic, it only enhanced his glory.

Returning to the question of whether it is better to be loved or feared, I say this: your subjects decide for themselves whether or not to love you, but you can control whether or not they fear you. A wise prince should secure his position with things that are under his control...he just needs to make sure that his subjects don't hate him.

CHAPTER XVIII: ON BEING TRUSTWORTHY

Everyone knows that it is praiseworthy for a prince to keep his word and live with integrity rather than duplicity. Nevertheless, the experience of our own age shows us that only untrustworthy princes accomplish great deeds. In the end, a liar will always outfox an honest man.

There are two different ways to play the game of politics: one is with the law, the other is with force. The first is properly human, the second is for the beasts. However, sometimes law alone does not work, and a wise prince will need to use force. Thus, a prince must learn how to act like a beast as well as a man...

Inasmuch as a prince must learn to act like a beast, he must know when to be a fox and when to be a lion. The lion is not savvy enough to steer clear of traps, but the fox is not strong enough to defend itself from the wolves. A prince, then, needs to be a fox who can escape from traps and a lion who can fight off the wolves. You can't just rely on strength like a lion. Thus, a prudent prince acts like the fox when he needs to and does not keep his word when it is no longer to his advantage.

If all men were good, this rule would not be good, but because people are evil, they will not keep their word with you, so you should not keep your word with them. This is okay because princes never lack legitimate reasons to break their promises...Men are so foolish that they think only about the present; thus, a liar can always find a dupe to fool.

There are many modern examples of this, but I must point out one specifically: Pope Alexander VI never did anything but lie and deceive, and he always found people to believe him. No one ever swore so thoroughly that he was telling the truth, and no one was ever quicker to break his word than he. Indeed, Pope Alexander VI knew the way the world works.

It is not necessary for a prince to have all the qualities that people think are good; it is only necessary to seem to have them. Though being too morally scrupulous will always cause a prince harm, the appearance of morality is very useful. A prince should appear clement, trustworthy, humane, upright, and religious, and by all means, a prince should actually be all these things, but he should not be afraid to abandon them if necessary. You must understand this: a prince, and especially a new prince, is not able to behave in all the ways that other men consider good. In order to maintain his position, a prince must frequently act against charity, against humanity, and against religion. He must be ready to change with the times and with his own fortune. He should be good if he can, but if necessary, he should be prepared to act in evil ways.

A prince should take care to appear pious, trustworthy, upright, humane, and most importantly, religious. For the most part, men judge on appearances. Everyone can see what you appear to be, but very few know what you really are, and the few who really know you will not dare to contradict the opinion of the mob, which in this case has the majesty of the state on its side. In the actions of all men, and especially of princes, when it is difficult to judge whether or not to protest, men look at his results. Thus, as long as the prince successfully defends his position, others will always approve his methods, and the common folk will praise him because they judge by appearances and outcomes.

CHAPTER XIX: ON AVOIDING CONTEMPT AND HATRED

In general, the prince should avoid doing things that will cause others to hate him. Avoid the people's hatred, and you will have nothing to fear. What can a prince do to make himself hateful? The worst possible thing is to take his subjects' goods or put his hands on their women. As long as a prince keeps his hands off his subjects' goods and their women, his subjects will remain peaceful. In that case, a prince only needs to worry about the ambitions of the few, which he can easily restrain. He should also avoid looking indecisive, weak, girly, mean-spirited, and irresolute. A prince must avoid this at all costs. Instead, he should give off the impression of greatness, spirit, gravitas, and fortitude. His decisions should be final, and his subjects should not think that they can deceive him or change his mind. Follow these rules, and you will gain a great reputation, which will make it difficult for others to overthrow you.

A prince must have two principal fears: he should keep one eye on his subjects and the other on foreign powers. He should defend himself from foreign nations with a strong military and good allies (and he will always have good allies if he has a strong military). As long as he is safe from foreign enemies, he will be safe from his own people, so long as there is no conspiracy against him. If he has built himself a reputation as a powerful prince, he will be able to defeat any attack from foreign powers.

Princes need to be wary of conspiracies, which is why a prince needs to avoid hatred. Conspirators always believe that the people will rejoice in the assassination of the prince; if they are not convinced of this, they will not dare raise their hand against him...Conspirators cannot act alone, but they can only join with others whom they think hate the prince; when one conspirator shares his plot with another, he puts himself in danger, for it takes either rare friendship or extreme hatred for someone to take sides with conspirators rather than just turn them in. Amongst conspirators there is nothing but fear, jealousy, and suspicion; on the prince's side are majesty, law, and the defense of friends and the state. When one adds the goodwill of the people to all those other things, no one will dare to harm the prince...

The best and most well-ordered monarchy in our time is France, which has many good institutions to secure the safety and liberty of the king. The most important of these is the authority of *parlement*.[8] The first lawgivers in France understood the ambition and insolence of the powerful and thought that someone would need to restrain them. They also knew that the common people would need to be protected from the wealthy and powerful, but they did not want this to be the king's duty, so they added a third judge, the *parlement*, which was in charge of protecting the people from the wealthy. This was prudent and helped to keep the French king safe. I should add one note here; the king needs to let his ministers do the unpleasant tasks of governance, but he should reserve the job of giving out benefits for himself. I conclude then that the prince

---

[8] The highest court in France.

needs the esteem of the wealthy and powerful, but he cannot be hated by the people.

It might seem that the lives and deaths of many Roman Emperors contradict my opinion since some of them lived outstanding lives and showed great *virtù* of soul, yet nevertheless lost their power or were killed by conspirators...However, we must note that whereas most princes only have to contend with the ambition and insolence of the people, the Roman Emperors had a third difficulty; they had to deal with the cruelty and greed of the soldiers. The difficulty in satisfying both the people and the soldiers led to the ruin of many emperors. The people love peace, and for this reason they love a peaceful prince, but the soldiers love war, and thus, they want a prince who is insolent, cruel, and rapacious. Moreover, they prefer that he be insolent, cruel, and rapacious to the people, so that they might double their pay and find an outlet for their own greed and cruelty. Thus it happened that unless an Emperor had a bellicose reputation already, he could not restrain the people or the army, and thus was ruined. Most Roman Emperors, especially those who were raised to their throne as new men, knew the difficulty of balancing these two different humors (*umore*),[9] and chose rather to satisfy the soldiers, since they did not care if they injured the people. This was necessary. Since princes will always be hated by someone, a prince needs to make sure that he is not hated by everyone, and when this is not possible, he needs to avoid the hatred of the most powerful. And those emperors who had only recently acquired power needed extraordinary help, so they cast their lot in with the soldiers more readily than with the people,

---

[9] Machiavelli borrows a term from medicine here. In early modern medicine, the human body was thought to contain four fluids, or humors, that regulated well-being. The four humors were thought to be blood, black bile, yellow bile, and phlegm. Good health consisted in keeping the humors in balance. Disease, on the other hand, represented humors that were not in balance (which makes a certain amount of sense if you consider what happens to your phlegm when you have a cold). This, incidentally, is the medical theory that underlies the practice of blood letting. In this case, Machiavelli is imagining the people and the soldiers as two competing humors who create a disease in the body politic if they get out of balance.

which was more or less useful for them inasmuch as they were more or less skilled at maintaining their reputation with the army.

Machiavelli examines this principle through a study of Roman Emperors.

CHAPTER XX: ON THE USEFULNESS OF FORTRESSES

Machiavelli argues that princes who have much to fear from their own people should build fortresses to keep them in check, but if they are worried about foreign invasions, they should arm their own people and not build fortresses. It is, however, better for a prince not to be hated by his own people than to rely on fortresses.

CHAPTER XXI: ON RESPECT

Nothing wins respect like doing great deeds. In our own day, we have the example of Ferdinand of Aragon, the King of Spain. Ferdinand was almost like a new prince because he inherited a weak monarchy, but on account of his glorious deeds, he became the most important king in Christendom...At the beginning of his reign, he assaulted Granada, which built the foundations of his power...With pious cruelty and using religion as an excuse, he expelled the Muslims from his lands and stole their goods. We should marvel at his example. He invaded Africa, Italy, and France, and he always accomplished stupendous feats, so that his subjects were astonished and admired him, caught up in the glory of his undertakings. In this way, he never gave them a chance to revolt.

Machiavelli gives other examples.

A prince should not sit on the sidelines when those around him are at war. It is always more useful to pick a side...Choose wisely, and you will be a friend to the winner; choose unwisely, and at least the loser will be your ally...If both of the states are weaker than you, you should ally with one side to destroy the other...However, a prince should never make alliances with more powerful states, except when he has no other choice. If his allies win, he will be at their mercy, and a prince should always avoid living at the mercy of others…In reality, no option is ever completely safe. As soon as you flee one danger, you run headlong into another; prudence consists in making the best choice amongst bad options.

A prince needs to show that he loves *virtù* and rewards excellence. He needs to persuade his people to work peacefully in their professions. People should not be afraid that the prince will take their land if they make improvements to it nor should they hesitate to engage in trade for fear of taxation. Rather, a prince should support these things and reward whomever makes the city or state better. He also needs to give the people festivals and spectacles. And because every city has its different groups, he needs to keep an eye on everything and to meet with everyone, to make himself an example of humanity and generosity. He should make sure that he never forgets the majesty of his office.

CHAPTER XXII: ON OFFICIALS

A prince should take great care in choosing his officials…A prince's officials are his first impression. If they are good and faithful, others will think him wise…If not, people will not trust his judgment…

There is one infallible way to test the quality of your officials. If you see one of them worrying more about himself than about you and always seeking his own profit rather than yours, you should know that he is neither good nor trustworthy. Officials should never think about themselves, only about their prince.

On the other hand, a prince needs to take care of his officials. He needs to honor them, make them rich, and give them duties and jobs. They must know that they rely on their prince and not let their appetite for riches and honors exceed due limits. They must be given many positions so as to make them content with the status quo. When the officials of a prince are like this, both the prince and his officials can trust each other; if not, either one or the other comes to harm.

CHAPTER XXIII: ON AVOIDING FLATTERY

All princes have difficulty avoiding flattery unless they are very prudent and choose their officials wisely. It is difficult to avoid flattery because men love themselves and are easily deceived about their own qualities. But a prince risks a different kind of danger in trying to avoid flattery, for he can only avoid flattery if his ministers feel free to tell him the truth; however, when everyone is allowed to speak his mind, no one gives the prince due reverence. Thus, a prince can neither completely restrict his officials' speech, nor give them all license to speak their minds. What then should he do? A prince should only allow a few of his wisest officials to speak freely, and he should only ask their opinions. Once he has heard their responses, he should think things over and make decisions on his own. He should encourage free speech amongst this group, but he should not listen to anything anyone else has to say, for whoever encourages flattery or changes his mind often will not be respected...

Machiavelli gives examples.

A prince should seek advice frequently, but only when he wants it, not when others want to give it to him. He should make others know that they are not to give him advice unless he asks for it, yet he should ask for advice often and listen to it patiently...

CHAPTER XXIV: ON WHY THE PRINCES OF ITALY HAVE LOST THEIR STATES

If a new prince observes all of my rules, he will be as secure as an hereditary prince in no time. People watch a new prince more closely than an hereditary prince, so when a new prince demonstrates competence, he is respected all the more. Men have short memories; they want to know what you have done for them recently. If the people are happy in the present, they will defend their prince rather than try to overthrow him. Thus, a new prince who secures his state will have a double glory: he will have given birth to a new monarchy and given his monarchy good laws, good arms, good allies, and a good example. The hereditary monarch who loses his state has a double shame: though born a prince, he loses his state for lack of prudence.

If we consider the Italian princes who have lost their realms in modern times, we will find that they have all neglected their militaries, and have antagonized either the people or the nobility. Without these missteps, they would never have lost their states, as long as they could keep an army in the field...

The princes who have lost their states in modern times should not blame fortune; they should blame their own laziness. They did not prepare for trouble during peacetime...then, when trouble came, they fled from it, hoping that the people would return them to power when they got tired of the new rulers. Such a strategy only works when one can rely on the incompetence of the conqueror, but leaving your fate in someone else's hands is a bad idea...

CHAPTER XXV: THE POWER OF FORTUNE AND HOW WE CAN RESIST IT

I realize that many people have held and continue to hold the opinion that political events are governed by fortune and by God and that even prudent men have no control over them. Thus, some people think that we should not fret too much about the events of the world, but rather leave them to chance. The ups and downs of the politics of our own time make this even more believable. Sometimes, I myself am even inclined to believe it. Nevertheless, I do not believe that we lack free will, and though fortune may dictate one half of our actions, even she lets us control the other half. Fortune, I think, is like a raging river; when she floods, she overflows her banks and knocks down all the trees and buildings...When this happens, everyone flees before her, succumbing to the power of the river's destructive force. Nevertheless, men can prepare for the storm by making dikes and digging ditches, so that when the flood arrives, it will be channeled into certain ditches and not be so ruinous. Fortune, then, is like a river, which shows its power where men have not prepared themselves to resist it.

Italy, which has been hit hard by fortune recently, is a land without ditches and a land without dikes. If we had defended Italy with military strength, like the Germans, French and Spanish, this flood would not have swept away so many princes, or indeed, would not have come at all. That is all I need to say about fortune in general.

If we come to particulars, we see that every day successful princes come to ruin without having changed anything in their own natures. This is because princes who rely on fortune come to ruin when their good luck changes. To be successful, a prince needs to change with the times...

How is it, then, that different tactics lead to success or failure at different times? One man wins riches and glory by acting cautiously, another by acting rashly. One wins them with violence, another with skill. One man with patience, another with impatience. Indeed, two people may follow the exact same course of action and end with different results... Why? Because success or failure depends on whether one's mode of action suits the times in which one lives...If the cautious and patient man lives in an age when such qualities are beneficial, he will be successful. But if the times change and he does not, he will come to ruin.

It is hard to find a man so prudent that he accommodates his actions to his circumstances. This is because it is hard to change one's nature. A successful man tends to stick with what has worked in the past, rather than change tactics for the future. Thus, the cautious man does not know how to act decisively when he needs to, and for that, he will be ruined, but if he knew how to change his character with the times, his fortune would not change.

Pope Julius II was rash in all of his undertakings, but he lived in a time when boldness was called for, and thus, he was always successful. Let us consider his takeover of Bologna...None of the great powers was in favor of it, but he personally and boldly led the invading force. Though neither Venice nor Spain favored Julius' plan, fear kept Venice from openly opposing him and the hope of gain neutralized the Spaniards. Even the French lent their aid because they wanted to humble the Venetians by making friends with the Pope. Thus, Julius' bold move, which no other pope would have even tried, led to a great success. If he had been as cautious as any other pope...he never would have succeeded. The French would have put him off with a thousand excuses, and others would have raised a thousand objections...He was lucky he did not live longer, however, because the times would have changed, but he would have not changed with them. This would have been his undoing.

I conclude that when fortune changes, men need to change with it. In general, however, it is better to be bold than cautious because fortune is a woman, and in order to keep her in her place, you need to beat her. Boldness succeeds more frequently than caution because as a woman, fortune favors young men.

CHAPTER XXVI: AN EXHORTATION TO LIBERATE ITALY FROM THE BARBARIANS[10]

Having read this work and considered the state of Italy, you must agree that the time is ripe for a new prince. Now is the time to establish a form of government that will bring honor to yourself and benefit the people. Indeed, Moses could only show his skill because the Israelites were slaves in Egypt, Cyrus could only demonstrate his excellence because the Persians were oppressed by the Medians, and Theseus could only show his leadership because the Athenians were disunited. At present, Italy is more enslaved than the Israelites, more oppressed than the Persians, and more disunited than the Athenians; we are without a head, without order—beaten, robbed, lacerated, worn out, and destroyed. Nevertheless, all of this will only prove the greatness of the Italian spirit all the more.

A short time ago, a leader appeared who seemed to be divinely ordained to redeem Italy, but fortune cut him down in the prime of his career.[11] Thus, Italy still awaits a savior who might heal its wounds[12] and cure those ills which have been festering for so long, putting an end to the pillaging of Lombardy and the taxing of Tuscany. Italy cries to God for a savior who can redeem it from the barbarism of the French, Spanish,

---

[10] In this case, barbarian refers to non-Italians: the French, Germans, and Spanish.

[11] Machiavelli is probably referring to Cesare Borgia here.

[12] Machiavelli is probably writing directly to Lorenzo dei Medici here (not Lorenzo the Magnificient, a different one); the Medici family name comes from the Italian word for doctor, so Machiavelli is playing on words with the phrase "heal its wounds."

and Germans. Everyone is ready to follow the banner, we just need someone to seize it and lead us.

All our hopes reside with your illustrious family.[13] You alone, with your fortune and *virtù*, are favored by God and by the Church, of which you are now the heads.[14] If you will follow the deeds of history's great men, you might easily become the saviors of Italy, for although those men were rare and marvelous, they were still only men. Each of them had less of an opportunity for greatness than you do at present. Their deeds were not more just nor their opportunities more ripe than yours. God was no more a friend to them than he is to you. The justice of your cause is great, for as Livy says, "that war is just whenever it is necessary, and strength of arms is pious when they are the only hope."

Moreover, where there is a will, there is a way, no matter the difficulties, if only you will follow the examples that I have given you. Moreover, we see that God has given us signs: the sea has opened, a cloud leads the way, water has flowed from a rock, manna rains down from heaven.[15] Everything points to your greatness; the rest is up to you. God does not want to do everything; he doesn't want to take away your free will or your part of the glory.

Do not be alarmed that no one has succeeded in liberating Italy yet. Do not fret that Italy seems to be without military valor of late. This is only because our old methods of governing were corrupt, and no one has been able to discover new ones. How much honor will the man gain, then, who finds new laws and makes new constitutions for Italy? Constitute the state well, and others will respect you. Italy still possesses enough strength in its members; all that is lacking is a head. Watch how Italians duel and brawl, and you will see how much strength, how much dexterity, and how much genius the Italians possess. Yet all of this disappears when they try to fight in an army because of the weakness of their leaders and because Italians don't know how to obey. As of yet, no

---

[13] The Medici.

[14] The Pope at this time, Leo X, was a Medici.

[15] Notice that Machiavelli puts signs of the Medici's prosperity in terms of miracles wrought by God in *Exodus* (remember Origins!), and that Moses is listed in *The Prince* as a man who gained power through his own *virtù* (Chapter VI).

one has so shined above others that he can make himself be obeyed. This is why armies composed entirely of Italians have so often failed in the wars of the last twenty years...

Thus, the first thing the Medici house must do is to establish its own army because you will never find soldiers more faithful, more true, or more capable than your own. And though each soldier may be individually capable, they will be better when they are commanded by a prince who honors them and maintains them. We need this army in order to defend Italy from the foreign barbarians...

You must not let this chance slip away. After so many years, Italy must see her savior. Those lands that have suffered under the floods of barbarian invasion would receive you with indescribable love, thirst for vengeance, obstinate faith, piety, and tears. What gates would be closed to you? Which peoples would not obey you? What jealousy could oppose you? What Italian would refuse his obedience? The barbarous foreigners are hateful to us all. Your illustrious house should take up this duty with the spirit and hope that animates all just undertakings, so that under your banners, our homeland might regain its nobility and under your watch, we might live up to that saying of Petrarch:

> *Virtù will take up arms against the furor*
> *And make the fighting short*
> *The ancient valor of Italy*
> *Is not yet dead* [16]

---

[16] Francesco Petrarcha (one of Machiavelli's favorite authors; see his "Letter to Francesco Vettori"), *Canzoniere* 128.93-96.

Discourses on Titus Livy
Niccolò Machiavelli, 1513-1519

HOW MANY TYPES OF REPUBLIC THERE ARE, AND WHAT TYPE THE ROMAN REPUBLIC WAS

I will leave off speaking of those cities that were subject to others and speak about free republics and free monarchies, which have had different laws and constitutions according to their different beginnings. In some cities, one man gave the city all its laws at its beginning, like Lycurgus in Sparta. Some city's constitutions developed gradually in response to various events, like in Rome. Happy is the republic that lives safely under a constitution that it receives from a prudent man, without any need to correct it. We see that Sparta kept its constitution for eight hundred years without any dangerous tumults. On the other hand, unhappy is the city that is not founded by a prudent man, for its constitution will need to be restructured. The further a city must depart from its original constitution, the unhappier it will be, for it gets off the path that leads to a perfect and true destination. If a city finds itself experimenting with new constitutional forms, it is almost impossible to get back on track. However, if a city has a good (though not perfect constitution), it is apt to improve and maybe even reach perfection. Nevertheless, no one ever made a constitution without danger, for most men will not agree to a new constitution unless it is absolutely necessary. As the only reason for such necessity is danger, it often happens that a republic is ruined before the constitution can be given perfect form. Florence gives testimony to this, for because of the war with Arezzo, it was given a new constitution in 1502 and then again in 1512 because of difficulties with Prato.

I want to speak about the Roman constitution and the events that led to its perfection. Others who have written about republics[1] call them one of three things: monarchy (*principato*), aristocracy (*ottimati*), and democracy (*popolare*). Lawgivers choose whichever one of these seems most suitable for their situation. More prudent men think that there are six different regime types: the three aforementioned and their corruptions; for the three I just mentioned are good but easily corrupted and made pernicious. The corrupt types match up with the good types, so a city can easily slide between the good form and the corrupt form. A monarchy can easily become tyrannical (*tirannico*), an aristocracy can easily become an oligarchy (*stato di pochi*), and a democracy easily becomes licentious (*licenzioso*). Thus, if a lawgiver establishes one of those three states, it will only last for a short time before it devolves into its corrupt form because of the small difference between virtue and vice.

In the beginning of the world, men were few, and they lived spread out, just like the beasts. As the number of people grew in each generation, they began to live together. To defend themselves, they made the fiercest among them into their leaders and obeyed them. From this was born the knowledge of good and right (*oneste*) and how goodness and right differed from pernicious and evil; for men saw that when someone harmed his benefactor, it aroused feelings of both hatred and compassion. Thus, they criticized ungrateful men and honored grateful men, since they were worried that the same injuries might be done to themselves. To avoid this, they made laws and ordered punishments for those who broke them. From this came the knowledge of justice. Finally, when they decided to make a prince, they chose the most prudent and most just, rather than the strongest. However, eventually the prince was made by succession rather than election, and the heirs started to degenerate from their ancestors. Forgetting virtuous works, these heirs thought that princes had nothing else to do but to live more sumptuously and lasciviously than others and to give in to every type of license. Thus, princes came to be hated and feared. Then, they started injuring their subjects, which led to tyranny. It is in this that we see the causes of the prince's

---

[1] As is customary for his time, Machiavelli here uses the word republics (*republiche*) to refer to all the regime types, even monarchies.

destruction, for soon there were conspiracies against them. These conspiracies were not made by the timid or the weak, but by those who excelled others in nobility (*generosità*), greatness of soul, riches and status; in short, those who could not tolerate the evil life of the prince. Following the authority of these powerful men, the multitude armed itself against the prince, and once they had conquered him, they obeyed these powerful conspirators as their liberators. The conspirators, who hated the name of king, made a government of themselves. Because of the past tyrannies, they governed according to constituted laws, putting the common utility ahead of their own and governing and conserving both private and public things (*cose de publico*) with great diligence. Then, they gave their power to their children, who did not understand the wheel of fortune, had never tasted evil, and were not content with civil equality. These children were swayed by greed, ambition, and lust; they changed the government of the best men into a government of a few, without any respect for civility. In a short time, this too was a tyranny. When the multitude got tired of this government, they raised up ministers and overthrew the oligarchy. However, they still remembered the injuries done to them by the prince, so they made a democracy (*stato popolare*), a constitution in which neither the powerful nor the prince had any authority. In the beginning all states garner some respect, and even this popular state maintained some respect for a short time, but not for long, especially not long after the generation that had drawn up the constitution, for the popular state immediately became shameless and licentious. Constrained by necessity or on the suggestion of one good man, they again returned to a monarchy and thus repeated the cycle. This is the cycle that governs all republics. However, the state rarely survives these changes for many cycles. They are usually taken over by a better constituted or stronger foreign power. However, if the republic were not conquered, it would whirl through this cycle indefinitely.

I say then that all of these regime types are bad because the good types are so unstable and the bad types so pernicious. Thus, a prudent and knowledgeable lawgiver will not establish any of these as a pure type, but rather use one that combines them all, since such a constitution is more solid and stable. When there is a prince, aristocracy, and popular government in one city, each one watches the other.

In this regard, Lycurgus, founder of Sparta, merits particular praise. The constitution of Sparta gave some power to the king, some to the aristocracy, and some to the people, and it lasted for 800 years and brought peace to the city. On the other hand, Solon gave a popular constitution to Athens, and it had such a brief life that it turned into the tyranny of Peisistratus before Solon had even died. Forty years later, the heirs of Peisistratus were overthrown and exiled, and Athens returned to its liberties and to the constitution of Solon, yet the Athenians could not preserve this constitution for more than a hundred years; rather, they experimented with many different types of constitutions to try to check the insolence of the rich and the license of the multitude. These were things that Solon had not considered, and because he never mixed the power of the prince and the aristocracy, Athenian regimes lasted a very short time compared to those of Sparta.

Finally, let us speak of Rome, which lived free for a very long time, even though it had no Lycurgus. Nonetheless, events gave cause for disunion between the plebs and the senate, so the tide of history [gave Rome a mixed constitution]. Rome was not lucky at first, but they were lucky shortly thereafter, for though the first constitution was not perfect, it had the potential to be. Romulus and all the other earliest kings made many good laws that were suitable for a free people, but because they sought to establish a reign rather than a republic, the city later lacked many things necessary for a constitution that favored liberty, which had not been provided for by the kings. When the kings lost their power, the new rulers immediately provided that there be two counsuls, who took the place of the king; thus, they eliminated the name of king, but not the power of the king. In the counsuls and the senate, Rome found that it had mixed two of the three regime types: principate and aristocracy. All that was left was to give some voice to the people. When the Roman nobility grew insolent…the people rose up against them; in order not to lose everything, the nobility was forced to give some authority to the people, though the senate and the counsuls retained enough authority to keep their position in the republic. Thus, the Romans created the Tribune of the Plebs, after which the republic was more stable since it then mixed all three regime types. In this way, the Romans were favored by fortune, for when the government passed from the king, to the aristocracy, to the people…the aristocracy did not take away all the authority from the king, nor did the people take away all the authority of the aristocracy. Rather, as the regime remained mixed, the Romans developed a perfect republic, whose perfection came from the disunion of the plebs and the senate…

The Visions of Saint Teresa

Teresa of Avila (1515-1582)

The Transverberation

Our Lord was pleased that I should sometimes see the vision of an angel close by me, on my left side, in bodily form. This did not usually happen to me, except when God miraculously allowed it. Though I frequently was in the presence of angels, I usually did not literally see them. It was the Lord's will that I should see this one in the flesh; he was not large, but short and most beautiful. His face was afire, and he seemed to be a Cherubim, a very high angel who seems to be made of fire. The angels never tell me their names; but I see that in heaven there is so great a difference between one angel and another, and between these and the others, that I cannot explain it.

I saw a long spear of gold in the Cherubim's hand, and at the point there seemed to be a little fire. He seemed to be thrusting it into my heart and to pierce my bowels themselves; when he removed it, he seemed to draw them out also, and to leave me all on fire with a great love of God. The pain was so great that I moaned, and yet the sweetness of this pain brought me such ecstasy that I did not want it to end nor for my soul to be satisfied by anything but God alone. The pain is not bodily, but spiritual, though there is a sharp bodily pain as well. The tenderness between God and the soul is so sweet that I pray God will give the same experience to whomever may think that I am lying.

During the days that this lasted, I went around as if beside myself. I did not wish to see or speak with anyone, but only to embrace my pain, which was to me a greater glory than any earthly thing. I was in this state from time to time, whenever it was our Lord's pleasure to throw me into a deep trance. I could not stop them from coming on even if others were present, even though it bothered me that they became publicly known... May He be blessed forever, who hath given such great graces to one who has not been worthy of them.

Visions of Heaven

One night I was so sick that I wanted to excuse myself from prayer, so I picked up a rosary to occupy myself, though I was not thinking about the words I was praying.

However, the Lord brings about whatever he wills. I had been praying for a short while when a sudden shaking of my spirit struck me with such force I was not able to resist it. It seemed to me that I was carried into heaven and saw my mother and father. I remained in this state for no longer than the time it takes to say a Hail Mary or perhaps a little longer, but I saw many things. This mercy seemed to be too much to bear.

I feared that I was seeing an illusion, though it seemed quite real to me. I did not know what to do because I was greatly ashamed to tell my confessor, not out of humility, it seemed to me, but because I was afraid that he would laugh at me and say, "What a Saint Paul she is, seeing heavenly visions! O Saint Jerome!"[1] Indeed, the glorious visions of these saints brought me even more fear. I cried a lot over it because it did not seem that I could have the same visions as they did. Though I was very afraid, I finally went to my confessor, for I dared not remain silent when I was so terrified that my vision was a deception (of the devil). When my confessor saw me so distressed, he gave me many good reasons for consolation.

I have had and continue to have similar sorts of visions, and each time the Lord shows me ever greater mysteries. The soul sees only what the Lord reveals to it, even if it desires to see more; thus, I never saw more

---

[1] St. Paul was considered to have received a heavenly vision, based on 2 Corinthians 12:1-10. The medieval *Golden Legend* (legends of saints' lives) recounts the story of St. Jerome having a vision of himself being scourged in heaven for his love of classical (pagan) literature.

than what the Lord wanted to show me each time. What I saw, however, was so great that it overwhelmed my soul and caused it to despise all the goods of this life.

I want to describe my vision, but I have found it impossible because there is no comparison between earthly light and the heavenly light I saw there; rather, the light of heaven makes the light of the sun itself seem dull by comparison. No one can imagine it, or indeed, imagine anything else that the Lord gave me to understand and which delighted me with an indescribably sovereign joy. In this state, the senses experience delight beyond all worth, and it is best to leave my description at that.

Once, I had been in such a state for more than an hour, with the Lord showing me wonderful things, when it seemed he was about to leave me. He said to me, "Look, daughter, see what my enemies give up. Be sure to tell them." O, Lord, how little profit my words are to those blinded by their sins, unless your majesty gives them light. Some have benefitted by the knowledge you have given them through me. But when others see that you have given these gifts to such a poor and miserable creature like me, I wonder how they have come to believe me. Blessed be your name and your mercy. For my own part, this knowledge has caused me to grow in virtue.

I wanted to remain in heaven forever and not return to this life. After this vision, the goods of this world seemed to me like nothing more than trash, which ensnares us when we occupy ourselves with things here below.

Once when I was sick at heart...a very charitable lady that I knew thought to cheer me up by giving me some expensive gold and stone pieces, including a very expensive diamond. I laughed quietly to myself, pained to see what men value. I was thinking to myself of the great treasures that the Lord is keeping in store for us, and how impossible it would be, even if I wanted, to value earthly things at all, unless the Lord caused me to forget those other heavenly things.

This proper and natural detachment from worldly things gives the soul great lordship over itself, though it is hard to understand it unless one has it. It is not accomplished by our labors; rather, God does all. His majesty shows us these truths, and they remain so impressed upon our mind that we can easily see that we would not be able to acquire them ourselves in such a brief span of life.

After these visions, I no longer feared death, which I had feared so much before. Now, death seems to me a simple thing for servants of God. In the moment of death, the soul is freed from its prison and given rest. My raptures seem a little like what happens when the soul leaves the body in death. In an instant, the soul finds itself in a place where all is well. Let us not speak of the sufferings associated with death, for death comes more softly for those who love God and have given up the things of this life.

I have benefitted greatly from having seen my true land and realized that I am a pilgrim here on earth. During a journey, it is a great help to think that you will one day come to your final destination. Thus, we should spend our time on earth thinking and speaking about heavenly things. This is done easily, for merely looking up to heaven puts the soul at peace.

At times, the Lord showed me companions who had gone to heaven, and I was consoled to know that they lived there. It seemed to me that they alone truly lived, and that those who live here on earth were dead, so that there seemed to me no companions in the entire world, especially when I was caught in those raptures.

Everything that I see with my bodily eyes seems like a dream or a joke. I desire only those things which I have seen with the eyes of my soul. Indeed, being so far from these things feels like death for my soul. Great is the mercy of God in giving these visions; for it is both a great help and a heavy cross, for after such visions, nothing on earth can ever satisfy one again. I do not know how one could live if the Lord did not allow them to occasionally forget their visions. Blessed and praised be the Lord forever.

Let it be pleasing to his Majesty, [2] by the blood that his Son shed for me, that I not follow the path of Lucifer[3] and throw away all those great blessings that it has pleased him to show me. For his own sake, may he not permit this. Indeed, the mercy of God gives me peace of mind, think-

---

[2] That is, God the Father
[3] Satan.

ing that he will not want to let me slip from his hands after having saved me from so many sins…

Visions of Divine Mercy

Great are the mysteries that I have just recounted, yet the Lord granted me the mercy to share even greater mysteries, each one of which is a treasure beyond compare and each one of which has given strength to my soul.

Once after the Pentecost vigil Mass, I retired to a quiet spot and began to read about the feast in a Carthusian book.[4] In this book, I was reading about the signs that "beginners," "improvers," and "perfects" should look for in order to know that the Holy Spirit is with them. It seemed to me, at least as far as I could say, that by God's grace, each of these signs was present in my own life. I praised God and thought back to the last time I had read this passage, a time in my life when I lacked all the signs of the Holy Spirit's presence. This moment gave me great insight into my progress, for my soul was barely recognizable to itself, and I knew that the Lord had taken great mercy on me. Then I began to consider the place in hell that my sins merited and praised God all the more. Thus mired in reflection, I was shaken by some unseen and irresistible force. My soul seemed to leap out of my body because it no longer fit into it and could not hold itself back from moving towards its great desire. Unlike during my other raptures, my soul was disoriented, and I swooned and tottered as my strength deserted me.

Then, I saw a dove hovering over my head. This dove was quite different from those on earth. He had no feathers; rather, his wings were made of dazzling little shells that shimmered and shone. It was bigger than a regular dove, and it seemed to me that I could hear the noise it made with its wings. It stayed for about the time it takes to say a Hail Mary, and then I lost sight of the bird.

---

[4] Pentecost is the solemnity that celebrates the descent of the Holy Spirit upon Jesus' apostles (Acts 2). The Carthusians are a particularly strict and pious religious order in the Catholic Church.

At first, this marvelous favor disturbed and alarmed my soul, but this beautiful guest gradually gave peace to it, and when I began to rejoice in the vision, the fear departed, and a great peace settled in my soul.

The glory of this rapture was so great that I remained in a stupor for most of the next day, not knowing what to do or understanding how I had merited such great favor and mercy. My great inner joy was so immense that I could neither see nor hear anything else. Now I see the progress I have made in feeling God's love and in practicing the virtues. Blessed and praised be God forever, Amen.

At another time, I saw the same dove hovering over the head of a Dominican priest, except that it seemed to me that the rays from the splendor of the wings extended much further. I understood that this was meant to draw souls to God.

Another time, I saw our Lady putting a pure, white cape on a teacher of theology...She told me that she did this to honor him for the services he had rendered to help build this house. She gave him that cloak as a sign that she would keep his soul pure thereafter and that he would not fall into mortal sin. I know for certain that he did not; a few years later, he died, and his life was so filled with penitence and his death with such sanctity, that as far as we are able to know, there can be no doubt that Our Lady spoke the truth. One eyewitness told me that the man had reported that Saint Thomas came to him on his deathbed. He died with great joy and desire to go to the next world. Afterwards, he appeared to me several times with great glory, and he told me many things.

When he grew too weak to pray on his deathbed, he had tried to excuse himself from prayer, but he had developed the habit of prayer so strongly in his life that he was enraptured in his prayers and could not leave them off, even when he was dying. Indeed, before he died, he had once asked me what he should do about the fact that upon finishing Mass, he would often remain ensnared in rapturous prayer. In the end, God gave him the reward that his service in life had merited.

I have seen the great mercies the Lord has made to the Rector of the Jesuits, which I will not recount here to keep things brief. Once the rector was undertaking a great work, in which he was much afflicted. When I was at Mass one day, I looked at Christ on the cross during the Elevation of the Host, and Christ gave me some words of consolation for the rector.

He gave me other predictions for the rector as well, reminding him of the sufferings that the rector had endured for him and preparing him to endure more. When I told the rector of these visions, they encouraged and consoled him greatly. Afterwards, all of the prophecies happened just as the Lord had foretold.

I have seen great things concerning the Jesuit Order; I have seen them in heaven with white banners in their hands. At times, as I have said, I see other wonderful things about them. I esteem this order greatly because I have had many dealings with them, and I see that they live according to the Lord's commands.

One night while I was at prayer, the Lord began to speak to me, reminding me of my former life. These words pained and confused me. Even though the Lord did not chastise me sternly, his words gave me a feeling that undid me. Just one of these words will show the soul's improvement more than months of considering the wickedness of one's former life, for the Lord draws the soul to him with truth that cannot be denied. He showed me how empty my desires had been and told me to put my crooked will in his hands and to let him into my heart.

At other times, he told me to reflect on the days when I thought it an honor to disobey his will. He told me to think about what I owed to him and to remember that when I so wounded him, he was always there, showing me mercy. Nowadays when I sin (and the Lord has given me to understand that I continue to sin a lot), I am immediately ashamed by it. Sometimes, when my confessor reprimands me for my sin, I run to pray, hoping to find consolation from God, but instead I find a real reprimand from him.

Now, returning to my train of thought. The Lord began to remind me how great had been my peril, and tears began to stream down my face. I wondered if the Lord was not preparing me for some mercy because I often find the feeling of shame precedes these visions, which I think the Lord gives me so that I can see more clearly how little I deserve them.

After a little while, my spirit was so enraptured that it almost seemed as if I was out of my body, or at least I did not sense that I inhabited it. I saw the Lord in his most sacred humanity, more glorious than I had ever seen before. Christ appeared in the midst of the Father's embrace, and though it is hard to put this into words, it seemed to me that I was present there too. It seemed to me that some days passed before I could come back to myself. During this whole time, the presence of Christ's majesty lingered in my mind, and it remained so sculpted on my imagination that for a long time after, I have not forgotten that brief glimpse. This vision has been a great consolation and a spur to improvement.

I have seen this vision three more times. It is, I think, the highest vision that the Lord has given me the favor to see, and I have drawn great profit from it. It seems that it purifies the soul in a great way, completely annihilating the power of our sensual nature and burning up our worldly desires. No longer do I cling to the vanities of this world, whose honors and glories I now see to be nothing at all. Rather, this vision raises our desires to pure truth, a truth who commands an obedience that is very difficult to describe, so different is it from the obedience that earthly powers command. Indeed, the soul shudders to see how it has dared, or that any soul has dared, to offend such majesty.

Eucharistic Visions

...When I went to receive communion, I remembered this vision, in which I had seen the majesty of the Lord directly. I saw that the same majesty was present there in the host (indeed, many times the Lord desired that I should physically see him in the host). Then, my hair stood on end, and I seemed to be completely overwhelmed. O my Lord. If you did not cover up your greatness in the host, what wretched and miserable creature would dare to combine with your majesty in Holy Communion? Blessed be the Lord. Let all the angels and creatures praise him! You measure all things by our weakness, veiling your sovereign majesties in the Eucharist, so that we weak and miserable beings do not grow too afraid of your great power and therefore fear to enjoy your presence in communion.

If God were to reveal himself openly to us in all his majesty, we might become like a certain peasant I know, who found a treasure that was too large to fit inside his lowly soul. Not knowing how to spend it, the peasant fell into a great sadness, from which he eventually died. If he had been given the treasure little by little, rather than all at once, he would have been relieved of his poverty without losing his life.

O riches of the poor! How wonderfully do you care for our souls, hiding such treasures in the Eucharist? When I see such majesty hidden in the little host, I admire your wisdom. Nor do I know how the Lord gives me the strength or courage to approach him.

How can I keep silent about these miracles? How shall I feel? A soul so heavy with sin and having shown so little fear of God in this life. How shall I feel when I see God's great majesty and see that he wants to join with me? How shall I put that glorious, pure, and compassionate body in a mouth that has so often spoken words against my Lord? To a soul that has not served the Lord, the love that shines through his faith is more painful than all of his terrible majesty.

What must I have felt, then, on the two occasions that I am about to describe?

...Once when I arrived at communion, the eyes of my soul saw two hideously shaped demons. They were clearer to me than if I had seen them with my bodily eyes. It seemed to me that their horns encircled the throat of the poor priest, and I saw my Lord in the wafer that the priest was about to give me. By this, I saw clearly that the priest had offended Christ, and I understood that his soul was in mortal sin.

Oh, to see your beauty between two such hideous figures, Lord! They seemed to be so frightened and alarmed by your presence, that it seemed they would have left willingly if you had given them leave to do so. The whole episode disturbed me so greatly that I did not know how I would take communion. I stood there, petrified by fear. However, since the vision came to me from God, I knew he would not let me be harmed by it. The Lord told me to pray for the priest, and that he had allowed me to see the vision so that I would know just how powerful the words of con-secration are. God's presence in communion does not fail just because of the sins of the priest who says the words. In his great goodness, God surrenders himself to the hands of his enemy, and all for my good and the good of others.

I understood how important it is for priests to live holy lives. I understood how evil it is to take this Holy Sacrament unworthily. Finally, I understood how powerfully a demon can become the master of a soul in mortal sin. It was of great profit to me and made me understand my debts to God. Blessed be God forever.

Visions of the Dead

On another occasion, I experienced a similar vision that frightened me very much. I was visiting a place, and in this place, a man whom I knew to have lived a very evil life had just died. He had been sick for the last two years, and towards the end, he had begun making some amends for his sins. Even though he had died without confession, I still thought there was a chance that he might have escaped the hellfires. However, when he died, I saw a throng of demons come for his body, and it seemed to me as if they were playing with it, tossing it amongst themselves with their large claws. This vision terrified me, and when I saw the body buried with great honor and ceremony, I was thinking of the goodness of God, and how he preferred to hide the fact that this man was his enemy rather than to dishonor him openly.

I was driven half-crazy by this vision. During the rest of the service, I did not see any demons, but when they put the body in the ground, there was such a horde of demons in the grave waiting to take him that I was nearly driven mad just looking at them, and it took all my courage to hide my fear from others. When I saw them make themselves the lords of his body, I considered what they would do to his soul. Let it please God to give such a terrifying vision to all who live such evil lives, for it would be a great spur for them to live better, it seems to me.

All this was done to make me recognize how much I owe the Lord and to see what he had saved me from. I kept this fear in my heart until I spoke of the matter with my confessor, thinking that it could perhaps be a demonic trick to defame the reputation of that man, even though he was not known for his Christianity. Illusion or not, it still terrifies me to think about it.

I have begun to speak about visions of the dead. I want to briefly share some visions of the dead that the Lord has wanted me to see. Once, I was told of the death of a prelate from another province. He was a very virtuous person who had done me many favors. When I heard that he had died, I was very disturbed because I feared for his salvation. He had been a prelate for twenty years and for all that time had the care of souls, which seems to me a dangerous and heavy responsibility. I prayed hard for him, offering up all the little merits that I had earned in my life and asking the Lord to supply what was still lacking with his own merits, so that the prelate's soul might ascend through purgatory.

As I was asking this of the Lord the best I could, the prelate seemed to rise from the ground on my right, and I saw him joyfully ascend to heaven. At the time he died, he had been very old, but in my vision he appeared to be about thirty years old or younger, and his face shone with a radiant glow. The vision was brief, but I remained consoled. His death gave me no more cause for pain, even though I saw many people very distressed by it because he was very well-liked. My soul was so consoled that I was no longer disturbed by his death, certain as I was that this was a true vision, and not an illusion.

By the time we heard of his death, he had been gone for more than fifteen days; nevertheless, I continued to pray for his soul and encouraged others to do so, though not as fervently as before I had the vision since praying for a soul that I knew to be in heaven seemed to me like giving alms to the rich. I learned afterwards that he edified many by his death, and witnesses at his bedside left astonished by the composure, tears, and humility with which he died.

There was a nun in our house who was a great servant of God. About a day and half after her death, we were reading an Office for the Dead, and I was helping with the verses.[5] In the middle of the reading, I saw her: it seemed to me that her soul rose up from the ground and went to heaven. This was no vision of the soul, like the last, but rather like the others I have described. I cannot at all doubt what I saw.

Once a younger nun died in our convent; she was a great friend of the house and a virtuous servant of God. I thought that she would go right to heaven because she had often been sick, and I thought that her tribulations would give her the merit to pass quickly through purgatory. While we were praying the liturgy of the hours (it would have been about four

---

[5] The Office for the Dead is a Catholic liturgy consisting of prayers for souls in Purgatory; hence Teresa's mention of "helping with the verses" —she is helping by reading verses of the Psalms.

hours after she died), ⁶ I saw her rise from the ground and ascend to heaven.

One time, I was visiting a Jesuit college and suffering in both soul and body, so much so that I doubted my ability to have a single positive thought. That night, a young Jesuit died, and while I was praying for him at Mass, I saw him ascending to heaven in great glory with Christ by his side.

Once, when I was at Mass, I had a vision of a very holy Carmelite friar, and I saw how he had died and risen to heaven without entering purgatory. He died the very same hour that my vision occurred, though I only learned of his death afterwards. I was amazed that he had not entered purgatory. I was given to understand that he had fulfilled his profession as a monk and had profited from the indulgences granted to the order by papal bull, so that he might be freed from purgatory. I did not understand why I understood this. It seemed to me that God showed me this vision to teach me that clothes alone do not make one a true friar.

The Lord has given me other visions, which I choose not to share here. But the only two souls that I knew who escaped purgatory completely were the friar that I mentioned and Father Peter Alcantara. It has pleased the Lord to show me the different grades of glory in heaven and the places in heaven that he has assigned to each. And there is a great difference between one and the other.

---

⁶ The Liturgy of the Hours (based on the Psalms) is the universal prayer of the Catholic Church; priests, monks, and nuns are required to pray the liturgy of the hours several times a day, every day of the year. Lay faithful are also encouraged to partake in this prayer.

Bernini, *Saint Teresa in Ecstasy*, courtesy of Dreamstime

Santa Maria Della Vittoria, Rome, 1647-1652

Letter to the Grand Duchess Christina, 1615

Galileo Galilei[1]

As you know, a few years ago, I discovered many bodies in the heavens that had not been visible before our age. Whether because of the novelty of my discoveries or because their existence contradicts commonly received scientific opinions, this discovery made me a target for many professors, almost as if I had placed those stars in the heavens with my own hands in order to upset science and nature. Forgetting that the discovery of facts strengthens rather than weakens the discipline of science and showing more affection for their own opinions than for truth, they rushed to deny my findings, which they would have seen were true if they had cared to look for themselves. Instead, they wrote a number of vain discourses and made a grave error by invoking Holy Scripture, citing passages that have nothing to do with science and which they did not fully understand. Perhaps they would not have made this error if they had known of a most useful tract written by Saint Augustine concerning matters that are difficult to understand. Speaking of certain conclusions about the stars, Augustine wrote, "Practicing moderation and a pious *gravitas*, we should not rush to conclusions about scientific matters, since we might later discover that we are in error and that the truths of science are not at all contrary to the Old and New Testament."

---

[1] Translated by Gregory Murry, all rights reserved.

Other astronomers who investigated the matter honestly have confirmed my findings, and the rancor has gradually died down. Many skilled astronomers were persuaded immediately, and the opponents who refused to believe me, either because of the novelty of my findings or because they had not had a chance to observe those bodies themselves, have quieted down as well. Others, however, seem to have a perverse vendetta against either myself or my discoveries. Because they can no longer deny my findings, they have grown even more bitter and try to attack me in any way they can. I would simply laugh at them, but they do not limit their attacks to my work as a scientist; rather, they have called me a name that I consider worse than death: heretic. Thus, I cannot sit idly by while they try to smear my reputation.

My opponents know that I believe the sun to be motionless and fixed in the center of the celestial orbs, and I believe that the Earth moves around the sun. They also know that I support my position not only by challenging Ptolemy and Aristotle, but by giving many reasons to support this opinion. Some of these are deduced from various aspects of nature, for the Copernican model explains many things about the natural world. Some of my reasons are astronomical and based on my new discoveries, which flatly contradict the Ptolemaic system and support Copernicus....Since my opponents cannot attack me on scientific grounds, they are determined to call me a heretic and use religion to dispute my findings. For this purpose, they have resorted to the authority of Holy Scripture, which they deploy with little intelligence and use to combat arguments that they cannot understand.

In the first place, my opponents have attempted to convince everyone that the heliocentric universe contradicts Sacred Scripture and thus is heretical. Since it is easier to find men who are ready to attack their neighbor unjustly than to find men ready to come to their neighbor's aid, it has not been difficult for my opponents to find preachers willing to call my ideas heretical and condemnable. In doing this, they not only harm my ideas, they harm mathematics and mathematicians everywhere. Thus, they grow ever more confident, hoping that the seeds that they have insincerely planted will grow and spread their branches everywhere, and the people go around murmuring that soon the heliocentric model will be condemned by the Pope. My opponents know that if this happens, it will not only destroy the heliocentric model but will make all the connected observations heretical, so they have tried to make it seem as if the heliocentric model is some new opinion that is only held by me alone. They intentionally ignore the fact that this idea was first proposed by Nicolas Copernicus, a Catholic priest and cathedral canon, who was so esteemed that during the Lateran Council under Leo X, he was called to Rome to help reform the calendar, which at that time was flawed because we did not know the exact length of the year and the lunar month. Bishop Sempronese gave him the task of overseeing the reform of the calendar and better understanding the motions of the celestial bodies. With his almost miraculous and amazing genius, he gave himself over to study, advanced his knowledge of astronomy, and uncovered the secrets of the celestial motions with such exactitude that he won the title of highest astronomer. Not only was the calendar reformed according to his findings, but so was the table of all the movements of the planets. And having compiled his learning, he published it in a book at the request of the Cardinal Capuano and Bishop Culmense. Because he had undertaken this work at the request of the Pope, he dedicated it to the Pope's successor, Paul III. After publication, the work was received by the Holy Church and read and studied by all the world without anyone expressing even a slight worry about his ideas. Now, it has been discovered that the idea is supported by clear observation and necessary proofs; nonetheless, there are many people, though they have never read the book, who reward Copernicus's efforts by declaring him a heretic, and this only to satisfy their unreasonable grudge against me, who has no other connection to Copernicus but to approve of his ideas.

Now I have thought it necessary to defend myself from these false accusations in the court of public opinion, which I value far more than the few who attack me and want to see Copernicus condemned. For these men not only want the heliocentric model to be declared false but even heretical; thus, they feign concern for religion and insincerely enlist the support of scriptures. By doing this (if I understand the doctors of the church correctly), they extend and abuse the authority of the Bible by making it to decide questions about the natural world rather than questions of faith and by forcing us to completely abandon our senses and our reason because of a few passages in scripture that might be interpreted in a contradictory way. I wish to demonstrate how much more pious and religious is my method when I suggest that Copernicus's book should not be condemned without understanding it, hearing it, or even seeing it, especially since he never treated matters of religion or faith, and none of his conclusions depend on Sacred Scripture. Because he might have misinterpreted scripture, he based his conclusions on a study of nature: observing celestial motion, using astronomical and geometrical demonstration, and utilizing sense experience and careful observation. It is not that he completely disregarded Sacred Scripture, but he understood acutely that the conclusions that he had demonstrated could not be contrary to scripture, as long as those scriptures were perfectly understood. In his dedication to the Pope he wrote:

> If perhaps one or two vain theologians who do not know any mathematics try to judge and condemn my work because of some passages in scripture whose meaning they distort, I pay no attention to them and consider their positions false. It is well known that Lactantius, a famous early Christian writer but poor mathematician, spoke very childishly about the form of the earth when he ridiculed those who held it to be a globe. Thus, it will not be a surprise if there are some who laugh at me. Math is written for mathematicians, by whose labors (if I am not mistaken) great good will be done for the church, whose most important office you now hold.

Some wish to see this author condemned without even reading his book, and they persuade themselves it is licit and even good to use passages of Holy Scripture and the Sacred Councils out of context. I revere scripture and the councils as the supreme authority, and I would consider it impudent and rash to contradict them in the senses that they have been adopted by the Holy Church. However, I do not commit an error by publishing my discoveries if all my opponents do is cite some passages from scripture and use them in ways that the Holy Church never intended. However, with self-evident sincerity, let me declare that I will remove from my writings any errors of religion into which I might have fallen. Also, let me declare that I do not want to engage in religious disputes with anyone, even on disputable points...Interpreting scripture is not my field of expertise, so if the Holy Church finds anything useful in my writings, let it do so. If not, let my writings be torn to pieces and burned since I do not want to earn anything from my writings if they are not pious and Catholic. Moreover, though I have heard many of these accusations with my own ears, I freely admit and concede to those who have said them that they may not have said them; perhaps, I have misunderstood them. Thus, I am not responding to anyone specifically, but to whomever holds such opinions.

The reason that some people condemn the heliocentric model is that they read in many parts of the Bible that the Sun moves, and the Earth stands still. Because the scriptures can never lie or error, it necessarily follows that the assertion that the Sun is immobile and the Earth moves is erroneous and condemnable.

I piously and prudently agree that Sacred Scripture can never lie, but only insofar as the true meanings of its words are understood. Frequently, the true sense of its meaning is obscure and very different from the plain sense of the words. Thus, it follows that in trying to understand Holy Scripture, we might error if we always understand the words in their plain, literal sense. If we did this, the Bible would not only contain contradictions and falsehoods, but also grave heresies and blasphemies, since we would need to say that God has feet and hands and eyes, as well as bodily needs and human emotions, such as wrath, penitence, and hatred. We would also need to affirm that God sometimes forgets things that happened in the past or does not know what will happen in the future. On the contrary, all these ideas were inspired by the Holy Spirit and were articulated with words that could be understood by the most uneducated and unintelligent men. Thus, if you want to be different than the common people, you must rely on wise theologians who can clarify the true sense of scripture and explain the reasons why it uses the words it does. This point is so well accepted in theology that it is hardly worth citing authorities on the point. Thus, it seems reasonable to suggest that whenever the Holy Bible seems to make any conclusions about the natural world, especially in matters that are obscure and difficult to understand, it uses common language, so as to not cause confusion in the minds of simple people and make them doubt the truths of the higher mysteries. As I have said, scripture uses common speech in order to accommodate itself to the intellectual capacities of simple people, by, for instance, assigning attributes to God that are far from his true being. Given this, why should we assume that scripture requires us to interpret the words land, water, sun and other creatures in the restricted, literal sense? Especially since these things have nothing to do with the primary concern of Sacred Scripture: the divine cult and the salvation of souls…

Thus, it seems to me that we should not begin scientific disputes by appealing to the authority of Sacred Scripture. Rather, science should be argued on the basis of sense experience and demonstrative proofs. Both sacred scripture and nature are dictated by the Holy Spirit, and both observe the laws of God; however, in scripture there are many things that are accommodated to the understanding of the common person and thus mean something different than the pure, literal sense of the words. On the other hand, because nature is unchangeable, never transcends the limits of the laws imposed on it, and does not care at all whether its hidden operations are knowable or not, it seems that we should make our conclusions based on the natural effects that sense experience and necessary demonstration put before our eyes.   These should not be doubted, much less condemned, by scriptural passages that have obscure meanings…Nor is it less excellent to discover God in the effects of nature than in the sacred words of scripture. As Tertullian writes, "We argue that God is first known through nature, then he is known by revelation: nature by its works, revelation, by preaching."

By asserting this, I do not want to imply that we should not value those parts of Sacred Scripture that speak of natural things; rather, once science has made conclusions about the natural world, we should use those conclusions to accommodate the true sense of scripture to the investigation of our sense experience. For the Bible must agree with scientific truth. Now, I think that scripture's primary purpose is to persuade men of the doctrines that mankind cannot discover by science because they exceed our intellectual capacity. We can only learn these truths from the mouth of the Holy Spirit herself. Even concerning those matters that are not properly matters of faith, we should prefer the authority of the Bible to all other human authorities that argue by narrative and probabilities rather than demonstrations and proofs, for the divine wisdom surpasses all human judgment and conjecture. Nevertheless, I do not believe that the same God who has given us sense, speech, and intellect forbids us to use them to acquire knowledge. I do not believe that God wants us to deny our senses, reason, intellect, experiences, and demonstrative proofs, especially in a field of science that is hardly mentioned in scripture at all. For the Bible doesn't even mention the names of the planets, except the sun, the moon, and Venus. If the sacred writers were trying to teach us about the planets and force us to get our knowledge of astronomy from the Bible, they would have said more about it, for the astronomy contained in the Bible is a tiny fraction of the discoveries to be made in the field.

It is the opinion of the Holy Fathers that the writers of scripture did not mean to teach us about the make-up and movement of the heavens and the stars, or their shape, size, and distance. Though all of these things were known to them, they said nothing about them. In Saint Augustine we read the following words:

> People have begun to ask about what form and figure of the heavens Christians must believe based on our scriptures. Many authors have debated about these things, but the most prudent of our authors do not speak about them at all, inasmuch as they have nothing to do with the question of everlasting life, and debating them takes up valuable time and impedes more salubrious things. What does it matter to me whether the heavens surround the earth on all sides like a sphere or whether they cover it like a disc? I have noted many times that the scriptures speak [only] about matters of faith in order to prevent anyone who does not understand the divine words to find anything in our scripture or hear anything in our doctrine that seems to contradict precepts or assertions that are not matters of faith and thus cause him to ignore scripture's many useful warnings and stories. Briefly put, our authors do not get the truth from the stars but from the Holy Spirit, and she only uses the scriptures to teach men things that are useful for their salvation.

Augustine says the same thing later, concerning the accidental qualities of the celestial bodies, when he asks whether the heavens move or stay in the same place, writing thus:

> Many brothers have asked me whether the heavens stay in one place or move. If they move, in what way are they a firmament? If however, they stand still, how do fixed stars move from the east to the west, with the more northerly making shorter rotations near the pole? Do the heavens have some other pole that is unknown to us, like a sphere? And if there is no other pole, like a disc, why does it seem to rotate? I respond to all this by stating that to discover the truth of this matter would be extremely difficult, and I do not have the time to do it, nor is it necessary to know this in order to fulfil my main duty: teaching others about their salvation and the Holy Church.

If the Holy Spirit did not mean to teach us whether the heavens move or not, nor whether the earth is a sphere or a disc, nor if the Earth is in the middle or on the side, she certainly did not mean to teach us other conclusions of this type...

And if the Holy Spirit has decided not to teach us about natural science, since it has nothing to do with our salvation, how can we then affirm that holding to this or that natural conclusion is necessary because of faith? Can an opinion be heretical if it has nothing to do with the salvation of souls? I repeat a saying that I have heard from an eminent priest: "The Holy Spirit meant to teach us how to go to heaven, not how the heavens go."

Let us consider how much we should value sense experience and demonstrative proofs in scientific matters. The doctors and theologians have given great weight to these matters when they say, amongst a hundred other things:

> We should diligently avoid affirming propositions that contradict manifest experiments or philosophical reason merely because we think we learned them from the teachings of Moses. Since truth can never contradict truth, the doctrine of the Bible can never be contrary to true reason and human learning.

And in Augustine we read:

> If a man uses the authority of sacred scripture against clear and certain reason, he does not understand what he does, for he sets up the sense of Sacred Scripture that he does not understand in contradiction to truth, so he does not use what is actually in Sacred Scripture but what he finds in himself through scripture.

Because two truths can never contradict one another, wise men must study and explain scripture in order to understand the true senses of the words; the true sense of the words will certainly agree with the conclusions of the sciences, when clear experience and demonstrative proof have rendered science's own conclusions certain. Because of all this, I believe it imprudent to limit scientists to the conclusions of Sacred Scripture or to force them to believe conclusions about the natural world that may be contrary to demonstrative proof and necessary reason. For, who would limit human ingenuity? Who would assert that he knows all there is to know...

A MODEST PROPOSAL

For preventing the children of poor people in Ireland,
from being a burden on their parents or country,
and for making them beneficial to the publick, 1729.

The Rev. Dr. Jonathan Swift, D.D.[1]

It is a melancholy object to those, who walk through this great town,[2] or travel in the country, when they see the streets, the roads and cabin-doors crowded with beggars of the female sex, followed by three, four, or six children, all in rags, and importuning every passenger for an alms. These mothers instead of being able to work for their honest livelihood, are forced to employ all their time in strolling to beg sustenance for their helpless infants who, as they grow up, either turn thieves for want of work, or leave their dear native country, to fight for the Pretender in Spain,[3] or sell themselves to the Barbadoes.[4]

I think it is agreed by all parties, that this prodigious number of children in the arms, or on the backs, or at the heels of their mothers, and frequently of their fathers, is in the present deplorable state of the

---

[1] Jonathan Swift was a minister in the Church of Ireland (Anglican) and dean of St. Patrick's Cathedral in Dublin.

[2] Dublin

[3] James Edward Stuart, son of the Catholic Stuart monarch who was ousted by Parliament in the Glorious Revolution of 1688.

[4] British colonies always in need of slaves

kingdom, a very great additional grievance; and therefore whoever could find out a fair, cheap and easy method of making these children sound and useful members of the common-wealth, would deserve so well of the publick, as to have his statue set up for a preserver of the nation.

But my intention is very far from being confined to provide only for the children of professed beggars: it is of a much greater extent, and shall take in the whole number of infants at a certain age, who are born of parents in effect as little able to support them, as those who demand our charity in the streets.

As to my own part, having turned my thoughts for many years, upon this important subject, and maturely weighed the several schemes of our projectors, I have always found them grossly mistaken in their computation. It is true, a child just dropt from its dam,[5] may be supported by her milk, for a solar year, with little other nourishment: at most not above the value of two shillings, which the mother may certainly get, or the value in scraps, by her lawful occupation of begging; and it is exactly at one year old that I propose to provide for them in such a manner, as, instead of being a charge upon their parents, or the parish, or wanting food and raiment for the rest of their lives, they shall, on the contrary, contribute to the feeding, and partly to the cloathing of many thousands.

There is likewise another great advantage in my scheme, that it will prevent those voluntary abortions, and that horrid practice of women murdering their bastard children, alas! too frequent among us, sacrificing the poor innocent babes, I doubt, more to avoid the expence than the shame, which would move tears and pity in the most savage and inhuman breast.

The number of souls in this kingdom being usually reckoned one million and a half, of these I calculate there may be about two hundred thousand couple whose wives are breeders;[6] from which number I subtract thirty thousand couple, who are able to maintain their own children, (although I apprehend there cannot be so many, under the

---

[5] Notice that these words usually refer to how farm animals give birth.

[6] More farm animal diction

present distresses of the kingdom) but this being granted, there will remain an hundred and seventy thousand breeders.[7] I again subtract fifty thousand, for those women who miscarry, or whose children die by accident or disease within the year. There only remain an hundred and twenty thousand children of poor parents annually born. The question therefore is, How this number shall be reared, and provided for? which, as I have already said, under the present situation of affairs, is utterly impossible by all the methods hitherto proposed. For we can neither employ them in handicraft or agriculture; we neither build houses, (I mean in the country) nor cultivate land: they can very seldom pick up a livelihood by stealing till they arrive at six years old; except where they are of towardly parts,[8] although I confess they learn the rudiments much earlier; during which time they can however be properly looked upon only as probationers: As I have been informed by a principal gentleman in the county of Cavan, who protested to me, that he never knew above one or two instances under the age of six, even in a part of the kingdom so renowned for the quickest proficiency in that art.[9]

I am assured by our merchants, that a boy or a girl before twelve years old, is no saleable commodity, and even when they come to this age, they will not yield above three pounds, or three pounds and half a crown at most, on the exchange; which cannot turn to account either to the parents or kingdom, the charge of nutriments and rags having been at least four times that value.[10]

I shall now therefore humbly propose my own thoughts, which I hope will not be liable to the least objection.

I have been assured by a very knowing American of my acquaintance in London, that a young healthy child well nursed, is, at a year old, a most delicious nourishing and wholesome food, whether stewed, roasted,

---

[7] Notice how logical and even scientific these calculations are: Swift is writing like an economist or social scientist.

[8] That is, quite clever

[9] County Cavan was known in the 18th century as having a high crime rate.

[10] Children are clearly a bad commodity in which to invest.

baked, or boiled; and I make no doubt that it will equally serve in a fricasie, or a ragoust.[11]

I do therefore humbly offer it to publick consideration, that of the hundred and twenty thousand children, already computed, twenty thousand may be reserved for breed, whereof only one fourth part to be males; which is more than we allow to sheep, black cattle, or swine, and my reason is, that these children are seldom the fruits of marriage, a circumstance not much regarded by our savages, therefore, one male will be sufficient to serve four females.[12] That the remaining hundred thousand may, at a year old, be offered in sale to the persons of quality and fortune, through the kingdom, always advising the mother to let them suck plentifully in the last month, so as to render them plump, and fat for a good table. A child will make two dishes at an entertainment for friends, and when the family dines alone, the fore or hind quarter will make a reasonable dish, and seasoned with a little pepper or salt, will be very good boiled on the fourth day, especially in winter.

I have reckoned upon a medium, that a child just born will weigh 12 pounds, and in a solar year, if tolerably nursed, encreaseth to 28 pounds.[13]

I grant this food will be somewhat dear, and therefore very proper for landlords, who, as they have already devoured most of the parents, seem to have the best title to the children.[14]

Infant's flesh will be in season throughout the year, but more plentiful in March, and a little before and after; for we are told by a grave author, an eminent French physician,[15] that fish being a prolifick diet, there are more children born in Roman Catholick countries about nine months after Lent, the markets will be more glutted than usual, because the number of Popish infants, is at least three to one in this kingdom, and

---

[11] A fricassee (modern spelling) is a dish of meat stewed in white sauce; a ragout (modern spelling) is another kind of stew.

[12] Swift's logic is sound . . .

[13] Weights in Swift's Ireland were not radically different from our own: do babies average 12 pounds at birth?

[14] What's the commentary on landlords here?

[15] Francois Rabelais (c. 1494-1553), a major French satirist

therefore it will have one other collateral advantage, by lessening the number of Papists among us.[16]

I have already computed the charge of nursing a beggar's child (in which list I reckon all cottagers, laborers, and four-fifths of the farmers) to be about two shillings *per annum*, rags included; and I believe no gentleman would repine to give ten shillings for the carcass of a good fat child, which, as I have said, will make four dishes of excellent nutritive meat, when he hath only some particular friend, or his own family to dine with him. Thus the squire will learn to be a good landlord, and grow popular among his tenants, the mother will have eight shillings neat profit, and be fit for work till she produces another child.[17]

Those who are more thrifty (as I must confess the times require) may flay the carcass; the skin of which, artificially dressed,[18] will make admirable gloves for ladies, and summer boots for fine gentlemen.

As to our City of Dublin, shambles[19] may be appointed for this purpose, in the most convenient parts of it, and butchers we may be assured will not be wanting; although I rather recommend buying the children alive, and dressing them hot from the knife, as we do roasting pigs.

A very worthy person, a true lover of his country, and whose virtues I highly esteem, was lately pleased, in discoursing on this matter, to offer a refinement upon my scheme.[20] He said, that many gentlemen of this kingdom, having of late destroyed their deer, he conceived that the want of venison might be well supply'd by the bodies of young lads and maidens, not exceeding fourteen years of age, nor under twelve;[21] so great

---

[16] Swift is reasoning as a good Irish Protestant here: Papists (Catholics) are a danger to the Crown because of their allegiance to Rome.

[17] Literally everyone involved profits from this plan!

[18] Skillfully prepared

[19] Slaughter-houses

[20] Here Swift is engaging in a Ciceronian *disgressio*, a brief digression on a side point to his argument.

[21] It is true that the nobles and gentry of Ireland drove the deer towards extinction. And deer hunting *is* a sport proper for the upper classes . . .

a number of both sexes in every country being now ready to starve for want of work and service: And these to be disposed of by their parents if alive, or otherwise by their nearest relations. But with due deference to so excellent a friend, and so deserving a patriot, I cannot be altogether in his sentiments; for as to the males, my American acquaintance assured me from frequent experience, that their flesh was generally tough and lean, like that of our school-boys, by continual exercise, and their taste disagreeable, and to fatten them would not answer the charge. Then as to the females, it would, I think, with humble submission, be a loss to the publick, because they soon would become breeders themselves: And besides, it is not improbable that some scrupulous people might be apt to censure such a practice, (although indeed very unjustly) as a little bordering upon cruelty, which, I confess, hath always been with me the strongest objection against any project, how well soever intended.[22]

But in order to justify my friend, he confessed, that this expedient was put into his head by the famous Salmanaazor,[23] a native of the island Formosa,[24] who came from thence to London, above twenty years ago, and in conversation told my friend, that in his country, when any young person happened to be put to death, the executioner sold the carcass to persons of quality, as a prime dainty; and that, in his time, the body of a plump girl of fifteen, who was crucified for an attempt to poison the Emperor, was sold to his imperial majesty's prime minister of state, and other great mandarins of the court in joints from the gibbet, at four hundred crowns. Neither indeed can I deny, that if the same use were made of several plump young girls in this town, who without one single groat to their fortunes, cannot stir abroad without a chair, and appear at a play-house and assemblies in foreign fineries which they never will pay for; the kingdom would not be the worse.

---

[22] Swift actually is quite compassionate: cruelty is to be avoided at all costs.

[23] George Psalmanazar (c. 1679-1763), famous for impersonating others and writing utterly fictional accounts of his journey to Taiwan.

[24] Taiwan

Some persons of a desponding spirit are in great concern about that vast number of poor people, who are aged, diseased, or maimed; and I have been desired to employ my thoughts what course may be taken, to ease the nation of so grievous an incumbrance. But I am not in the least pain upon that matter, because it is very well known, that they are every day dying, and rotting, by cold and famine, and filth, and vermin, as fast as can be reasonably expected. And as to the young laborers, they are now in almost as hopeful a condition. They cannot get work, and consequently pine away from want of nourishment, to a degree, that if at any time they are accidentally hired to common labor, they have not strength to perform it, and thus the country and themselves are happily delivered from the evils to come.

I have too long digressed, and therefore shall return to my subject. I think the advantages by the proposal which I have made are obvious and many, as well as of the highest importance.

For *first*, as I have already observed, it would greatly lessen the number of Papists, with whom we are yearly over-run, being the principal breeders of the nation, as well as our most dangerous enemies, and who stay at home on purpose with a design to deliver the kingdom to the Pretender,[25] hoping to take their advantage by the absence of so many good Protestants, who have chosen rather to leave their country, than stay at home and pay tithes against their conscience to an episcopal curate.[26]

Secondly, The poorer tenants will have something valuable of their own, which by law may be made liable to a distress,[27] and help to pay their landlord's rent, their corn and cattle being already seized, and money a thing unknown.

Thirdly, Whereas the maintainance of an hundred thousand children, from two years old, and upwards, cannot be computed at less than ten

---

[25] Again, James Stuart.

[26] That is, members of Protestant denominations (such as the Presbyterians) who object to having an episcopacy (bishops).

[27] "Distraint," that is, having their property forcibly seized to pay debts.

shillings a piece per annum, the nation's stock will be thereby encreased fifty thousand pounds per annum, besides the profit of a new dish, introduced to the tables of all gentlemen of fortune in the kingdom, who have any refinement in taste. And the money will circulate among our selves, the goods being entirely of our own growth and manufacture.

Fourthly, The constant breeders, besides the gain of eight shillings sterling per annum by the sale of their children, will be rid of the charge of maintaining them after the first year.

Fifthly, This food would likewise bring great custom to taverns, where the vintners will certainly be so prudent as to procure the best receipts[28] for dressing it to perfection; and consequently have their houses frequented by all the fine gentlemen, who justly value themselves upon their knowledge in good eating; and a skilful cook, who understands how to oblige his guests, will contrive to make it as expensive as they please.

Sixthly, This would be a great inducement to marriage, which all wise nations have either encouraged by rewards, or enforced by laws and penalties. It would encrease the care and tenderness of mothers towards their children, when they were sure of a settlement for life to the poor babes, provided in some sort by the publick, to their annual profit instead of expence. We should soon see an honest emulation among the married women, which of them could bring the fattest child to the market. Men would become as fond of their wives, during the time of their pregnancy, as they are now of their mares in foal, their cows in calf, or sow when they are ready to farrow; nor offer to beat or kick them (as is too frequent a practice) for fear of a miscarriage.[29]

Many *other advantages* might be enumerated. For instance, the addition of some thousand carcasses in our exportation of barrel'd beef: the propagation of swine's flesh, and improvement in the art of making good bacon, so much wanted among us by the great destruction of pigs, too frequent at our tables; which are no way comparable in taste or

---

[28] Recipes

[29] In addition to all of the economic benefits, this proposal would prevent domestic violence against women: what's not to like?

magnificence to a well grown, fat yearly child, which roasted whole will make a considerable figure at a Lord Mayor's feast, or any other publick entertainment. But this, and many others, I omit, being studious of brevity.

Supposing that one thousand families in this city, would be constant customers for infants flesh, besides others who might have it at merry meetings, particularly at weddings and christenings,[30] I compute that Dublin would take off annually about twenty thousand carcasses; and the rest of the kingdom (where probably they will be sold somewhat cheaper) the remaining eighty thousand.

I can think of no one objection, that will possibly be raised against this proposal, unless it should be urged, that the number of people will be thereby much lessened in the kingdom. This I freely own, and 'twas indeed one principal design in offering it to the world. I desire the reader will observe, that I calculate my remedy for this one individual Kingdom of Ireland, and for no other that ever was, is, or, I think, ever can be upon Earth.[31] Therefore let no man talk to me of other expedients: Of taxing our absentees at five shillings a pound: Of using neither cloaths, nor houshold furniture, except what is of our own growth and manufacture: Of utterly rejecting the materials and instruments that promote foreign luxury: Of curing the expensiveness of pride, vanity, idleness, and gaming in our women: Of introducing a vein of parsimony, prudence and temperance: Of learning to love our country, wherein we differ even from Laplanders,[32] and the inhabitants of Topinamboo:[33] Of quitting our animosities and factions, nor acting any longer like the Jews, who were

---

[30] That is, infant flesh would be particularly well-suited for Wedding Receptions and parties celebrating Baptisms.

[31] Based on the information in this Proposal, what makes colonial Ireland so unique?

[32] Inhabitants of Northern Scandinavia

[33] The Tupinambá people of Brazil

murdering one another at the very moment their city was taken:[34] Of being a little cautious not to sell our country and consciences for nothing: Of teaching landlords to have at least one degree of mercy towards their tenants. Lastly, of putting a spirit of honesty, industry, and skill into our shop-keepers, who, if a resolution could now be taken to buy only our native goods, would immediately unite to cheat and exact upon us in the price, the measure, and the goodness, nor could ever yet be brought to make one fair proposal of just dealing, though often and earnestly invited to it.[35]

Therefore I repeat, let no man talk to me of these and the like expedients, 'till he hath at least some glympse of hope, that there will ever be some hearty and sincere attempt to put them into practice.

But, as to my self, having been wearied out for many years with offering vain, idle, visionary thoughts, and at length utterly despairing of success, I fortunately fell upon this proposal, which, as it is wholly new, so it hath something solid and real,[36] of no expence and little trouble, full in our own power, and whereby we can incur no danger in disobliging England. For this kind of commodity will not bear exportation, and flesh being of too tender a consistence, to admit a long continuance in salt,

---

[34] This is a reference to Josephus' *The Antiquities of the Jew*, which reported that the Jewish people killed one another rather than be taken captive during the destruction of Jerusalem by Titus in 70 A.D..

[35] Jonathan Swift had published many pamphlets before this Modest Proposal trying to address the problems of the poor in Ireland. All of the measures rejected in this paragraph were ones that he had previously proposed to try to alleviate the plight of the Irish poor. The upper class of Ireland politely ignored these pamphlets.

[36] Compare these words to Machiavelli's in *The Prince*: other people have proposed fantasies, but *this* plan will treat the way things *really* are. Hobbes might also be in the background: don't consider how humans *ought* to act: they *actually* are brutish. How lucky that we have such social scientists to let us know the way things *actually* are, providing us with solid, real solutions for the problems facing humanity!

although perhaps I could name a country,[37] which would be glad to eat up our whole nation without it.

After all, I am not so violently bent upon my own opinion, as to reject any offer, proposed by wise men, which shall be found equally innocent, cheap, easy, and effectual. But before something of that kind shall be advanced in contradiction to my scheme, and offering a better, I desire the author or authors will be pleased maturely to consider two points. *First*, As things now stand, how they will be able to find food and raiment for a hundred thousand useless mouths and backs. And *secondly*, There being a round million of creatures in humane figure throughout this kingdom, whose whole subsistence put into a common stock, would leave them in debt two million of pounds sterling, adding those who are beggars by profession, to the bulk of farmers, cottagers and laborers, with their wives and children, who are beggars in effect; I desire those politicians who dislike my overture, and may perhaps be so bold to attempt an answer, that they will first ask the parents of these mortals, whether they would not at this day think it a great happiness to have been sold for food at a year old, in the manner I prescribe, and thereby have avoided such a perpetual scene of misfortunes, as they have since gone through, by the oppression of landlords, the impossibility of paying rent without money or trade, the want of common sustenance, with neither house nor cloaths to cover them from the inclemencies of the weather, and the most inevitable prospect of intailing the like, or greater miseries, upon their breed for ever.

I profess, in the sincerity of my heart, that I have not the least personal interest in endeavouring to promote this necessary work, having no other motive than the publick good of my country, by advancing our trade, providing for infants, relieving the poor, and giving some pleasure to the rich. I have no children, by which I can propose to get a single penny; the youngest being nine years old, and my wife past child-bearing.[38]

---

[37] That is, England

[38] Mark how selfless Swift is here: he would not profit *at all*. Also note that Jonathan Swift never married . . . Although Swift was a Protestant clergyman, he

cared deeply about the problems affecting poverty-ridden Irish Catholics, and his serious proposals for reducing poverty were ignored. "A Modest Proposal" was not, causing quite a stir, though British colonial rule of Ireland continued to oppress the Catholic majority.

Declaration of the Rights of Man and Citizen, 1789[1]

Inasmuch as the ignorance, disregard, and scorn of the Rights of Man are the sole causes of public ill and governmental corruption, the representatives of the French people, duly constituted in the National Assembly, have resolved to solemnly declare the natural, inalienable, and sacred Rights of Man, so that all the members of this social body can see them and bring them to their mind at any time, constantly recalling their rights and their duties; so that all the acts of the legislative and executive power can be instantly compared to the ends of all political institutions and to be more respected; and so that the complaints of the citizens, founded now on simple and incontestable principles, redound always to the maintenance of the Constitution and the happiness of all.

Therefore, the National Assembly recognizes and declares, in the presence and under the auspices of the Supreme Being, the following rights of Man and Citizen:

1. Man is born and remains free and equal in rights. Social distinctions can only be founded on the common utility.

---

[1] Translation by Gregory Murry © 2016.

2.   The goal of all political association is the maintenance of the natural and unwritten rights of man.   These rights are life, liberty, security, and resistance to oppression.

3.   Sovereignty remains with the Nation. No body or individual can exercise authority unless expressly authorized by the nation.

4. Liberty consists in being able to do all that does not harm others; thus, man is only limited in his natural rights when they infringe on the rights of other members of society. These limits can only be determined by law.

5. The law only has the right to forbid actions that harm society. All that is not forbidden by law cannot be impeded, and no one can be forced to do what the law does not command.

6.   The law is the expression of the general will. All Citizens have the right to participate in the formation of the law, either personally or by their representatives. The law should be the same for all, whether it concerns what the law protects or what the law punishes. Because all citizens are equal in the eyes of the law, they are equally admissible to all dignities, stations, and public employments, according to no other measure than their capabilities, virtues, and talents.

7.   No man can be accused, arrested, or detained, except in cases determined by the law and according to the forms that it has prescribed. Those who ask for, aid in, execute, or cause to be executed arbitrary orders should be punished, but all citizens called forth or seized by the power of the law must obey immediately. Those who do not render themselves guilty by their resistance.

8. The law should only establish penalties that are strictly and evidently necessary, and no one should be punished by a law established and promulgated after the crime.

9. Because all men are innocent until they have been declared guilty, anyone whom it is judged necessary to arrest shall have protection from any force or harm beyond that which is necessary to secure their person.

10. No one should be harassed for their opinions, including religious views, provided that the manifestation of said opinions not disturb the public order established by Law.

11. The free communication of thoughts and opinions is one of the most precious rights of Man. All citizens can thus, speak, write, and print freely, but shall be responsible for abuses of said liberty as determined by Law.

12. The guarantee of the rights of Man and Citizen necessitates a public force; this public force is thus instituted for the advantage of all, and not for the particular utility of those to whom it is entrusted.

13. A common contribution is necessary for the maintenance of this public force as well as for the expenses of public administration; it should be equally shared by all citizens in accordance with their faculties.

14. All Citizens, either by themselves or by their representatives, have the right to ascertain the necessity of the public contribution, to consent to it freely, to know what it is used for, and to determine its amount, assessment, collection method, and duration.

15. Society has the right to demand an account from every public agent of his administration.

16. A society in which the guarantee of rights is not assured, nor the separation of powers determined, has no constitution.

17. Property being a sacred and inviolable right, no one can be deprived of it, except when there is a legally-ascertained, manifestly-evident, public necessity and when a just indemnity has been made.

A Vindication of the Rights of Woman, 1792.

Mary Wollstonecraft

AFTER considering the historic page, and viewing the living world with anxious solicitude, the most melancholy emotions of sorrowful indignation have depressed my spirits, and I have sighed when obliged to confess, that either nature has made a great difference between man and man, or that the civilization which has hitherto taken place in the world has been very partial. I have turned over various books written on the subject of education, and patiently observed the conduct of parents and the management of schools; but what has been the result?—a profound conviction that the neglected education of my fellow-creatures is the grand source of the misery I deplore; and that women, in particular, are rendered weak and wretched by a variety of concurring causes, originating from one hasty conclusion. The conduct and manners of women, in fact, evidently prove that their minds are not in a healthy state; for, like the flowers which are planted in too rich a soil, strength and usefulness are sacrificed to beauty; and the flaunting leaves, after having pleased a fastidious eye, fade, disregarded on the stalk, long before the season when they ought to have arrived at maturity.—One cause of this barren blooming I attribute to a false system of education, gathered from the books written on this subject by men who, considering females rather as women than human creatures, have been more anxious to make them alluring mistresses than wives; and the understanding of the sex has been so bubbled by this specious homage, that the civilized women of the present century, with a few exceptions, are only anxious to inspire love, when they ought to cherish a nobler ambition, and by their abilities and virtues exact respect.

In a treatise, therefore, on female rights and manners, the works which have been particularly written for their improvement must not be overlooked; especially when it is asserted, in direct terms, that the minds of women are enfeebled by false refinement; that the books of instruction, written by men of genius, have had the same tendency as more frivolous productions; and that, in the true style of Mahometanism,[1] they are only considered as females, and not as a part of the human species, when improvable reason is allowed to be the dignified distinction which raises men above the brute creation, and puts a natural sceptre in a feeble hand.

Yet, because I am a woman, I would not lead my readers to suppose that I mean violently to agitate the contested question respecting the equality or inferiority of the sex; but as the subject lies in my way, and I cannot pass it over without subjecting the main tendency of my reasoning to misconstruction, I shall stop a moment to deliver, in a few words, my opinion.—In the government of the physical world it is observable that the female, in general, inferior to the male. The male pursues, the female yields—this is the law of nature; and it does not appear to be suspended or abrogated in favor of woman. This physical superiority cannot be denied—and it is a noble prerogative! But not content with this natural pre-eminence, men endeavour to sink us still lower, merely to render us alluring objects for a moment; and women, intoxicated by the adoration which men, under the influence of their senses, pay them, do not seek to obtain a durable interest in their hearts, or to become the friends of the fellow creatures who find amusement in their society.

---

[1] The religion of Mohammed, or Islam. European writers in Wollstonecraft's time identified Islam and Muslim countries of the Eastern Orient as despotic and tyrannical. The seraglio, or harem, where women were thought to be held in bondage as sexual slaves under the rule of a tyrannical man, served as a central image of such despotism. It was also commonly (and mistakenly) believed that Muslims thought of their women as soulless creatures, little better than animals.

I am aware of an obvious inference: — from every quarter have I heard exclamations against masculine women;[2] but where are they to be found? If by this appellation men mean to inveigh against their ardour in hunting, shooting, and gaming, I shall most cordially join in the cry; but if it be against the imitation of manly virtues, or, more properly speaking, the attainment of those talents and virtues, the exercise of which ennobles the human character, and which raises females in the scale of animal being, when they are comprehensively termed mankind; — all those who view them with a philosophical eye must, I should think, wish with me, that they may every day grow more and more masculine.

This discussion naturally divides the subject. I shall first consider women in the grand light of human creatures, who, in common with men, are placed on this earth to unfold their faculties; and afterwards I shall more particularly point out their peculiar designation.

I wish also to steer clear of an error which many respectable writers have fallen into; for the instruction which has hither been addressed to women, has rather been applicable to ladies, if the little indirect advice, that is scattered through Sanford and Merton be excepted;[3] but, addressing my sex in a firmer tone, I pay particular attention to those in the middle class, because they appear to be in the most natural state. Perhaps the seeds of false refinement, immorality, and vanity, have ever been shed by the great. Weak, artificial beings, raised above the common wants and affections of their race, in a premature unnatural manner, undermine the very foundation of virtue, and spread corruption through the whole mass of society! As a class of mankind they have the strongest claim to pity; the education of the rich tends to render them vain and helpless, and the

---

[2] Pamphlets printed in early modern England regularly bemoaned the problem of "masculine women," which could include women "scolds" who spoke out against authority on issues such as politics or religion, women who refused to obey their husbands or fathers, or women who dressed like men and participated in macho activities (fighting, swearing, etc.).

[3] Thomas Day's *The History of Sandford and Merton* (1783-89) was a bestselling series of children's books in England. Intended to teach good morals, the books contained a series of tales about a spoiled, six-year old aristocratic boy named Tommy Merton, who eventually became educated and virtuous through his friendship with Harry Sandford, a plain, honest farmer's son.

unfolding mind is not strengthened by the practice of those duties which dignify the human character.—They only live to amuse themselves, and by the same law which in nature invariably produces certain effects, they soon only afford barren amusement.

But as I purpose taking a separate view of the different ranks of society, and of the moral character of women, in each, this hint is, for the present, sufficient; and I have only alluded to the subject, because it appears to me to be the very essence of an introduction to give a cursory account of the contents of the work it introduces.

My own sex, I hope, will excuse me, if I treat them like rational creatures, instead of flattering their fascinating graces, and viewing them as if they were in a state of perpetual childhood, unable to stand alone. I earnestly wish to point out in what true dignity and human happiness consists—I wish to persuade women to endeavour to acquire strength, both of mind and body, and to convince them that the soft phrases, susceptibility of heart, delicacy of sentiment, and refinement of taste, are almost synonymous with epithets of weakness, and that those beings who are only the objects of pity and that kind of love, which has been termed its sister, will soon become objects of contempt.

Dismissing then those pretty feminine phrases, which the men condescendingly use to soften our slavish dependence, and despising that weak elegancy of mind, exquisite sensibility, and sweet docility of manners, supposed to be the sexual characteristics of the weaker vessel, I wish to show that elegance is inferior to virtue, that the first object of laudable ambition is to obtain a character as a human being, regardless of the distinction of sex; and that secondary views should be brought to this simple touchstone.

This is a rough sketch of my plan; and should I express my conviction with the energetic emotions that I feel whenever I think of the subject, the dictates of experience and reflection will be felt by some of my readers. Animated by this important object, I shall disdain to cull my phrases or polish my style;—I aim at being useful, and sincerity will render me unaffected; for, wishing rather to persuade by the force of my arguments, than dazzle by the elegance of my language, I shall not waste my time in rounding periods, nor in fabricating the turgid bombast of artificial feelings, which, coming from the head, never reach the heart.—

I shall be employed about things, not words!—and, anxious to render my sex more respectable members of society, I shall try to avoid that flowery diction which has slided from essays into novels, and from novels into familiar letters and conversation.[4]

These pretty nothings—these caricatures of the real beauty of sensibility, dropping glibly from the tongue, vitiate the taste, and create a kind of sickly delicacy that turns away from simple unadorned truth; and a deluge of false sentiments and overstretched feelings, stifling the natural emotions of the heart, render the domestic pleasures insipid, that ought to sweeten the exercise of those severe duties, which educate a rational and immortal being for a nobler field of action.

The education of women has, of late, been more attended to than formerly; yet they are still reckoned a frivolous sex, and ridiculed or pitied by the writers who endeavor by satire or instruction to improve them. It is acknowledged that they spend many of the first years of their lives in acquiring a smattering of accomplishments:[5] meanwhile strength of body and mind are sacrificed to libertine notions of beauty, to the desire of establishing themselves,—the only way women can rise in the world,—by marriage. And this desire making mere animals of them, when they marry they act as such children may be expected to act:—they dress; they paint, and nickname God's creatures.—Surely these weak beings are only fit for a seraglio![6] —Can they govern a family, or take care of the poor babes whom they bring into the world?

If then it can be fairly deduced from the present conduct of the sex, from the prevalent fondness for pleasure which takes place of ambition and those nobler passions that open and enlarge the soul; that the instruction which women have received has only tended, with the constitution of civil society, to render them insignificant objects of desire—

---

[4] Here Wollstonecraft is mocking the polite and flowery writing-style women were encouraged to use when penning letters. To her eighteenth-century audience, her prose would have sounded forceful, argumentative, and indeed "masculine."

[5] These accomplishments might include needlework, embroidery and sewing; singing and/or playing an instrument, such as the piano or harp; speaking some French; drawing or painting with watercolors

[6] Harem. See footnote 1 above.

mere propagators of fools!—if it can be proved that in aiming to accomplish them, without cultivating their understandings, they are taken out of their sphere of duties, and made ridiculous and useless when the short-lived bloom of beauty is over, I presume that rational men will excuse me for endeavouring to persuade them to become more masculine and respectable.

Indeed the word masculine is only a bugbear:[7] there is little reason to fear that women will acquire too much courage or fortitude; for their apparent inferiority with respect to bodily strength, must render them, in some degree, dependent on men in the various relations of life; but why should it be increased by prejudices that give a sex to virtue, and confound simple truths with sensual reveries?

Women are, in fact, so much degraded by mistaken notions of female excellence, that I do not mean to add a paradox when I assert, that this artificial weakness produces a propensity to tyrannize, and gives birth to cunning, the natural opponent of strength, which leads them to play off those contemptible infantile airs that undermine esteem even whilst they excite desire. Do not foster these prejudices, and they will naturally fall into their subordinate, yet respectable station, in life.

It seems scarcely necessary to say, that I now speak of the sex in general. Many individuals have more sense than their male relatives; and, as nothing preponderates where there is a constant struggle for an equilibrium, without it has naturally more gravity, some women govern their husbands without degrading themselves, because intellect will always govern.[8]

---

[7] Literally, this was an imaginary creature who devoured naughty children; nannies told stories of bugbears to frighten children into good behavior. More generally, the term meant any imaginary terror or object of needless dread.

[8] Although her suggestion here about wives ruling less-intelligent husbands was probably unpopular for an eighteenth-century audience, Wollstonecraft was not the first to make such a claim. Several Enlightenment authors in the decades preceding Wollstonecraft had argued as much. An example is Loius, chevalier de Jaucourt, whose article defining "wife (femme)" for *The Encyclopedia of Diderot & d'Alembert* (1756) contended that a woman with more judgment or greater fortune than her husband should, with her husband's consent, have authority over him in the governance of their family.

Observations on the State of Degradation to Which Woman Is Reduced by Various Causes.

THAT woman is naturally weak, or degraded by a concurrence of circumstances, is, I think, clear. But this position I shall simply contrast with a conclusion, which I have frequently heard fall from sensible men in favor of an aristocracy: that the mass of mankind cannot be anything, or the obsequious slaves, who patiently allow themselves to be penned up, would feel their own consequence, and spurn their chains. Men, they further observe, submit everywhere to oppression, when they have only to lift up their heads to throw off the yoke; yet, instead of asserting their birthright, they quietly lick the dust, and say, let us eat and drink, for to-morrow we die. Women, I argue from analogy, are degraded by the same propensity to enjoy the present moment; and, at last, despise the freedom which they have not sufficient virtue to struggle to attain. But I must be more explicit....

I shall not go back to the remote annals of antiquity to trace the history of woman; it is sufficient to allow that she has always been either a slave, or a despot, and to remark, that each of these situations equally retards the progress of reason. The grand source of female folly and vice has ever appeared to me to arise from narrowness of mind; and the very constitution of civil governments has put almost insuperable obstacles in the way to prevent the cultivation of the female understanding:—yet virtue can be built on no other foundation! The same obstacles are thrown in the way of the rich, and the same consequences ensue.

Necessity has been proverbially termed the mother of invention—the aphorism may be extended to virtue. It is an acquirement, and an acquirement to which pleasure must be sacrificed—and who sacrifices pleasure when it is within the grasp, whose mind has not been opened and strengthened by adversity, or the pursuit of knowledge goaded on by necessity?—Happy is it when people have the cares of life to struggle with; for these struggles prevent their becoming a prey to enervating vices, merely from idleness! But, if from their birth men and women are placed in a torrid zone,[9] with the meridian sun of pleasure darting

---

[9] The hottest region of the earth, located between the tropics, through which the equator runs.

directly upon them, how can they sufficiently brace their minds to discharge the duties of life, or even to relish the affections that carry them out of themselves?

Pleasure is the business of woman's life, according to the present modification of society, and while it continues to be so, little can be expected from such weak beings. Inheriting, in a lineal descent from the first fair defect in nature, the sovereignty of beauty, they have, to maintain their power, resigned the natural rights, which the exercise of reason might have procured them, and chosen rather to be short-lived queens than labor to obtain the sober pleasures that arise from equality. Exalted by their inferiority (this sounds like a contradiction) they constantly demand homage as women, though experience should teach them that the men who pride themselves upon paying this arbitrary insolent respect to the sex, with the most scrupulous exactness, are most inclined to tyrannize over, and despise, the very weakness they cherish....

Ah! why do women, I write with affectionate solicitude, condescend to receive a degree of attention and respect from strangers, different from that reciprocation of civility which the dictates of humanity and the politeness of civilization authorise between man and man? And, why do they not discover, when 'in the noon of beauty's power,' that they are treated like queens only to be deluded by hollow respect, till they are led to resign, or not assume, their natural prerogatives? Confined then in cages like the feathered race, they have nothing to do but to plume themselves, and stalk with mock majesty from perch to perch. It is true they are provided with food and raiment, for which they neither toil nor spin; but health, liberty, and virtue, are given in exchange. But, where, amongst mankind has been found sufficient strength of mind to enable a being to resign these adventitious prerogatives; one who, rising with the calm dignity of reason above opinion, dared to be proud of the privileges inherent in man? And it is vain to expect it whilst hereditary power chokes the affections and nips reason in the bud.

The passions of men have thus placed women on thrones, and, till mankind become more reasonable, it is to be feared that women will avail themselves of the power which they attain with the least exertion, and which is the most indisputable. They will smile,—yes, they will smile, though told that—

'In beauty's empire is no mean,
And woman, either slave or queen,
Is quickly scorn'd when not ador'd.'[10]

But the adoration comes first, and the scorn is not anticipated....

On National Education.

THE good effects resulting from attention to private education will ever be very confined, and the parent who really puts his own hand to the plow, will always, in some degree, be disappointed, till education becomes a grand national concern. A man cannot retire into a desert with his child, and if he did he could not bring himself back to childhood, and become the proper friend and play-fellow of an infant or youth. And when children are confined to the society of men and women, they very soon acquire that kind of premature manhood which stops the growth of every vigorous power of mind or body. In order to open their faculties they should be excited to think for themselves; and this can only be done by mixing a number of children together, and making them jointly pursue the same objects....

...[T]o improve both sexes they ought, not only in private families, but in public schools, to be educated together. If marriage be the cement of society, mankind should all be educated after the same model, or the intercourse of the sexes will never deserve the name of fellowship, nor will women ever fulfil the peculiar duties of their sex, till they become enlightened citizens, till they become free by being enabled to earn their own subsistence, independent of men; in the same manner, I mean, to

---

[10] These lines were taken from "Song V" of Anna Laetitia Barbauld's *Poems* (1773). An important early Romantic poet, Barbauld associated closely with the same group of radical Dissenters as Wollstonecraft, and was a lifelong friend of Wollstonecraft's publisher. While both women advocated for the advancement of women, their relationship seems to have been complicated. In some sections of the *Vindication*, Wollstonecraft cited Barbauld's poems admiringly (such as in this instance); in other sections, however, she blasted her, and especially her poem, "To a Lady, with some painted flowers."

prevent misconstruction, as one man is independent of another. Nay, marriage will never be held sacred till women, by being brought up with men, are prepared to be their companions rather than their mistresses; for the mean doublings of cunning will ever render them contemptible, whilst oppression renders them timid. So convinced am I of this truth, that I will venture to predict that virtue will never prevail in society till the virtues of both sexes are founded on reason; and, till the affections common to both are allowed to gain their due strength by the discharge of mutual duties.

Were boys and girls permitted to pursue the same studies together, those graceful decencies might early be inculcated which produce modesty without those sexual distinctions that taint the mind. Lessons of politeness, and that formulary of decorum, which treads on the heels of falsehood, would be rendered useless by habitual propriety of behaviour. Not indeed, put on for visitors like the courtly robe of politeness, but the sober effect of cleanliness of mind. Would not this simple elegance of sincerity be a chaste homage paid to domestic affections, far surpassing the meretricious compliments that shine with false lustre in the heartless intercourse of fashionable life? But, till more understanding preponderate in society, there will ever be a want of heart and taste, and the harlot's rouge will supply the place of that celestial suffusion which only virtuous affections can give to the face. Gallantry,[11] and what is called love, may subsist without simplicity of character; but the main pillars of friendship, are respect and confidence—esteem is never founded on it cannot tell what!...

To render this practicable, day schools, for particular ages, should be established by government, in which boys and girls might be educated together. The school for the younger children, from five to nine years of age, ought to be absolutely free and open to all classes.....

...[I]n an elementary day school, ...boys and girls, the rich and poor, should meet together. And to prevent any of the distinctions of vanity, they should be dressed alike, and all obliged to submit to the same

---

[11] Flirting and dallying with women in a big, showy manner. Wollstonecraft, like many writers in the period, criticized gallants for making a game of leading women on.

discipline, or leave the school. The school-room ought to be surrounded by a large piece of ground, in which the children might be usefully exercised, for at this age they should not be confined to any sedentary employment for more than an hour at a time. But these relaxations might all be rendered a part of elementary education, for many things improve and amuse the senses, when introduced as a kind of show, to the principles of which, dryly laid down, children would turn a deaf ear. For instance, botany, mechanics, and astronomy. Reading, writing, arithmetic, natural history, and some simple experiments in natural philosophy, might fill up the day; but these pursuits should never encroach on gymnastic plays in the open air. The elements of religion, history, the history of man, and politics, might also be taught, by conversations, in the socratic form.

After the age of nine, girls and boys, intended for domestic employments, or mechanical trades, ought to be removed to other schools, and receive instruction, in some measure appropriated to the destination of each individual, the two sexes being still together in the morning; but in the afternoon, the girls should attend a school, where plain-work, mantua-making, millinery, &c. would be their employment.[12]

The young people of superiour abilities, or fortune, might now be taught, in another school, the dead and living languages, the elements of science, and continue the study of history and politics, on a more extensive scale, which would not exclude polite literature.

Girls and boys still together? I hear some readers ask: yes. And I should not fear any other consequence than that some early attachment might take place; which, whilst it had the best effect on the moral character of the young people, might not perfectly agree with the views of the parents, for it will be a long time, I fear, before the world is so far

---

12 These were all typical female professions. "Plain-work" refers to simple needlework or sewing; "mantua-making" is dressmaking; "milliners" made women's clothing and accessories, especially hats. As skills which could bring women employment and an income, Wollstonecraft understood them to be much more useful than acquiring the "smattering of accomplishments" she criticized above.

enlightened that parents, only anxious to render their children virtuous, will let them choose companions for life themselves.

Besides, this would be a sure way to promote early marriages, and from early marriages the most salutary physical and moral effects naturally flow. What a different character does a married citizen assume from the selfish coxcomb, who lives, but for himself, and who is often afraid to marry lest he should not be able to live in a certain style.[13] Great emergencies excepted, which would rarely occur in a society of which equality was the basis, a man could only be prepared to discharge the duties of public life, by the habitual practice of those inferiour ones which form the man.

In this plan of education the constitution of boys would not be ruined by the early debaucheries, which now makes men so selfish, nor girls rendered weak and vain, by indolence, and frivolous pursuits.[14] But, I presuppose, that such a degree of equality should be established between the sexes as would shut out gallantry and coquetry,[15] yet allow friendship and love to temper the heart for the discharge of higher duties.

These would be schools of morality—and the happiness of man, allowed to flow from the pure springs of duty and affection, what advances might not the human mind make? Society can only be happy and free in proportion as it is virtuous; but the present distinctions, established in society, corrode all private, and blast all public virtue.

I have already inveighed against the custom of confining girls to their needle, and shutting them out from all political and civil employments; for by thus narrowing their minds they are rendered unfit to fulfil the peculiar duties which nature has assigned them.

Only employed about the little incidents of the day, they necessarily grow up cunning. My very soul has often sickened at observing the sly

---

[13] Coxcomb means a vain fool or simpleton; it literally refers to the hat that professional fools wore in the courts of kings.

[14] In modern-day terms, she's saying that young men would no longer be ruined by one-night stands, STDs, and heavy drinking (i.e. frat culture), nor young women by laziness and playing silly games to get attention from men.

[15] Gallantry here would mean male flirting and coquetry female flirting. In both cases, the flirt would seek to arouse admiration or love in another without any intention of responding to the feelings awakened.

tricks practised by women to gain some foolish thing on which their silly hearts were set. Not allowed to dispose of money, or call anything their own, they learn to turn the market penny; or, should a husband offend, by staying from home, or give rise to some emotions of jealousy—a new gown, or any pretty bauble, smooths Juno's angry brow.[16]

But these littlenesses would not degrade their character, if women were led to respect themselves, if political and moral subjects were opened to them; and, I will venture to affirm, that this is the only way to make them properly attentive to their domestic duties.—An active mind embraces the whole circle of its duties, and finds time enough for all. It is not, I assert, a bold attempt to emulate masculine virtues; it is not the enchantment of literary pursuits, or the steady investigation of scientific subjects, that lead women astray from duty. No, it is indolence and vanity—the love of pleasure and the love of sway, that will rain paramount in an empty mind. I say empty emphatically, because the education which women now receive scarcely deserves the name. For the little knowledge that they are led to acquire, during the important years of youth, is merely relative to accomplishments; and accomplishments without a bottom, for unless the understanding be cultivated, superficial and monotonous is every grace. Like the charms of a made up face, they only strike the senses in a crowd; but at home, wanting mind, they want variety. The consequence is obvious; in gay scenes of dissipation we meet the artificial mind and face, for those who fly from solitude dread, next to solitude, the domestic circle; not having it in their power to amuse or interest, they feel their own insignificance, or find nothing to amuse or interest themselves....

To render mankind more virtuous, and happier of course, both sexes must act from the same principle; but how can that be expected when only one is allowed to see the reasonableness of it? To render also the social compact truly equitable, and in order to spread those enlightening principles, which alone can meliorate the fate of man, women must be allowed to found their virtue on knowledge, which is scarcely possible unless they be educated by the same pursuits as men. For they are now

---

[16] Remember back in *Origins* how angry Juno became with Aeneas because he did not pick her as the most beautiful goddess?

made so inferiour by ignorance and low desires, as not to deserve to be ranked with them; or, by the serpentine wrigglings of cunning they mount the tree of knowledge, and only acquire sufficient to lead men astray.

It is plain from the history of all nations, that women cannot be confined to merely domestic pursuits, for they will not fulfil family duties, unless their minds take a wider range, and whilst they are kept in ignorance they become in the same proportion the slaves of pleasure as they are the slaves of man. Nor can they be shut out of great enterprises, though the narrowness of their minds often make them mar, what they are unable to comprehend....

....In short, in whatever light I view the subject, reason and experience convince me that the only method of leading women to fulfil their peculiar duties, is to free them from all restraint by allowing them to participate in the inherent rights of mankind.

Make them free, and they will quickly become wise and virtuous, as men become more so; for the improvement must be mutual, or the injustice which one half of the human race are obliged to submit to, retorting on their oppressors, the virtue of man will be worm-eaten by the insect whom he keeps under his feet.

Let men take their choice, man and woman were made for each other, though not to become one being; and if they will not improve women, they will deprave them!

....The conclusion which I wish to draw, is obvious; make women rational creatures, and free citizens, and they will quickly become good wives, and mothers; that is—if men do not neglect the duties of husbands and fathers.

What to a Slave is the Fourth of July?

Frederick Douglass[1]

Mr. President, Friends and Fellow Citizens:

He who could address this audience without a quailing sensation, has stronger nerves than I have. I do not remember ever to have appeared as a speaker before any assembly more shrinkingly, nor with greater distrust of my ability, than I do this day. A feeling has crept over me, quite unfavorable to the exercise of my limited powers of speech. The task before me is one which requires much previous thought and study for its proper performance. I know that apologies of this sort are generally considered flat and unmeaning. I trust, however, that mine will not be so considered. Should I seem at ease, my appearance would much misrepresent me. The little experience I have had in addressing public meetings, in country schoolhouses, avails me nothing on the present occasion.

The papers and placards say, that I am to deliver a 4th [of] July oration. This certainly sounds large, and out of the common way, for it is true that I have often had the privilege to speak in this beautiful Hall, and to address many who now honor me with their presence. But neither

---

[1] This speech was originally given on July 5, 1852 to a Ladies' Abolitionist Society in Rochester, New York.

their familiar faces, nor the perfect gage I think I have of Corinthian Hall, seems to free me from embarrassment.

The fact is, ladies and gentlemen, the distance between this platform and the slave plantation, from which I escaped, is considerable — and the difficulties to be overcome in getting from the latter to the former, are by no means slight. That I am here to-day is, to me, a matter of astonishment as well as of gratitude. You will not, therefore, be surprised, if in what I have to say I evince no elaborate preparation, nor grace my speech with any high sounding exordium. With little experience and with less learning, I have been able to throw my thoughts hastily and imperfectly together; and trusting to your patient and generous indulgence, I will proceed to lay them before you.[2]

This, for the purpose of this celebration, is the 4th of July. It is the birthday of your National Independence, and of your political freedom.[3] This, to you, is what the Passover was to the emancipated people of God.[4] It carries your minds back to the day, and to the act of your great deliverance; and to the signs, and to the wonders, associated with that act, and that day. This celebration also marks the beginning of another year of your national life; and reminds you that the Republic of America is now 76 years old. I am glad, fellow-citizens, that your nation is so young. Seventy-six years, though a good old age for a man, is but a mere speck in the life of a nation. Three score years and ten is the allotted time for individual men;[5] but nations number their years by thousands. According to this fact, you are, even now, only in the beginning of your national career, still lingering in the period of childhood. I repeat, I am glad this is so. There is hope in the thought, and hope is much needed, under the dark clouds which lower above the horizon. The eye of the reformer is met with angry flashes, portending disastrous times; but his heart may well beat lighter at the thought that America is young, and that she is still in the impressible stage of her existence. May he not hope that

---

[2] Note to all readers: Douglass is characterizing himself as being unlearned, but could you write sentences as eloquent and stylistically balanced?

[3] Notice how Douglass is using *pronouns* here.

[4] Recall the Passover narrative in Exodus 12, studied in Origins of the West.

[5] Psalm 90:10

high lessons of wisdom, of justice and of truth, will yet give direction to her destiny? Were the nation older, the patriot's heart might be sadder, and the reformer's brow heavier. Its future might be shrouded in gloom, and the hope of its prophets go out in sorrow. There is consolation in the thought that America is young. Great streams are not easily turned from channels, worn deep in the course of ages. They may sometimes rise in quiet and stately majesty, and inundate the land, refreshing and fertiliz-ing the earth with their mysterious properties. They may also rise in wrath and fury, and bear away, on their angry waves, the accumulated wealth of years of toil and hardship. They, however, gradually flow back to the same old channel, and flow on as serenely as ever. But, while the river may not be turned aside, it may dry up, and leave nothing behind but the withered branch, and the unsightly rock, to howl in the abyss-sweeping wind, the sad tale of departed glory. As with rivers so with nations.

Fellow-citizens, I shall not presume to dwell at length on the associations that cluster about this day. The simple story of it is that, 76 years ago, the people of this country were British subjects. The style and title of your "sovereign people" (in which you now glory) was not then born. You were under the British Crown. Your fathers esteemed the English Government as the home government; and England as the fatherland. This home government, you know, although a considerable distance from your home, did, in the exercise of its parental prerogatives, impose upon its colonial children, such restraints, burdens and limit-ations, as, in its mature judgment, it deemed wise, right and proper.

But, your fathers, who had not adopted the fashionable idea of this day, of the infallibility of government, and the absolute character of its acts, presumed to differ from the home government in respect to the wisdom and the justice of some of those burdens and restraints. They went so far in their excitement as to pronounce the measures of govern-ment unjust, unreasonable, and oppressive, and altogether such as ought not to be quietly submitted to. I scarcely need say, fellow-citizens, that my opinion of those measures fully accords with that of your fathers. Such a declaration of agreement on my part would not be worth much to anybody. It would, certainly, prove nothing, as to what part I might have taken, had I lived during the great controversy of 1776. To say now that

America was right, and England wrong, is exceedingly easy. Everybody can say it; the dastard, not less than the noble brave, can flippantly discant on the tyranny of England towards the American Colonies. It is fashionable to do so; but there was a time when to pronounce against England, and in favor of the cause of the colonies, tried men's souls. They who did so were accounted in their day, plotters of mischief, agitators and rebels, dangerous men. To side with the right, against the wrong, with the weak against the strong, and with the oppressed against the oppressor! here lies the merit, and the one which, of all others, seems unfashionable in our day. The cause of liberty may be stabbed by the men who glory in the deeds of your fathers. But, to proceed.

Feeling themselves harshly and unjustly treated by the home government, your fathers, like men of honesty, and men of spirit, earnestly sought redress. They petitioned and remonstrated; they did so in a decorous, respectful, and loyal manner. Their conduct was wholly unexceptionable. This, however, did not answer the purpose. They saw themselves treated with sovereign indifference, coldness and scorn. Yet they persevered. They were not the men to look back.

As the sheet anchor takes a firmer hold, when the ship is tossed by the storm, so did the cause of your fathers grow stronger, as it breasted the chilling blasts of kingly displeasure. The greatest and best of British statesmen admitted its justice, and the loftiest eloquence of the British Senate came to its support. But, with that blindness which seems to be the unvarying characteristic of tyrants, since Pharaoh and his hosts were drowned in the Red Sea, the British Government persisted in the exactions complained of.

The madness of this course, we believe, is admitted now, even by England; but we fear the lesson is wholly lost on our present ruler.

Oppression makes a wise man mad. Your fathers were wise men, and if they did not go mad, they became restive under this treatment. They felt themselves the victims of grievous wrongs, wholly incurable in their colonial capacity. With brave men there is always a remedy for oppression. Just here, the idea of a total separation of the colonies from the crown was born! It was a startling idea, much more so, than we, at this distance of time, regard it. The timid and the prudent (as has been intimated) of that day, were, of course, shocked and alarmed by it.

Such people lived then, had lived before, and will, probably, ever have a place on this planet; and their course, in respect to any great change, (no matter how great the good to be attained, or the wrong to be redressed by it), may be calculated with as much precision as can be the course of the stars. They hate all changes, but silver, gold and copper change! Of this sort of change they are always strongly in favor.

These people were called Tories in the days of your fathers; and the appellation, probably, conveyed the same idea that is meant by a more modern, though a somewhat less euphonious term, which we often find in our papers, applied to some of our old politicians.

Their opposition to the then dangerous thought was earnest and powerful; but, amid all their terror and affrighted vociferations against it, the alarming and revolutionary idea moved on, and the country with it.

On the 2d of July, 1776, the old Continental Congress, to the dismay of the lovers of ease, and the worshipers of property, clothed that dreadful idea with all the authority of national sanction. They did so in the form of a resolution; and as we seldom hit upon resolutions, drawn up in our day whose transparency is at all equal to this, it may refresh your minds and help my story if I read it. "Resolved, That these united colonies are, and of right, ought to be free and Independent States; that they are absolved from all allegiance to the British Crown; and that all political connection between them and the State of Great Britain is, and ought to be, dissolved."

Citizens, your fathers made good that resolution. They succeeded; and to-day you reap the fruits of their success. The freedom gained is yours; and you, therefore, may properly celebrate this anniversary. The 4th of July is the first great fact in your nation's history — the very ring-bolt in the chain of your yet undeveloped destiny.

Pride and patriotism, not less than gratitude, prompt you to celebrate and to hold it in perpetual remembrance. I have said that the Declaration of Independence is the ring-bolt to the chain of your nation's destiny; so, indeed, I regard it. The principles contained in that instrument are saving principles. Stand by those principles, be true to them on all occasions, in all places, against all foes, and at whatever cost.

From the round top of your ship of state, dark and threatening clouds may be seen.[6] Heavy billows, like mountains in the distance, disclose to the leeward huge forms of flinty rocks! That bolt drawn, that chain broken, and all is lost. Cling to this day — cling to it, and to its principles, with the grasp of a storm-tossed mariner to a spar at midnight.

The coming into being of a nation, in any circumstances, is an interesting event. But, besides general considerations, there were peculiar circumstances which make the advent of this republic an event of special attractiveness.

The whole scene, as I look back to it, was simple, dignified and sublime.

The population of the country, at the time, stood at the insignificant number of three millions. The country was poor in the munitions of war. The population was weak and scattered, and the country a wilderness unsubdued. There were then no means of concert and combination, such as exist now. Neither steam nor lightning had then been reduced to order and discipline.[7] From the Potomac to the Delaware was a journey of many days. Under these, and innumerable other disadvantages, your fathers declared for liberty and independence and triumphed.

Fellow Citizens, I am not wanting in respect for the fathers of this republic. The signers of the Declaration of Independence were brave men. They were great men too — great enough to give fame to a great age. It does not often happen to a nation to raise, at one time, such a number of truly great men. The point from which I am compelled to view them is not, certainly, the most favorable; and yet I cannot contemplate their great deeds with less than admiration. They were statesmen, patriots and heroes, and for the good they did, and the principles they contended for, I will unite with you to honor their memory.

They loved their country better than their own private interests; and, though this is not the highest form of human excellence, all will concede that it is a rare virtue, and that when it is exhibited, it ought to command

---

[6] Recall Creon's formulation of the state as a ship with him at the helm in *Antigone*, 180.

[7] That is to say, steam engines and electricity had not yet been utilized. Douglass is referencing the Industrial Revolution in the United States.

respect. He who will, intelligently, lay down his life for his country, is a man whom it is not in human nature to despise. Your fathers staked their lives, their fortunes, and their sacred honor, on the cause of their country. In their admiration of liberty, they lost sight of all other interests.

They were peace men; but they preferred revolution to peaceful submission to bondage. They were quiet men; but they did not shrink from agitating against oppression. They showed forbearance; but that they knew its limits. They believed in order; but not in the order of tyranny. With them, nothing was "settled" that was not right. With them, justice, liberty and humanity were "final;" not slavery and oppression. You may well cherish the memory of such men. They were great in their day and generation. Their solid manhood stands out the more as we contrast it with these degenerate times.

How circumspect, exact and proportionate were all their movements! How unlike the politicians of an hour! Their statesmanship looked beyond the passing moment, and stretched away in strength into the distant future. They seized upon eternal principles, and set a glorious example in their defense. Mark them![8]

Fully appreciating the hardship to be encountered, firmly believing in the right of their cause, honorably inviting the scrutiny of an on-looking world, reverently appealing to heaven to attest their sincerity, soundly comprehending the solemn responsibility they were about to assume, wisely measuring the terrible odds against them, your fathers, the fathers of this republic, did, most deliberately, under the inspiration of a glorious patriotism, and with a sublime faith in the great principles of justice and freedom, lay deep the corner-stone of the national super-structure, which has risen and still rises in grandeur around you.

Of this fundamental work, this day is the anniversary. Our eyes are met with demonstrations of joyous enthusiasm. Banners and pennants wave exultingly on the breeze. The din of business, too, is hushed. Even Mammon seems to have quitted his grasp on this day.[9] The ear-piercing fife and the stirring drum unite their accents with the ascending peal of a thousand church bells. Prayers are made, hymns are sung, and sermons

---

[8] What specific eternal principles does Douglass find true?

[9] Mammon was Riches personified as a demonic god. Cf. Matthew 6:24

are preached in honor of this day; while the quick martial tramp of a great and multitudinous nation, echoed back by all the hills, valleys and mountains of a vast continent, bespeak the occasion one of thrilling and universal interest — a nation's jubilee.

Friends and citizens, I need not enter further into the causes which led to this anniversary. Many of you understand them better than I do. You could instruct me in regard to them. That is a branch of knowledge in which you feel, perhaps, a much deeper interest than your speaker. The causes which led to the separation of the colonies from the British crown have never lacked for a tongue. They have all been taught in your common schools, narrated at your firesides, unfolded from your pulpits, and thundered from your legislative halls, and are as familiar to you as household words. They form the staple of your national poetry and eloquence.[10]

I remember, also, that, as a people, Americans are remarkably familiar with all facts which make in their own favor. This is esteemed by some as a national trait — perhaps a national weakness. It is a fact, that whatever makes for the wealth or for the reputation of Americans, and can be had cheap! will be found by Americans. I shall not be charged with slandering Americans, if I say I think the American side of any question may be safely left in American hands.

I leave, therefore, the great deeds of your fathers to other gentlemen whose claim to have been regularly descended will be less likely to be disputed than mine!

My business, if I have any here to-day, is with the present. The accepted time with God and his cause is the ever-living now.

Trust no future, however pleasant,
Let the dead past bury its dead;
Act, act in the living present,
Heart within, and God overhead.[11]

---

[10] In other words, this narration of Liberty is a "background story," taken for granted by most white Americans.

[11] These lines are from Henry Wordsworth Longfellow's "A Psalm of Life."

We have to do with the past only as we can make it useful to the present and to the future. To all inspiring motives, to noble deeds which can be gained from the past, we are welcome. But now is the time, the important time. Your fathers have lived, died, and have done their work, and have done much of it well. You live and must die, and you must do your work. You have no right to enjoy a child's share in the labor of your fathers, unless your children are to be blest by your labors. You have no right to wear out and waste the hard-earned fame of your fathers to cover your indolence. Sydney Smith tells us that men seldom eulogize the wisdom and virtues of their fathers, but to excuse some folly or wickedness of their own. This truth is not a doubtful one. There are illustrations of it near and remote, ancient and modern. It was fashionable, hundreds of years ago, for the children of Jacob to boast, we have "Abraham to our father," when they had long lost Abraham's faith and spirit. That people contented themselves under the shadow of Abraham's great name, while they repudiated the deeds which made his name great. Need I remind you that a similar thing is being done all over this country to-day? Need I tell you that the Jews are not the only people who built the tombs of the prophets, and garnished the sepulchres of the righteous? Washington could not die till he had broken the chains of his slaves. Yet his monument is built up by the price of human blood, and the traders in the bodies and souls of men shout — "We have Washington to *our father*." — Alas! that it should be so; yet so it is.

> *The evil that men do, lives after them, The good is oft-interred with their bones.*[12]

Fellow-citizens, pardon me, allow me to ask, why am I called upon to speak here to-day? What have I, or those I represent, to do with your national independence? Are the great principles of political freedom and of natural justice, embodied in that Declaration of Independence, ex-tended to us? and am I, therefore, called upon to bring our humble offering to the national altar, and to confess the benefits and express

---

[12] Shakespeare, *Julius Caesar* 3.2.74-75

devout gratitude for the blessings resulting from your independence to us?

Would to God, both for your sakes and ours, that an affirmative answer could be truthfully returned to these questions! Then would my task be light, and my burden easy and delightful. For who is there so cold, that a nation's sympathy could not warm him? Who so obdurate and dead to the claims of gratitude, that would not thankfully acknowledge such priceless benefits? Who so stolid and selfish, that would not give his voice to swell the hallelujahs of a nation's jubilee, when the chains of servitude had been torn from his limbs? I am not that man. In a case like that, the dumb might eloquently speak, and the "lame man leap as an hart."[13]

But, such is not the state of the case. I say it with a sad sense of the disparity between us. I am not included within the pale of this glorious anniversary! Your high independence only reveals the immeasurable distance between us. The blessings in which you, this day, rejoice, are not enjoyed in common. — The rich inheritance of justice, liberty, prosperity and independence, bequeathed by your fathers, is shared by you, not by me. The sunlight that brought life and healing to you, has brought stripes and death to me. This Fourth [of] July is *yours*, not *mine*. *You* may rejoice, *I* must mourn. To drag a man in fetters into the grand illuminated temple of liberty, and call upon him to join you in joyous anthems, were inhuman mockery and sacrilegious irony. Do you mean, citizens, to mock me, by asking me to speak to-day? If so, there is a parallel to your conduct. And let me warn you that it is dangerous to copy the example of a nation whose crimes, lowering up to heaven, were thrown down by the breath of the Almighty, burying that nation in irrecoverable ruin! I can to-day take up the plaintive lament of a peeled and woe-smitten people!

"By the rivers of Babylon, there we sat down. Yea! we wept when we remembered Zion. We hanged our harps upon the willows in the midst thereof. For there, they that carried us away captive, required of us a song; and they who wasted us required of us mirth, saying, Sing us one of the songs of Zion. How can we sing the Lord's song in a strange land?

---

[13] Isaiah 35:6

If I forget thee, O Jerusalem, let my right hand forget her cunning. If I do not remember thee, let my tongue cleave to the roof of my mouth."[14]

Fellow-citizens; above your national, tumultuous joy, I hear the mournful wail of millions! whose chains, heavy and grievous yesterday, are, to-day, rendered more intolerable by the jubilee shouts that reach them. If I do forget, if I do not faithfully remember those bleeding children of sorrow this day, "may my right hand forget her cunning, and may my tongue cleave to the roof of my mouth!" To forget them, to pass lightly over their wrongs, and to chime in with the popular theme, would be treason most scandalous and shocking, and would make me a reproach before God and the world. My subject, then fellow-citizens, is AMERICAN SLAVERY. I shall see, this day, and its popular characteristics, from the slave's point of view. Standing, there, identified with the American bondman, making his wrongs mine, I do not hesitate to declare, with all my soul, that the character and conduct of this nation never looked blacker to me than on this 4th of July! Whether we turn to the declarations of the past, or to the professions of the present, the conduct of the nation seems equally hideous and revolting. America is false to the past, false to the present, and solemnly binds herself to be false to the future. Standing with God and the crushed and bleeding slave on this occasion,[15] I will, in the name of humanity which is outraged, in the name of liberty which is fettered, in the name of the constitution and the Bible, which are disregarded and trampled upon, dare to call in question and to denounce, with all the emphasis I can command, everything that serves to perpetuate slavery — the great sin and shame of America! "I will not equivocate; I will not excuse;"[16] I will use the severest language I can command; and yet not one word shall escape me

---

[14] Psalm 137:1-6: Why do you suppose Douglass quotes so much of this Psalm? Notice how he uses Psalm 137 to interpret the current state of affairs in the United States.

[15] Notice how Douglass asserts that God is on the side of the crushed and bleeding slave. This is not far removed from Jean Vanier's comments on Christ being with the poorest and weakest in "From Brokenness to Community," back in Freshman Symposium.

[16] William Lloyd Garrison (1807-1879), abolitionist and social reformer

that any man, whose judgment is not blinded by prejudice, or who is not at heart a slaveholder, shall not confess to be right and just.

But I fancy I hear some one of my audience say, it is just in this circumstance that you and your brother abolitionists fail to make a favorable impression on the public mind. Would you argue more, and denounce less, would you persuade more, and rebuke less, your cause would be much more likely to succeed. But, I submit, where all is plain there is nothing to be argued. What point in the anti-slavery creed would you have me argue? On what branch of the subject do the people of this country need light? Must I undertake to prove that the slave is a man? That point is conceded already. Nobody doubts it. The slaveholders themselves acknowledge it in the enactment of laws for their government. They acknowledge it when they punish disobedience on the part of the slave. There are seventy-two crimes in the State of Virginia, which, if committed by a black man, (no matter how ignorant he be), subject him to the punishment of death; while only two of the same crimes will subject a white man to the like punishment. What is this but the acknowledgement that the slave is a moral, intellectual and responsible being? The manhood of the slave is conceded. It is admitted in the fact that Southern statute books are covered with enactments forbidding, under severe fines and penalties, the teaching of the slave to read or to write. When you can point to any such laws, in reference to the beasts of the field, then I may consent to argue the manhood of the slave. When the dogs in your streets, when the fowls of the air, when the cattle on your hills, when the fish of the sea, and the reptiles that crawl, shall be unable to distinguish the slave from a brute, *then* will I argue with you that the slave is a man!

For the present, it is enough to affirm the equal manhood of the Negro race. Is it not astonishing that, while we are ploughing, planting and reaping, using all kinds of mechanical tools, erecting houses, constructing bridges, building ships, working in metals of brass, iron, copper, silver and gold; that, while we are reading, writing and cyphering, acting as clerks, merchants and secretaries, having among us lawyers, doctors, ministers, poets, authors, editors, orators and teachers; that, while we are engaged in all manner of enterprises common to other men, digging gold in California, capturing the whale in the Pacific, feeding sheep and cattle on the hill-side, living, moving, acting, thinking, planning, living in families as husbands, wives and children, and, above all, confessing and worshipping the Christian's God, and looking hopefully for life and immortality beyond the grave, we are called upon to prove that we are men!

Would you have me argue that man is entitled to liberty? that he is the rightful owner of his own body? You have already declared it. Must I argue the wrongfulness of slavery? Is that a question for Republicans? Is it to be settled by the rules of logic and argumentation, as a matter beset with great difficulty, involving a doubtful application of the principle of justice, hard to be understood? How should I look to-day, in the presence of Americans, dividing, and subdividing a discourse, to show that men have a natural right to freedom? speaking of it relatively, and positively, negatively, and affirmatively. To do so, would be to make myself ridiculous, and to offer an insult to your understanding. — There is not a man beneath the canopy of heaven, that does not know that slavery is wrong *for him.*

What, am I to argue that it is wrong to make men brutes, to rob them of their liberty, to work them without wages, to keep them ignorant of their relations to their fellow men, to beat them with sticks, to flay their flesh with the lash, to load their limbs with irons, to hunt them with dogs, to sell them at auction, to sunder their families, to knock out their teeth, to burn their flesh, to starve them into obedience and submission to their masters? Must I argue that a system thus marked with blood, and stained with pollution, is *wrong?*[17] No! I will not. I have better employments for my time and strength than such arguments would imply.

What, then, remains to be argued? Is it that slavery is not divine; that God did not establish it; that our doctors of divinity are mistaken? There is blasphemy in the thought. That which is inhuman, cannot be divine! Who can reason on such a proposition? They that can, may; I cannot. The time for such argument is passed.

----

[17] Notice how Douglass is not simply concerned with the evil of individuals or communities, but the entire *system* of oppression in the United States, a system from which even those who do not own slaves benefit.

At a time like this, scorching irony, not convincing argument, is needed. O! had I the ability, and could I reach the nation's ear, I would, to-day, pour out a fiery stream of biting ridicule, blasting reproach, withering sarcasm, and stern rebuke.[18] For it is not light that is needed, but fire; it is not the gentle shower, but thunder. We need the storm, the whirlwind, and the earthquake.[19] The feeling of the nation must be quickened; the conscience of the nation must be roused; the propriety of the nation must be startled; the hypocrisy of the nation must be exposed; and its crimes against God and man must be proclaimed and denounced.

What, to the American slave, is your 4th of July? I answer: a day that reveals to him, more than all other days in the year, the gross injustice and cruelty to which he is the constant victim. To him, your celebration is a sham; your boasted liberty, an unholy license; your national great-ness, swelling vanity; your sounds of rejoicing are empty and heartless; your denunciations of tyrants, brass fronted impudence; your shouts of liberty and equality, hollow mockery; your prayers and hymns, your sermons and thanksgivings, with all your religious parade, and solemn-ity, are, to him, mere bombast, fraud, deception, impiety, and hypocrisy — a thin veil to cover up crimes which would disgrace a nation of savages. There is not a nation on the earth guilty of practices, more shocking and bloody, than are the people of these United States, at this very hour.

Go where you may, search where you will, roam through all the monarchies and despotisms of the old world, travel through South America, search out every abuse, and when you have found the last, lay your facts by the side of the everyday practices of this nation, and you will say with me, that, for revolting barbarity and shameless hypocrisy, America reigns without a rival.

Take the American slave-trade, which, we are told by the papers, is especially prosperous just now. Ex-Senator Benton tells us that the price

---

[18] Here Douglass is adopting the diction (though not quoting exactly) of Shakespeare's Marc Antony in his Funeral Oration; consider especially *Julius Caesar* 3.2.239-43.

[19] These sublime and powerful natural phenomena are commonly encountered in Romantic art, music, and literature.

of men was never higher than now. He mentions the fact to show that slavery is in no danger. This trade is one of the peculiarities of American institutions. It is carried on in all the large towns and cities in one-half of this confederacy; and millions are pocketed every year, by dealers in this horrid traffic. In several states, this trade is a chief source of wealth. It is called (in contradistinction to the foreign slave-trade) "*the internal slave trade.*" It is, probably, called so, too, in order to divert from it the horror with which the foreign slave-trade is contemplated. That trade has long since been denounced by this government, as piracy. It has been denounced with burning words, from the high places of the nation, as an execrable traffic. To arrest it, to put an end to it, this nation keeps a squadron, at immense cost, on the coast of Africa. Everywhere, in this country, it is safe to speak of this foreign slave-trade, as a most inhuman traffic, opposed alike to the laws of God and of man. The duty to extirpate and destroy it, is admitted even by our DOCTORS OF DIVINITY.[20] In order to put an end to it, some of these last have consented that their colored brethren (nominally free) should leave this country, and establish themselves on the western coast of Africa![21] It is, however, a notable fact that, while so much execration is poured out by Americans upon those engaged in the foreign slave-trade, the men engaged in the slave-trade between the states pass without condemnation, and their business is deemed honorable.

Behold the practical operation of this internal slave-trade, the American slave-trade, sustained by American politics and America religion. Here you will see men and women reared like swine for the market. You know what is a swine-drover?[22] I will show you a man-drover. They inhabit all our Southern States. They perambulate the country, and crowd the highways of the nation, with droves of human stock. You will see one of these human flesh-jobbers, armed with pistol, whip and bowie-knife, driving a company of a hundred men, women,

---

[20] That is to say, clergymen. A Doctor of Divinity (D.D.) is the Protestant equivalent of a Doctor of Sacred Theology (S.T.D.) in the Catholic world.

[21] The notion of sending slaves back to Africa may sound odd, but it actually was a serious proposition by the American Colonization Society. If you don't know the history of the African nation of Liberia, now is the time to look it up.

[22] That is, a swineherd or swine-driver.

and children, from the Potomac to the slave market at New Orleans. These wretched people are to be sold singly, or in lots, to suit purchasers.[23] They are food for the cotton-field, and the deadly sugar-mill. Mark the sad procession, as it moves wearily along, and the inhuman wretch who drives them. Hear his savage yells and his blood-chilling oaths, as he hurries on his affrighted captives! There, see the old man, with locks thinned and gray. Cast one glance, if you please, upon that young mother, whose shoulders are bare to the scorching sun, her briny tears falling on the brow of the babe in her arms. See, too, that girl of thirteen, weeping, *yes*! weeping, as she thinks of the mother from whom she has been torn! The drove moves tardily. Heat and sorrow have nearly consumed their strength; suddenly you hear a quick snap, like the discharge of a rifle; the fetters clank, and the chain rattles simultaneously; your ears are saluted with a scream, that seems to have torn its way to the center of your soul! The crack you heard, was the sound of the slave-whip; the scream you heard, was from the woman you saw with the babe. Her speed had faltered under the weight of her child and her chains! that gash on her shoulder tells her to move on. Follow the drove to New Orleans. Attend the auction; see men examined like horses; see the forms of women rudely and brutally exposed to the shocking gaze of American slave-buyers. See this drove sold and separated forever; and never forget the deep, sad sobs that arose from that scattered multitude. Tell me citizens, WHERE, under the sun, you can witness a spectacle more fiendish and shocking. Yet this is but a glance at the American slave-trade, as it exists, at this moment, in the ruling part of the United States.

I was born amid such sights and scenes. To me the American slave-trade is a terrible reality. When a child, my soul was often pierced with a sense of its horrors. I lived on Philpot Street, Fell's Point, Baltimore, and have watched from the wharves, the slave ships in the Basin, anchored from the shore, with their cargoes of human flesh, waiting for favorable winds to waft them down the Chesapeake.[24] There was, at that time, a

---

[23] Note the vivid narration that follows and compare it to the litany of abuses Martin Luther King, Jr. catalogues in his "Letter from Birmingham Jail."

[24] Many of you have probably visited Fell's Point in Baltimore, which is now known more for bars and restaurants than human trafficking.

grand slave mart kept at the head of Pratt Street, by Austin Woldfolk. His agents were sent into every town and county in Maryland, announcing their arrival, through the papers, and on flaming *"hand-bills,"* headed CASH FOR NEGROES. These men were generally well dressed men, and very captivating in their manners. Ever ready to drink, to treat, and to gamble. The fate of many a slave has depended upon the turn of a single card; and many a child has been snatched from the arms of its mother by bargains arranged in a state of brutal drunkenness.

The flesh-mongers gather up their victims by dozens, and drive them, chained, to the general depot at Baltimore. When a sufficient number have been collected here, a ship is chartered, for the purpose of conveying the forlorn crew to Mobile, or to New Orleans. From the slave prison to the ship, they are usually driven in the darkness of night; for since the antislavery agitation, a certain caution is observed.

In the deep still darkness of midnight, I have been often aroused by the dead heavy footsteps, and the piteous cries of the chained gangs that passed our door. The anguish of my boyish heart was intense; and I was often consoled, when speaking to my mistress in the morning, to hear her say that the custom was very wicked; that she hated to hear the rattle of the chains, and the heart-rending cries. I was glad to find one who sympathized with me in my horror.

Fellow-citizens, this murderous traffic is, to-day, in active operation in this boasted republic. In the solitude of my spirit, I see clouds of dust raised on the highways of the South; I see the bleeding footsteps; I hear the doleful wail of fettered humanity, on the way to the slave-markets, where the victims are to be sold like *horses*, *sheep*, and *swine*, knocked off to the highest bidder.[25] There I see the tenderest ties ruthlessly broken, to gratify the lust, caprice and rapacity of the buyers and sellers of men. My soul sickens at the sight.

Is this the land your Fathers loved,
The freedom which they toiled to win?

---

[25] Compare this passage to the ways in which the narrator of Swift's "A Modest Proposal" talks about the poor Irish Catholics in dehumanizing terms.

Is this the earth whereon they moved?
Are these the graves they slumber in?[26]

But a still more inhuman, disgraceful, and scandalous state of things remains to be presented. By an act of the American Congress, not yet two years old, slavery has been nationalized in its most horrible and revolting form. By that act, Mason and Dixon's line has been obliterated;[27] New York has become as Virginia; and the power to hold, hunt, and sell men, women, and children as slaves remains no longer a mere state institution, but is now an institution of the whole United States. The power is co-extensive with the Star-Spangled Banner and American Christianity. Where these go, may also go the merciless slave-hunter. Where these are, man is not sacred. He is a bird for the sportsman's gun. By that most foul and fiendish of all human decrees, the liberty and person of every man are put in peril. Your broad republican domain is hunting ground for *men*. Not for thieves and robbers, enemies of society, merely, but for men guilty of no crime. Your lawmakers have commanded all good citizens to engage in this hellish sport. Your President, your Secretary of State, our *lords*, *nobles*, and ecclesiastics,[28] enforce, as a duty you owe to your free and glorious country, and to your God, that you do this accursed thing. Not fewer than forty Americans have, within the past two years, been hunted down and, without a moment's warning, hurried away in chains, and consigned to slavery and excruciating torture. Some of these have had wives and children, dependent on them for bread; but of this, no account was made. The right of the hunter to his prey stands superior to the right of marriage, and to *all* rights in this republic, the rights of God included! For black men there are neither law, justice, humanity, not religion. The Fugitive Slave *Law* makes mercy to them a crime; and bribes the judge who tries them. An American judge gets ten dollars for every victim he consigns to slavery, and five, when he fails to

---

[26] These lines are from John Greenleaf Whittier's anti-slavery poem "Stanzas for the Times."

[27] And, remember, this Mason-Dixon line is about four miles north of Mount St. Mary's University.

[28] Notice how Douglass is characterizing these people in terms similar to the British during the American Revolution.

do so. The oath of any two villains is sufficient, under this hell-black enactment, to send the most pious and exemplary black man into the remorseless jaws of slavery! His own testimony is nothing. He can bring no witnesses for himself. The minister of American justice is bound by the law to hear but *one* side; and *that* side, is the side of the oppressor. Let this damning fact be perpetually told. Let it be thundered around the world, that, in tyrant-killing, king-hating, people-loving, democratic, Christian America, the seats of justice are filled with judges, who hold their offices under an open and palpable *bribe*, and are bound, in deciding in the case of a man's liberty, *hear only his accusers!*[29]

In glaring violation of justice, in shameless disregard of the forms of administering law, in cunning arrangement to entrap the defenseless, and in diabolical intent, this Fugitive Slave Law stands alone in the annals of tyrannical legislation. I doubt if there be another nation on the globe, having the brass and the baseness to put such a law on the statute-book. If any man in this assembly thinks differently from me in this matter, and feels able to disprove my statements, I will gladly confront him at any suitable time and place he may select.

I take this law to be one of the grossest infringements of Christian Liberty, and, if the churches and ministers of our country were not stupidly blind, or most wickedly indifferent, they, too, would so regard it.[30]

At the very moment that they are thanking God for the enjoyment of civil and religious liberty, and for the right to worship God according to the dictates of their own consciences, they are utterly silent in respect to a law which robs religion of its chief significance, and makes it utterly worthless to a world lying in wickedness. Did this law concern the "*mint, anise, and cumin*"[31] — abridge the right to sing psalms, to partake of the sacrament, or to engage in any of the ceremonies of religion, it would be

---

[29] Let the horrible irony of this sentence sink in.

[30] "Christian Liberty" was a central concept for Protestant and Evangelical Christians during the Reformation. One of Martin Luther's major works was *De Libertate Christiana / Von der Freiheit eines Christenmenschen*, "On Christian Liberty".

[31] Matthew 23:23; Douglass will return to the rest of this verse at the end of this paragraph.

smitten by the thunder of a thousand pulpits. A general shout would go up from the church, demanding *repeal, repeal, instant repeal!* — And it would go hard with that politician who presumed to solicit the votes of the people without inscribing this motto on his banner. Further, if this demand were not complied with, another Scotland would be added to the history of religious liberty, and the stern old Covenanters would be thrown into the shade.[32] A John Knox would be seen at every church door,[33] and heard from every pulpit, and Fillmore would have no more quarter than was shown by Knox, to the beautiful, but treacherous queen Mary of Scotland.[34] The fact that the church of our country, (with fractional exceptions), does not esteem "the Fugitive Slave Law" as a declaration of war against religious liberty, implies that that church regards religion simply as a form of worship, an empty ceremony, and *not* a vital principle, requiring active benevolence, justice, love and good will towards man.[35] It esteems sacrifice above mercy; psalm-singing above right doing; solemn meetings above practical righteousness. A worship that can be conducted by persons who refuse to give shelter to the houseless, to give bread to the hungry, clothing to the naked, and who enjoin obedience to a law forbidding these acts of mercy, is a curse, not a blessing to mankind. The Bible addresses all such persons as "scribes, Pharisees, hypocrites, who pay tithe of *mint, anise,* and *cumin,* and have omitted the weightier matters of the law, judgment, mercy and faith."

But the church of this country is not only indifferent to the wrongs of the slave, it actually takes sides with the oppressors. It has made itself the bulwark of American slavery, and the shield of American slave-hunters. Many of its most eloquent Divines. who stand as the very lights of the

---

[32] The Covenanters were 17th-century Scottish Presbyterians who objected to the interference of the Stuart monarchy into the practices of the Church of Scotland (Presbyterian).

[33] John Knox (1513-1572) was the leading figure in the Protestant Reformation in Scotland, founder of Scottish Presbyterianism.

[34] Mary Stuart ("Queen of Scots," 1542-1587), Catholic cousin to Queen Elizabeth I of England and opponent to Protestantism

[35] How would this sentence have affected a Protestant American audience? American Christianity is more about external ceremonies than active faith, which was the exact criticism of Catholicism during the Reformation.

church, have shamelessly given the sanction of religion and the Bible to the whole slave system. They have taught that man may, properly, be a slave; that the relation of master and slave is ordained of God; that to send back an escaped bondman to his master is clearly the duty of all the followers of the Lord Jesus Christ; and this horrible blasphemy is palmed off upon the world for Christianity.[36]

For my part, I would say, welcome infidelity! welcome atheism! welcome anything! in preference to the gospel, *as preached by those Divines*! They convert the very name of religion into an engine of tyranny, and barbarous cruelty, and serve to confirm more infidels, in this age, than all the infidel writings of Thomas Paine, Voltaire, and Bolingbroke, put together, have done! These ministers make religion a cold and flinty-hearted thing, having neither principles of right action, nor bowels of compassion. They strip the love of God of its beauty, and leave the throng of religion a huge, horrible, repulsive form. It is a religion for oppressors, tyrants, man-stealers, and *thugs*. It is not that *"pure and undefiled religion"*[37] which is from above, and which is *"first pure, then peaceable, easy to be entreated*, full of mercy and good fruits, *without partiality, and without hypocrisy."*[38] But a religion which favors the rich against the poor; which exalts the proud above the humble; which divides mankind into two classes, tyrants and slaves; which says to the man in chains, *stay there*; and to the oppressor, *oppress on*; it is a religion which may be professed and enjoyed by all the robbers and enslavers of mankind; it makes God a respecter of persons, denies his fatherhood of the race, and tramples in the dust the great truth of the brotherhood of man. All this we affirm to be true of the popular church, and the popular worship of our land and nation — a religion, a church, and a worship which, on the authority of inspired wisdom, we pronounce to be an abomination in the sight of God. In the language of Isaiah, the American church might be well addressed, "Bring no more vain ablations; incense is an abomination unto me: the new moons and Sabbaths, the calling of assemblies, I cannot away with;

---

[36] St. Paul's epistle to Philemon was the most frequent source of Christian arguments in favor of slavery.

[37] James 1:27

[38] Both of the other phrases are from James 3:17

it is iniquity even the solemn meeting. Your new moons and your appointed feasts my soul hateth. They are a trouble to me; I am weary to bear them; and when ye spread forth your hands I will hide mine eyes from you. Yea! when ye make many prayers, I will not hear. YOUR HANDS ARE FULL OF BLOOD; cease to do evil, learn to do well; seek judgment; relieve the oppressed; judge for the fatherless; plead for the widow."[39]

The American church is guilty, when viewed in connection with what it is doing to uphold slavery; but it is superlatively guilty when viewed in connection with its ability to abolish slavery. The sin of which it is guilty is one of omission as well as of commission. Albert Barnes but uttered what the common sense of every man at all observant of the actual state of the case will receive as truth, when he declared that "There is no power out of the church that could sustain slavery an hour, if it were not sustained in it."[40]

Let the religious press, the pulpit, the Sunday school, the conference meeting, the great ecclesiastical, missionary, Bible and tract associations of the land array their immense powers against slavery and slave-holding; and the whole system of crime and blood would be scattered to the winds; and that they do not do this involves them in the most awful responsibility of which the mind can conceive.

In prosecuting the anti-slavery enterprise, we have been asked to spare the church, to spare the ministry; but *how*, we ask, could such a thing be done? We are met on the threshold of our efforts for the redemption of the slave, by the church and ministry of the country, in battle arrayed against us; and we are compelled to fight or flee. From *what* quarter, I beg to know, has proceeded a fire so deadly upon our ranks, during the last two years, as from the Northern pulpit? As the champions of oppressors, the chosen men of American theology have appeared — men, honored for their so-called piety, and their real learning. The Lords of Buffalo, the Springs of New York, the Lathrops of Auburn, the Coxes and Spencers of Brooklyn, the Gannets and Sharps of

---

[39] Isaiah 1:13-17

[40] Barnes (1798-1870) was a Protestant theologian and professor at Princeton University's Divinity School.

Boston, the Deweys of Washington, and other great religious lights of the land have, in utter denial of the authority of *Him* by whom they professed to be called to the ministry, deliberately taught us, against the example or the Hebrews and against the remonstrance of the Apostles, they teach *that we ought to obey man's law before the law of God*.[41]

My spirit wearies of such blasphemy; and how such men can be supported, as the "standing types and representatives of Jesus Christ," is a mystery which I leave others to penetrate. In speaking of the American church, however, let it be distinctly understood that I mean the great mass of the religious organizations of our land. There are exceptions, and I thank God that there are. Noble men may be found, scattered all over these Northern States, of whom Henry Ward Beecher of Brooklyn, Samuel J. May of Syracuse, and my esteemed friend (Rev. R. R. Raymond) on the platform, are shining examples; and let me say further, that upon these men lies the duty to inspire our ranks with high religious faith and zeal, and to cheer us on in the great mission of the slave's redemption from his chains.

One is struck with the difference between the attitude of the American church towards the anti-slavery movement, and that occupied by the churches in England towards a similar movement in that country.[42] There, the church, true to its mission of ameliorating, elevating, and improving the condition of mankind, came forward promptly, bound up the wounds of the West Indian slave, and restored him to his liberty. There, the question of emancipation was a high religious question. It was demanded, in the name of humanity, and according to the law of the living God. The Sharps, the Clarksons, the Wilberforces, the Buxtons, and Burchells and the Knibbs, were alike famous for their piety, and for their philanthropy. The anti-slavery movement *there* was not an anti-church movement, for the reason that the church took its full share in pro-secuting that movement: and the anti-slavery movement in this country

---

[41] This line is a parody of Acts 5:29: "Then Peter and the other apostles answered and said, We ought to obey God rather than men."

[42] Remember that this is a speech for *The Fourth of July*, and Douglass is pointing out that, in 1852, Great Britain has outlawed slavery (since the Slavery Abolition Act of 1833), while the United States still allows it and profits from it . . .

will cease to be an anti-church movement, when the church of this country shall assume a favorable, instead of a hostile position towards that movement.

Americans! your republican politics, not less than your republican religion, are flagrantly inconsistent. You boast of your love of liberty, your superior civilization, and your pure Christianity, while the whole political power of the nation (as embodied in the two great political parties), is solemnly pledged to support and perpetuate the enslavement of three millions of your countrymen. You hurl your anathemas at the crowned headed tyrants of Russia and Austria, and pride yourselves on your Democratic institutions, while you yourselves consent to be the mere *tools* and *body-guards* of the tyrants of Virginia and Carolina. You invite to your shores fugitives of oppression from abroad, honor them with banquets, greet them with ovations, cheer them, toast them, salute them, protect them, and pour out your money to them like water; but the fugitives from your own land you advertise, hunt, arrest, shoot and kill. You glory in your refinement and your universal education yet you maintain a system as barbarous and dreadful as ever stained the character of a nation — a system begun in avarice, supported in pride, and perpetuated in cruelty. You shed tears over fallen Hungary, and make the sad story of her wrongs the theme of your poets, statesmen and orators, till your gallant sons are ready to fly to arms to vindicate her cause against her oppressors; but, in regard to the ten thousand wrongs of the American slave, you would enforce the strictest silence, and would hail him as an enemy of the nation who dares to make those wrongs the subject of public discourse! You are all on fire at the mention of liberty for France or for Ireland; but are as cold as an iceberg at the thought of liberty for the enslaved of America. You discourse eloquently on the dignity of labor; yet, you sustain a system which, in its very essence, casts a stigma upon labor. You can bare your bosom to the storm of British artillery to throw off a threepenny tax on tea; and yet wring the last hard-earned farthing from the grasp of the black laborers of your country. You profess to believe "that, of one blood, God made all nations of men to dwell on the face of all the earth,"[43] and hath commanded all men, everywhere to

---

[43] Acts 17:26

love one another; yet you notoriously hate, (and glory in your hatred), all men whose skins are not colored like your own. You declare, before the world, and are understood by the world to declare, that you *"hold these truths to be self evident, that all men are created equal; and are endowed by their Creator with certain inalienable rights; and that, among these are, life, liberty, and the pursuit of happiness;"* and yet, you hold securely, in a bondage which, according to your own Thomas Jefferson, *"is worse than ages of that which your fathers rose in rebellion to oppose,"* a *seventh* part of the inhabitants of your country.

Fellow-citizens! I will not enlarge further on your national inconsistencies. The existence of slavery in this country brands your republicanism as a sham, your humanity as a base pretence, and your Christianity as a lie. It destroys your moral power abroad; it corrupts your politicians at home. It saps the foundation of religion; it makes your name a hissing, and a bye-word to a mocking earth. It is the antagonistic force in your government, the only thing that seriously disturbs and endangers your *Union*. It fetters your progress;[44] it is the enemy of improvement, the deadly foe of education; it fosters pride; it breeds insolence; it promotes vice; it shelters crime; it is a curse to the earth that supports it; and yet, you cling to it, as if it were the sheet anchor of all your hopes. Oh! be warned! be warned! a horrible reptile is coiled up in your nation's bosom; the venomous creature is nursing at the tender breast of your youthful republic; *for the love of God*, tear away, and fling from you the hideous monster, and *let the weight of twenty millions crush and destroy it forever*!

But it is answered in reply to all this, that precisely what I have now denounced is, in fact, guaranteed and sanctioned by the Constitution of the United States; that the right to hold and to hunt slaves is a part of that Constitution framed by the illustrious Fathers of this Republic.

Then, I dare to affirm, notwithstanding all I have said before, your fathers stooped, basely stooped

---

[44] Notice that Douglass' argument is that slavery holds back *Progress*.

To palter with us in a double sense:
And keep the word of promise to the ear,
But break it to the heart.[45]

And instead of being the honest men I have before declared them to be, they were the veriest imposters that ever practiced on mankind. This is the inevitable conclusion, and from it there is no escape. But I differ from those who charge this baseness on the framers of the Constitution of the United States. It is a slander upon their memory, at least, so I believe. There is not time now to argue the constitutional question at length — nor have I the ability to discuss it as it ought to be discussed. The subject has been handled with masterly power by Lysander Spooner, Esq., by William Goodell, by Samuel E. Sewall, Esq., and last, though not least, by Gerritt Smith, Esq. These gentlemen have, as I think, fully and clearly vindicated the Constitution from any design to support slavery for an hour.

Fellow-citizens! there is no matter in respect to which, the people of the North have allowed themselves to be so ruinously imposed upon, as that of the pro-slavery character of the Constitution. In that instrument I hold there is neither warrant, license, nor sanction of the hateful thing; but, interpreted as it ought to be interpreted, the Constitution is a GLORIOUS LIBERTY DOCUMENT. Read its preamble, consider its purposes. Is slavery among them? Is it at the gateway? or is it in the temple? It is neither. While I do not intend to argue this question on the present occasion, let me ask, if it be not somewhat singular that, if the Constitution were intended to be, by its framers and adopters, a slave-holding instrument, why neither slavery, slaveholding, nor slave can anywhere be found in it. What would be thought of an instrument, drawn up, legally drawn up, for the purpose of entitling the city of Rochester to a track of land, in which no mention of land was made? Now, there are certain rules of interpretation, for the proper understanding of all legal instruments. These rules are well established. They are plain, common-

---

[45] Shakespeare, *Macbeth* 5.8.20-22; Douglass slightly misquotes Shakespeare, whose last phrase is "And break it to our hope" (this variant is not noted in the textual criticism in *The Riverside Shakespeare*).

sense rules, such as you and I, and all of us, can understand and apply, without having passed years in the study of law. I scout the idea that the question of the constitutionality or unconstitutionality of slavery is not a question for the people. I hold that every American citizen has a right to form an opinion of the constitution, and to propagate that opinion, and to use all honorable means to make his opinion the prevailing one. Without this right, the liberty of an American citizen would be as insecure as that of a Frenchman. Ex-Vice-President Dallas tells us that the Constitution is an object to which no American mind can be too attentive, and no American heart too devoted. He further says, the Constitution, in its words, is plain and intelligible, and is meant for the home-bred, unsophisticated understandings of our fellow-citizens. Senator Berrien tell us that the Constitution is the fundamental law, that which controls all others. The charter of our liberties, which every citizen has a personal interest in understanding thoroughly. The testimony of Senator Breese, Lewis Cass, and many others that might be named, who are everywhere esteemed as sound lawyers, so regard the constitution. I take it, therefore, that it is not presumption in a private citizen to form an opinion of that instrument.

Now, take the Constitution according to its plain reading, and I defy the presentation of a single pro-slavery clause in it. On the other hand it will be found to contain principles and purposes, entirely hostile to the existence of slavery.[46]

I have detained my audience entirely too long already. At some future period I will gladly avail myself of an opportunity to give this subject a full and fair discussion.

Allow me to say, in conclusion, notwithstanding the dark picture I have this day presented of the state of the nation, I do not despair of this country. There are forces in operation, which must inevitably work the downfall of slavery. "The arm of the Lord is not shortened,"[47] and the doom of slavery is certain. I, therefore, leave off where I began, with hope.

---

[46] Notice how this problem is similar to the problem of the Reformation: who has Authority to interpret the Text? Douglass' insistence on "plain reading" has Protestant resonances.

[47] Isaiah 59:1

While drawing encouragement from the Declaration of Independence, the great principles it contains, and the genius of American Institutions, my spirit is also cheered by the obvious tendencies of the age. Nations do not now stand in the same relation to each other that they did ages ago.[48] No nation can now shut itself up from the surrounding world, and trot round in the same old path of its fathers without interference. The time was when such could be done. Long established customs of hurtful character could formerly fence themselves in, and do their evil work with social impunity. Knowledge was then confined and enjoyed by the privileged few, and the multitude walked on in mental darkness. But a change has now come over the affairs of mankind. Walled cities and empires have become unfashionable. The arm of commerce has borne away the gates of the strong city. Intelligence is penetrating the darkest corners of the globe. It makes its pathway over and under the sea, as well as on the earth. Wind, steam, and lightning are its chartered agents. Oceans no longer divide, but link nations together. From Boston to London is now a holiday excursion. Space is comparatively annihilated. Thoughts expressed on one side of the Atlantic, are distinctly heard on the other. The far off and almost fabulous Pacific rolls in grandeur at our feet. The Celestial Empire, the mystery of ages, is being solved.[49] The fiat of the Almighty, "Let there be Light," has not yet spent its force. No abuse, no outrage whether in taste, sport or avarice, can now hide itself from the all-pervading light. The iron shoe, and crippled foot of China must be seen, in contrast with nature. Africa must rise and put on her yet unwoven garment. "Ethiopia shall stretch out her hand unto God."[50] In the fervent aspirations of William Lloyd Garrison, I say, and let every heart join in saying it:

> *God speed the year of jubilee*
> *The wide world o'er*

---

[48] Note that what follows is an anthem to Progress, containing homages to Globalization, Industrialization, and Capitalism.

[49] Notice how Apocalyptic this sentence is: American Progress is bringing about a Heaven on Earth.

[50] Psalm 68:31

When from their galling chains set free,
Th' oppress'd shall vilely bend the knee,
And wear the yoke of tyranny
Like brutes no more.
That year will come, and freedom's reign,
To man his plundered fights again
Restore.
God speed the day when human blood
Shall cease to flow!
In every clime be understood,
The claims of human brotherhood,
And each return for evil, good,
Not blow for blow;
That day will come all feuds to end.
And change into a faithful friend
Each foe.
God speed the hour, the glorious hour,
When none on earth
Shall exercise a lordly power,
Nor in a tyrant's presence cower;
But all to manhood's stature tower,
By equal birth!
That hour will come, to each, to all,
And from his prison-house, the thrall
Go forth.
Until that year, day, hour, arrive,
With head, and heart, and hand I'll strive,
To break the rod, and rend the gyve,
The spoiler of his prey deprive —
So witness Heaven!
And never from my chosen post,
Whate'er the peril or the cost,
Be driven.

God's Grandeur

Gerard Manley Hopkins

The world is charged with the grandeur of God.

It will flame out, like shining from shook foil;

It gathers to a greatness, like the ooze of oil

Crushed. Why do men then now not reck his rod?

Generations have trod, have trod, have trod;

And all is seared with trade; bleared, smeared with toil;

And wears man's smudge and shares man's smell: the soil

Is bare now, nor can foot feel, being shod.

And for all this, nature is never spent;

There lives the dearest freshness deep down things;

And though the last lights off the black West went

Oh, morning, at the brown brink eastward, springs—

Because the Holy Ghost over the bent

World broods with warm breast and with ah! bright wings.

Made in the USA
Middletown, DE
03 August 2020